A review of British mammals:
population estimates and conservation status of British mammals other than cetaceans

Stephen Harris, *Pat Morris, Stephanie Wray and +Derek Yalden

School of Biological Sciences, University of Bristol, Woodland Road, Bristol, BS8 1UG,
*Department of Biology, Royal Holloway, University of London, Egham, Surrey, TW20 OEX
and +School of Biological Sciences, 3.239 Stopford Building, University of Manchester,
Oxford Road, Manchester, M13 9PL

Published by JNCC, Peterborough
Copyright JNCC 1995
ISBN 1 873701 68 3

Page layout: Sue Wenlock
Cover design: the Art Company, Over, Cambridge
Printing: Peter Fretwell & Sons Ltd, Keighley, West Yorkshire

Foreword

Historically, the health of the British fauna has been characterised by its distribution, with dots on maps denoting the presence of a particular species. In cases of drastic decline this sometimes proved an adequate tool - the disappearance of the otter from most of England, for example, was well illustrated by comparison of maps made at different times. For many widespread and common species, however, there can be serious declines in numbers that are not, until it is too late, mirrored in changes in distribution - a dot on a map can represent ten animals in a square where once there were a thousand.

Nature conservationists are increasingly asked to quantify their statements - *how many* otters, red squirrels or lesser horseshoe bats do we have and how many must we conserve? These simple questions identify the immediate problem: we often have little idea how many mammals there are, nor how their numbers change in annual (or longer) cycles.

For all but the rarest and most visible species, it is impossible to count the actual number of animals. Instead, one has to rely on extrapolation from empirical estimates of density for a particular habitat. Accuracy depends, therefore, on good field-derived estimates for that habitat and good estimates of the amount of the habitat. In some cases we have neither of these, and in many cases we have just one. In both these instances, we then turn to the opinions of experts.

For all the reasons outlined above, this report provides an estimate of population size, trends, threats and conservation status for every terrestrial mammal in Britain. Producing this report has been a considerable task - the authors have consulted widely and canvassed the opinions and data (both of which have been given voluntarily) of many mammal experts, all of whom deserve a great deal of thanks for their generous support.

Actually putting a figure on the number of some species that exist in Great Britain will inevitably be a controversial step - the exercise is certainly easier to criticise than it has been to do. We hope that this report will act as a focus for constructive debate on ways of improving the information for each species, and for initiating dedicated surveys of both species and habitats.

I am sure this report will be of great interest to all mammalogists; I hope it will further the conservation of British mammals by promoting discussion on the reliability of the figures, what they mean and how they can be improved.

Dr T. E. Tew
Vertebrate Ecology & Conservation Branch
Joint Nature Conservation Committee

Executive summary

1. This review covers 64 species and one sub species of terrestrial mammal known, or believed, to breed in Britain. It includes those feral species that have persisted as breeding populations for at least fifteen years, but excludes the cetaceans.

2. For each species there is an assessment of the current status, historical and recent changes in numbers, population trends and population threats. For most species these assessments are based on subjective rather than objective criteria because there are few species for which there are long-term population data.

3. For each species except Nathusius' pipistrelle a pre-breeding population estimate was calculated to provide a base-line against which to measure future changes. Estimates are provided for Great Britain as a whole and separately for England, Scotland and Wales. The results are summarised in Table 14. The minimum aim was to achieve a population estimate with an accuracy to within an order of magnitude, but most are thought to be more accurate. A code is used to identify the level of confidence for each estimate. For nine species the estimate was graded 1 (most reliable), for 11 it was graded 2, for 20 it was graded 3, for 19 it was graded 4, and for five the estimate was graded 5.

4. Several problems were highlighted in the course of making these estimates. First, there are very few species for which an estimate of total population size was available; for most, population size was calculated either by estimating their abundance relative to other species and/or by multiplying the amount of suitable habitat by known population density estimates for those habitats However, even this approach proved problematical for many species, either because density estimates were not available from Britain, or because these estimates were only available for a limited number of habitat types. Furthermore, most population sizes calculated in this way will tend to be over-estimates, because density estimates so derived are invariably based on a limited number of studies in some of the more suitable habitats for that particular species.

5. The review highlights the paucity of population data for many species of mammal, and density data are few or non-existent even for a number of common and/or widespread species such as the hedgehog, house mouse and common rat. Thus, further field studies are needed to improve our knowledge of the distribution and density of most species; only then will it be possible to refine many of the population estimates.

6. Absolute numbers of mammals are perhaps less important than trends in population size and degree of population fragmentation. The known or believed changes in British mammal populations over the last thirty years are summarised: two species have become extinct; eight are known, or believed, to have undergone substantial increases in range and/or numbers; nine have undergone some increase; for 23, population size was believed to have remained approximately stable; nine have undergone small declines in range and/or numbers; and for 14 there have been substantial declines. The species known, or believed, to be increasing in numbers include several already, or potentially, damaging to agriculture or silviculture, such as the rabbit, red deer, sika deer, roe deer and muntjac

and several species which are of conservation concern and which previously had been reduced to low levels, e.g. otter and polecat.

7. The population estimates for mammals are compared to those for other vertebrates. Few species of mammal are as rare as the species of bird listed on Schedule 1 of the Wildlife and Countryside Act 1981. However, mammals are less mobile, and minimum viable populations are likely to be larger. The commonest species of mammal have population sizes an order of magnitude larger than those of the commonest species of bird; the same relationship applies for the rarest species of mammals and birds.

8. There are a number of population threats faced by British mammals. Of the 65 mammals included in the review, seven are known, or believed, to be threatened by competitors, seven by climate change and/or adverse weather conditions, four by disease, seven by population fragmentation or isolation, 31 by habitat changes, five by inter-breeding, 18 by deliberate killing, 25 by pesticides, pollution or poisoning, four by predation and seven by road deaths.

9. The conservation status and legal protection afforded to all species of mammal in Britain are summarised. See Table 15.

10. The conservation status of each species is discussed from a European perspective. On this basis, most of the species of mammal that are rare in Britain have larger populations in Europe. The insectivores are generally about as common in Britain as in the rest of their European range; other than the Bechstein's and barbastelle bats, which are rare throughout Europe, the British populations of bats contribute only a small proportion of the European population; of the lagomorphs, the brown hare and rabbit populations are important in a European context; of the rodents, the grey squirrel and field vole populations constitute a significant proportion of the total European population; of the carnivores and pinnipeds, the otter, badger, common seal and grey seal populations are important in a European context; of the artiodactyls, the red, sika, fallow, muntjac and Chinese water deer populations constitute a major proportion of the European population, and the Soay sheep and wild goats that are of ancient origin are of particular interest because the populations in Britain are unique and constitute about half the ancient feral caprines in Europe.

11. The monitoring of endangered wild mammal populations is now a statutory responsibility under European Union legislation. This review identifies those species of particular conservation concern from both a British and a European perspective and provides a basis on which to develop a comprehensive monitoring scheme for British mammals.

Contents

Introduction 1

Methods 2

    Basis of the calculations 2

    Problems with producing the population estimates 3

    Reliability of the population estimates 4

    Population trends and factors likely to affect population size 5

Species accounts

    Order: Marsupialia 6

        Red-necked wallaby *Macropus rufogriseus* 6

    Order: Insectivora 7

        Hedgehog *Erinaceus europaeus* 7

        Mole *Talpa europaea* 9

        Common shrew *Sorex araneus* 10

        Pygmy shrew *Sorex minutus* 11

        Water shrew *Neomys fodiens* 12

        Lesser white-toothed shrew *Crocidura suaveolens* 13

    Order: Chiroptera 14

        Greater horseshoe bat *Rhinolophus ferrumequinum* . . . 17

        Lesser horseshoe bat *Rhinolophus hipposideros* 19

        Whiskered bat *Myotis mystacinus* 21

        Brandt's bat *Myotis brandtii* 21

        Natterer's bat *Myotis nattereri* 22

        Bechstein's bat *Myotis bechsteinii* 23

        Greater mouse-eared bat *Myotis myotis* 24

        Daubenton's bat *Myotis daubentonii* 24

        Serotine *Eptesicus serotinus* 25

        Noctule *Nyctalus noctula* 26

        Leisler's bat *Nyctalus leisleri* 27

        Pipistrelle *Pipistrellus pipistrellus* 27

        Nathusius' pipistrelle *Pipistrellus nathusii* 29

        Barbastelle *Barbastella barbastellus* 30

        Brown long-eared bat *Plecotus auritus* 30

        Grey long-eared bat *Plecotus austriacus* 31

    Order: Lagomorpha 32

        Rabbit *Oryctolagus cuniculus* 32

        Brown hare *Lepus europaeus* 34

        Mountain hare *Lepus timidus* 37

    Order: Rodentia 39

        Red squirrel *Sciurus vulgaris* 39

        Grey squirrel *Sciurus carolinensis* 41

        Bank vole *Clethrionomys glareolus* 43

        Skomer vole *Clethrionomys glareolus skomerensis* . . . 45

        Field vole *Microtus agrestis* 45

        Orkney vole *Microtus arvalis orcadensis* 48

        Water vole *Arvicola terrestris* 49

        Wood mouse *Apodemus sylvaticus* 51

        Yellow-necked mouse *Apodemus flavicollis* 52

        Harvest mouse *Micromys minutus* 54

        House mouse *Mus domesticus* 56

Common rat *Rattus norvegicus* 58
Ship rat *Rattus rattus* 62
Common dormouse *Muscardinus avellanarius* 63
Fat dormouse *Glis glis* 65
Coypu *Myocastor coypus* 66
- Order: Carnivora 67
Red fox *Vulpes vulpes* 67
Pine marten *Martes martes* 70
Stoat *Mustela erminea* 72
Weasel *Mustela nivalis* 73
Polecat *Mustela putorius* 74
Feral ferret *Mustela furo* 76
American mink *Mustela vison* 77
Badger *Meles meles* 80
Otter *Lutra lutra* 81
Wildcat *Felis silvestris* 85
Feral cat *Felis catus* 87
Order: Pinnipedia 89
Common seal *Phoca vitulina* 89
Grey seal *Halichoerus grypus* 92
Order: Artiodactyla 95
Red deer *Cervus elaphus* 95
Sika deer *Cervus nippon* 97
Fallow deer *Dama dama* 98
Roe deer *Capreolus capreolus* 100
Chinese muntjac *Muntiacus reevesi* 102
Chinese water deer *Hydropotes inermis* 104
Reindeer *Rangifer tarandus* 105
Park cattle *Bos taurus* 105
Feral goat *Capra hircus* 106
Feral sheep *Ovis aries* 107
Discussion 110
Current status 110
Changing status 110
Relative status 111
European status 111
Tables 115
Acknowledgements 139
References 140
Appendix: vagrant species recorded since 1900 168
Order: Chiroptera 168
Particoloured bat *Vespertilio murinus* 168
Northern bat *Eptesicus nilssonii* 168
Order: Pinnipedia 168
Ringed seal *Phoca hispida* 168
Harp seal *Phoca groenlandica* 168
Bearded seal *Erignathus barbatus* 168
Hooded seal *Cystophora cristata* 168
Walrus *Odobenus rosmarus* 169

Introduction

There are few data on population sizes and/or population trends for most British mammals, although the National Game Bag Census data provide an indication of population trends for some species (Tapper 1992). For many others, however, even such basic data as population densities are absent for more than a few habitats (see review in Corbet & Harris 1991). Detailed surveys have been undertaken for a few species, e.g. badger *Meles meles* (Cresswell, Harris & Jefferies 1990) and wildcat *Felis silvestris* (Easterbee, Hepburn & Jefferies 1991), and for others there are periodic monitoring exercises, e.g. otter *Lutra lutra* (Andrews & Crawford 1986; Green & Green 1987; Strachan *et al.* 1990), or annual counts over much of their range, e.g. red deer *Cervus elaphus*; see Clutton-Brock & Albon (1989) for an analysis of the data collected for red deer. Overall, however, unlike the regular monitoring of bird populations (e.g. Stroud & Glue 1991), there is no comprehensive monitoring scheme for British mammals. Neither has there been any attempt to estimate the population size for most species of British mammal, unlike the British avifauna (Morris 1993a), although the status of some of the rarer species has now been reviewed (Morris 1993b). Thus for many species of mammal substantial population changes could go unrecorded, as has occurred for the water vole *Arvicola terrestris* (Strachan & Jefferies 1993) and may have occurred for the hedgehog *Erinaceus europaeus* (P.A. Morris unpubl.). Whilst there are data on the number of hedgehogs killed by gamekeepers, these are not suitable for monitoring changes in hedgehog populations (Tapper 1992). This comparative lack of information on British mammal populations is largely due to the difficulties of counting mammals. For birds, counts are often based on habitat type (e.g. gardens), and hence include large numbers of species, whereas for mammals, survey or census techniques need to be tailored to suit the ecology of individual species or, more rarely, groups of species.

Despite the hitherto rather fragmented approach, there is now an increasing amount of information available on the status of many British mammals and, for a small number, good population estimates are available. This review attempts to assess the abundance of all British mammals, to show where deficiencies in knowledge exist, to highlight their status and population trends, and to comment on any potential population threats or other factors that may affect future population size. Finally, the importance of the British mammal fauna is assessed in a European context.

Methods

Basis of the calculations: This review covers all 63 species of native and introduced mammal that are known to have bred in Great Britain in the last thirty years and one species that may have bred in Britain; it also includes one sub species for which there are data on population size, but excludes the cetaceans. The review covers an area of 230,367 km², and includes off-shore islands but not the Channel Islands and Isle of Man (Table 1). Records for vagrant or migratory species, and those not known, or not believed, to have bred in Britain, are also summarised. However, introduced species that have not persisted as breeding populations for at least 15 years, such as Mongolian gerbil *Meriones unguiculatus*, golden hamster *Mesocricetus auratus*, raccoon *Procyon lotor* and Himalayan porcupine *Hystrix brachyura* (Smallshire & Davey 1989; Baker 1990), have been excluded. The selection of species included in the review was largely based on the third edition of *The handbook of British mammals* (Corbet & Harris 1991). Where historical records are quoted, the county name used is that given in the original report, and these have not been adjusted to take account of any changes in county names.

Data have been collated from published sources or from specialists for each species, with the minimum goal of producing an 'order of magnitude' population estimate. For many species, there are significant inter-seasonal or inter-annual changes in population size and so, for comparisons between species, we have estimated the size of the overwintering or pre-breeding population. For some species, where accurate population estimates were already available, minimum/maximum figures are given or, where appropriate, estimates with 95% confidence limits. Where no published data on population size were available, for some species these have been provided by key workers. For species where no other population estimates were available, population densities and/or home range sizes for different habitat types were extracted from the literature or supplied by workers on that

species, and were used to estimate the total population size, based on the distribution of the species and the area of suitable habitats available. As a general rule, only data from mainland Britain were used for these calculations, since information from the rest of Europe, where there are likely to be differences in both habitat and faunal composition, are unlikely to be representative of Britain.

To estimate habitat availability, data on 42 main habitat types in each of the 32 land classes devised by the Institute of Terrestrial Ecology (Bunce, Barr & Whittaker 1981a, 1981b) were used. The distribution of land classes within England, Scotland and Wales is shown in Table 2. When calculating population size of some species, four land class groups, rather than individual land classes, were used. Thus land classes 2, 3, 4, 9, 11, 12, 14, 25 and 26 formed the arable land class group, land classes 1, 5, 6, 7, 8, 10, 13, 15, 16 and 27 formed the pastoral land class group, land classes 17, 18, 19, 20, 28 and 31 formed the marginal upland land class group and land classes 21, 22, 23, 24, 29, 30 and 32 formed the upland land class group (Barr *et al.* 1993). The habitat data were collected by surveying 2455 1 x 1 km squares during the period November 1985 to February 1988 as part of a national badger survey; full details of the habitat data recorded are given in Cresswell, Harris & Jefferies (1990). In addition, a further 165 1 x 1 km squares from land classes on the Scottish islands, not included in the original badger survey, were subsequently surveyed for habitat data only, to ensure that the habitat data were not biased due to the exclusion of islands uninhabited by badgers. For the habitat data, all areas over 0·5 ha or linear features over 50 m long were included. For each land class, mean areas of each habitat type were calculated, excluding areas of sea. Details of the area of the main habitat types in the area covered by this review are given in Table 3. For aquatic species such as water voles, mink *Mustela vison* and otters, data on abundance were available for water authority regions, and so figures for the lengths of riparian habitats in each authority region are given in Table 4. Data on the rates of habitat change in Britain are given by Barr *et al.* (1993).

When the calculations included in this review were undertaken, there were no habitat data available for Britain as a whole, although there were some data on the land-use changes in England (Sinclair 1992). Subsequent to the calculations being completed, a report was published on the pattern of land use in Britain in 1990 (Barr *et al.* 1993). This presented land cover data from two different sources: satellite imagery and a very detailed survey of 508 1 x 1 km squares, stratified by land class, with a greater number of squares surveyed within larger land classes. Habitat classifications for these two surveys differed slightly from those used here, and so direct comparisons are difficult. However, the broad results are very similar. For example, in this survey it was estimated that there were 528,000 km of hedgerow, compared to 549,000 km estimated by Barr *et al.* (1993). Thus the habitat data used here provide a reliable basis for estimating the size of the mammal populations in Britain.

Problems with producing the population estimates: There are very few, if any, species for which the population estimates presented here could not be improved. Counting mammals is notoriously difficult, and even for well-monitored species there are uncertainties inherent in the estimates. For example, for the seals, there will be uncertainties about what proportion of the population is hauled-out when the counts are undertaken. Some of the weakest population estimates are those based on population density figures and the area of suitable habitat available. The problem with such an approach is that inevitably there are few density estimates, and those are for a limited range of habitat types, even for the commonest species. Since most workers base their study of a particular species in an area where that species is common and hence easiest to catch, it is difficult to know how typical such density estimates are for the rest

of that species' range. For this reason, population estimates using this approach were generally based on density estimates slightly below those reported in autecological studies.

Of particular difficulty in this respect are all the small mammals, the bats and the deer. Hence for the small mammals and the bats, the relative proportions of the different species in a variety of samples were used as a cross-check to determine if at least the relative size of the population estimates were correct, and that the rank order of abundance for the species was appropriate. Thus for small mammals, data were collated from a variety of pellet analyses (Table 5), bottle studies (Table 6) and trapping studies (Table 7); the relative proportions from these studies are summarised in Table 8. These tables are not comprehensive in that they deliberately do not include all the data that were available, since these were strongly biased to southern England, and there were few samples from Scotland or Wales. Thus the samples included in these tables were designed to provide as wide a coverage as was possible, both geographically and by habitat, without excessively biasing the data to a few habitats in southern England. For species such as the water shrew *Neomys fodiens*, for which few, if any, density estimates were available, population size could only be calculated by comparing abundance relative to a common species in a variety of samples from different habitats; in the case of the water shrew, abundance relative to common shrew *Sorex araneus* and pygmy shrew *Sorex minutus* was used. For the bats, few density estimates were available. For greater horseshoe bat *Rhinolophus ferrumequinum* and lesser horseshoe bat *Rhinolophus hipposideros*, total population size was reasonably well known, but for most others there were few data on which to base a population estimate. Thus relative abundance was the only approach available for calculating population size for most bats, and the estimates had to be based on the subjective assessment of relative abundance by experienced bat workers.

For the deer, with the exception of red and to some extent sika *Cervus nippon*, there were few density estimates because counting deer, even in a small area, is notoriously difficult. Most deer census figures tend to be an under-estimate (Springthorpe & Myhill 1985), and using these to calculate total population size is therefore inherently unreliable. The problem is compounded for those species where the latest distribution maps (Arnold 1993) were used to provide an estimate of the occupied range, since these maps provided at best only the minimum distribution for a species. For instance, a survey into the distribution of muntjac *Muntiacus reevesi* increased the number of 10 x 10 km square records from 417 (Arnold 1993) to 745 (Chapman, Harris & Stanford 1994), an increase of 79%. Whilst muntjac may be an extreme example, in that they were still expanding their range, even species with established ranges were likely to have been under-recorded, and probably by a significant amount.

For each species, a separate population estimate was also calculated for each of England, Scotland and Wales. Where there were regional counts, e.g. for the seals and some of the deer, the three estimates were based on these counts. Where the estimate was based on the area of suitable habitat and known population densities, the figures were based on the availability of suitable habitats in each country. For total population estimates based on abundance relative to other species, e.g. many of the bats, the estimates for each country were based on the proportion of the 10 x 10 km square records in each of the three countries (Arnold 1993), excluding the Channel Islands and the Isle of Man. There are problems with each approach. For instance, the quality of counts from different regions often varied. When using density estimates, it had to be assumed that the same population density occurred in similar habitats throughout the range. Using the proportion of 10 x 10 km square records in different parts of a species' range of necessity placed equal weight on squares with one record and those with many. Thus these regional figures are intended only

to give an indication of the relative status of a species in different regions of the British Isles.

Since there are limitations in the data used to produce any of the estimates in this review, they must be viewed as the first stage in a process of estimating the population size for British mammals, and in monitoring population changes and trends. With better data on the distribution and ecology of each species, the estimates for most, if not all, species will be improved.

Reliability of the population estimates:
Since there were limitations in the data used to produce the population estimates, a reliability score is provided to give some indication of the level of accuracy that is thought to have been achieved. The scores are as follows:-

1. A widely distributed species for which there had been a recent census or for which there were regular counts that were believed to have a high degree of accuracy, or a rare species for which most of the populations were thought to be known and regularly monitored. For these species it was believed that any improvements in census techniques were unlikely to alter the population estimate by more than 10% either way.

2. A widely distributed species for which the population estimate was based on good data on population densities in different habitat types, or a rare or local species for which the estimate was based on a good understanding of the factors that were limiting its distribution or numbers, and good information on population densities in a reasonable range of habitat types. For these species, there was scope for improving the population estimate, but any improvements were unlikely to be substantial, and any resulting change in the population estimate would probably be less than 25%.

3. A widely distributed species for which the population estimate was based on a

limited amount of data on population densities in different habitat types, or for which the population estimate was obtained by scaling abundance relative to a species for which there was a reasonable population estimate. For rare species, the estimate was based on only a limited knowledge of the factors limiting its distribution or numbers, or on only a few density estimates from a limited range of habitats. Any improvement in the population estimate could result in a change of up to 50%, but on current knowledge it was considered unlikely that the estimate would be wrong by a greater margin.

4. An estimate based on a very limited amount of information on the species, for which there was a need for much more information on either its distribution in Britain, or population densities in a variety of habitat types, or relative abundance. Any improvement in knowledge would greatly improve the basis on which the estimate was achieved, but may not necessarily have made a substantial difference to the estimate presented here, since all species have been ranked in order of relative abundance and its position in the rankings was thought to be correct.

5. A species for which there was so little information on its distribution and/or abundance in different habitat types, and for which the data were so inadequate or biased, that it was not possible to scale its abundance relative to other species reliably. For these species the estimate was believed on subjective criteria to be within the right order of magnitude, but no greater degree of accuracy was thought to have been achieved.

Of the 65 species and sub species covered in the review, for one there was no population estimate, for nine the estimate was graded 1, for 11 it was graded 2, for 20 it was graded 3, for 19 it was graded 4, and for five it was graded 5.

Population trends and factors likely to affect population size: Population size *per se* is not the only, nor necessarily the major, factor to consider when assessing the status of British mammals, and population trends and factors likely to affect future population size are at least as important. Thus absolute numbers are often considered to be less important than the degree of habitat, and hence population, fragmentation (see review by Bright 1993). So for each species the available information on population trends, and significant factors that might affect future population size either locally or nationally, are reviewed. For the latter, only factors likely to have an impact on population size, rather than normal mortality factors, were considered. Since there are so few data on population size or trends for many species, any assessment of the factors likely to have an impact on population size are, of necessity, based on subjective, rather than objective, criteria. Hence the sections on population threats for each species must be viewed as a preliminary assessment of perceived, rather than known, risk. Methods of assessing change in population size, and the value of conservation measures to improve the status of threatened species of mammal, are discussed by Jefferies & Mitchell-Jones (1993).

Species accounts

Order: Marsupialia

Red-necked wallaby *Macropus rufogriseus*

Status: Introduced; two recent populations in England were founded in 1940 and a third in about 1985, and one in Scotland in 1975.

Distribution: Colonies are still present in the Peak District and on the island of Inchconachan, Loch Lomond, Scotland; the colony in Ashdown Forest, Sussex, and that near Teignmouth, Devon, are now extinct. In addition there are occasional escapes from wildlife collections.

Population data: The last record from the Sussex colony was in 1972 and this population is assumed to be extinct. The Teignmouth population originated from an unknown number of animals that escaped, probably early in 1985; an animal killed on the road in 1994 was believed to be the last survivor (C.J. Wilson pers. comm.). Survey techniques for the Peak District population are detailed in Yalden (1988). The population was divided into two, and each sub-population counted on a separate day. The total population size is based on 'best counts'. Intensive field work in 1978 showed that, with enough visits, 'best counts' seemed to provide a total population estimate, and no other individuals were known to occur away from the two sub-populations. In January 1993 the Peak District colony stood at only three animals (D.W. Yalden unpubl.). The size of the Loch Lomond population in 1992 was 26 (Weir, McLeod & Adams 1995).

Population estimates: The total free-living population of wallabies in 1993 was 29 individuals: 3 in England, 28 in Scotland and none in Wales. In addition, there is a free-ranging colony of 400-600 animals at Whipsnade Park, Bedfordshire. **Reliability of population estimate:** 1.

Historical changes: A number of other populations have existed in the past. In the 1850s several escaped into woods near Cromer, Norfolk; there were rumours of feral wallabies in the Pennines early this century; and several were released near Rothesay on the Isle of Bute about 1912, one of which was self-supporting for about three years. In the 1920s a number were released on Lundy; they were later accidentally drowned (Lever 1977). The present colony in the Peak District originated from five animals that were released from a collection at Leek, Staffordshire in 1939 or 1940; the early history of this population is described by Lever (1977). The Sussex colony originated from a captive colony at Lower Beeding, near Horsham, and by 1940 there was a small but apparently fully naturalized and breeding colony in the Ashdown Forest and St Leonard's Forest district (Lever 1977). The population at Loch Lomond started with two pairs from Whipsnade that were introduced in 1975 (Weir, McLeod & Adams 1995).

Population trends: Although four free-living populations have become established in recent times, one is certainly extinct, one is probably extinct, one no longer appears viable, and there is no evidence that the Scottish population is spreading. Overall, the number of feral wallabies in Britain appears to be declining. Most data on population trends are for the Peak District population, which increased from five in 1940 to around 50 in 1962. Thereafter numbers declined, ranging between 10 and 20 during 1970-1985, followed by a further recent decline (Yalden 1988).

Population threats: Harsh winters reduce numbers and they suffer heavy mortality in severe snow falls. Traffic and other accidents are also a significant cause of death in the Peak District, and many of these may result from animals fleeing following disturbance by dogs or people (Yalden 1991). In the Peak District, disturbance appeared to be a significant factor limiting their distribution (Yalden 1990).

Order: Insectivora

Hedgehog *Erinaceus europaeus*

Status: Native; locally common.

Distribution: Found throughout mainland Britain up to the treeline, but scarce or absent from very wet habitats, areas of large arable fields and conifer plantations. Although there are occasional records of animals foraging at higher altitudes (Arnold 1993), they are probably absent from many upland areas, especially in Scotland. They are also found on many islands, often as a result of introductions; for details see Morris (1991). Recent (1970s and 1980s) introductions include North Ronaldsay (Orkney) and St Mary's (Isles of Scilly).

Population data: Hedgehogs are most abundant where there is close proximity of grassland to woodland, scrub or hedgerow, and they are present in virtually all lowland habitats where there is sufficient cover for nesting. They are common in suburban areas, but generally scarce in coniferous woods and marshy and moorland areas (Morris 1991). Hedgehogs appear to be patchily distributed, and the National Game Bag Census suggests that hedgehogs are more regionally aggregated than species such as the stoat *Mustela erminea* and the weasel *Mustela nivalis* (Tapper 1992), a finding also supported by the distribution of road-deaths (P.A. Morris unpubl.). Road-kill data collected during July-September for 1989-1992 inclusive showed large regional differences, with a rank order of decreasing abundance of: north-east England, north-west England, East Anglia, Wales, east midlands, south England, Scotland, south-west England, west midlands and south-east England. There was a four-fold difference in the number of dead hedgehogs recorded per 100 km of road between north-east and south-east England

(P.A. Morris unpubl.). Doncaster (1992) suggested that predation by badgers may account for this patchy distribution; he showed that high densities of badgers in one area in Oxfordshire appeared to enhance dispersal and mortality of introduced hedgehogs. The regional differences in hedgehog numbers indicated by the road-kill survey seem to support the suggestion that hedgehogs are most common where badgers are rarer (cf. Cresswell *et al*. 1989).

Approximately 1 per ha were recorded on a golf course with a particularly high density of hedgehogs (Reeve 1982). In north-east London a minimum density for the urban area, based on public sightings and road mortality figures, was 0·0735 per ha (Plant 1979). In a woodland in the Yorkshire Dales, Morris, Munn & Craig-Wood (1993) recorded 1 per 1·5 ha. In an ancient field system with a mosaic of hedgerows, small copses and unimproved grassland, the density was 1 per 4·5 ha (Morris 1988). Studies elsewhere have suggested that this density is probably typical for mixed farmland in southern England (P.A. Morris unpubl.), although numbers are likely to be lower in areas with large fields, where there may be a shortage of nesting sites (Reeve 1994).

The few data on hedgehog population densities were collected during the summer, and so are greater than would be expected for the pre-breeding population at the end of hibernation. Thus the following densities were used to estimate population size: 1 per 2·5 ha for semi-natural broadleaved, mixed and recently felled woodlands, parkland, scrub, lowland unimproved grasslands and amenity grasslands; 1 per 10 ha for built-up areas; and 1 per 20 ha for broadleaved, coniferous and mixed plantations, semi-natural mixed woodlands, bracken, semi-improved and improved grasslands and arable areas.

Population estimates: A total pre-breeding population of about 1,555,000; 1,100,000 in England, 310,000 in Scotland and 145,000 in Wales. This clearly is an approximate figure, because there were few data available on

hedgehog densities in different habitat types.
Reliability of population estimate: 4.

Historical changes: At the turn of the century hedgehogs were described as plentiful throughout the greater part of Great Britain, in spite of constant persecution by farmers and gamekeepers, though scarce in the northern highlands of Scotland (Millais 1904-1906; Thorburn 1920). They were said to have been introduced to western Ross-shire in 1890 in baled hay and were also introduced to the eastern parts of Sutherland and Caithness (Millais 1904-1906). Hence it would appear that hedgehogs were extending their range in Scotland in the second half of the 19th century (Millais 1904-1906).

Burton (1969) suggested an average density in the early 1950s of 1 per acre, i.e. 1 per 0·405 ha, throughout the country, although he admitted this was derived largely from guess work. Excluding the marginal upland and upland land classes, this would still give a population of around 36,500,000 hedgehogs for the arable and pastoral land classes, or more than twenty times the present population estimate. Based on his subjective impressions of hedgehog numbers in a rural area of Surrey, Burton (1969) suggested that 1947 was a year of particular abundance, and that hedgehog numbers had fallen in the 1960s when compared with the 1950s. However, he also suggested that there had been little change in the numbers living in the vicinity of small towns and in the suburbs of larger towns.

Population trends: The National Game Bag Census data suggest a steady reduction in the numbers killed, possibly dating from before the 1960s. Whether this denotes a population decline due to an increasing loss of suitable habitats, or a change in gamekeeping practice, is unclear (Tapper 1992). In an attempt to get a subjective assessment of whether hedgehog numbers were changing, P.A. Morris & S. Wroot (unpubl.) sent a questionnaire survey to the National Federation of Women's Institutes in 1990; over 1200 members participated. Of these, 36% thought that hedgehog road kills were less common than

10 years previously, compared with 25% who thought they were more common; the rest either did not know or thought they were about the same. However, in the south-west, significantly more people thought that hedgehogs had become less common, and in the south-east more respondents thought there were fewer hedgehogs in 1989 than in previous years. The south-west and south-east were two of the areas the road-kill survey (see above) identified as currently having the lowest hedgehog densities. Whilst it is difficult to draw firm conclusions from opinion surveys, it is clear that only a minority of people felt that hedgehogs were becoming more numerous, and it is probable that in the 1980s the hedgehog population was either static or declining.

Estimating population trends is further complicated because in some years hedgehogs may be particularly abundant. It has been suggested that this may occur when conditions are suitable for a significant proportion of the population to rear second litters successfully (Jefferies & Pendlebury 1968). However, this is unlikely to be the case because few second litters attain sufficient body weight to survive the winter (Morris 1984). A study in southern Sweden showed that annual mortality varied greatly between seasons, and that population size was influenced predominantly by environmental factors such as food availability, the availability of suitable winter nest sites and winter climate (Kristiansson 1990); thus adult population size in an area of 50 ha varied by a factor of 2·7.

The rate of growth for island populations is largely unknown. Two hedgehogs were introduced to North Ronaldsay in 1972; the population is now thought to be about 500, but may be as low as 100 (H. Warwick pers. comm.). An unknown number of hedgehogs was introduced to the Isles of Scilly before the mid-1980s; the current population size is also unknown.

Population threats: These have been discussed in general terms by Burton (1969). The effects of predation by badgers (see above) are unclear, but if this does lead to population declines, then any increase in badger numbers is likely to have an impact on hedgehog populations. Mortality on roads may also be a significant population threat. A survey during July-September suggested an average count of 2·26 killed per 100 km of roads in 1990, 1·88 per 100 km in 1991 and 2·14 per 100 km in 1992 (P.A. Morris unpubl.). It is not clear how these figures should be used to estimate the total killed on the whole road network. The 1990 survey suggested at least 20,000 hedgehogs are killed annually, but figures up to 100,000 have been quoted (Stocker 1987). A similar figure (102,400) is obtained by extrapolating the results of a five-year survey in Surrey (R. Ramage pers. comm.), where 49 km of road were travelled daily and all road kills recorded. The survey included a wide variety of habitats, but was confined to major roads. The figure of around 100,000 is obtained by extrapolating the data to all principal, trunk, motorway, minor and unclassified roads in Britain. Whilst this ignores lower hedgehog densities in parts of Britain, this is offset by the fact that the Surrey results were very much minimum figures. Only animals seen whilst driving were recorded, and so some casualties would have been missed, as would all animals that had managed to crawl off the carriageway. Also, the survey in Surrey was undertaken in a part of Britain having the lowest recorded density of hedgehog road deaths (see above). Whether losses on the roads constitute a significant threat to long-term survival is unclear; Reichholf (1983) has suggested that in Germany road mortality can lead to the extinction of isolated populations. In Sweden, however, Kristiansson (1990) found that while sub-adult and adult hedgehog mortality averaged 47% per annum over seven years, the majority (average 33%) was winter mortality; winter temperatures much lower than normal were associated with higher mortality. In contrast, road deaths were less important.

Rural habitat changes probably constitute a more significant threat to hedgehog populations, particularly the change from permanent grassland and rough grazing to arable land, which is less suitable for hedgehogs because of its lower earthworm population. In addition, the removal of hedgerows and concomitant increase in field sizes limits the availability of nesting sites, further reducing the suitability of arable land for hedgehogs; a shortage of suitable nesting sites generally may be a factor limiting hedgehog numbers. Such landscape changes may account for the decline in hedgehog numbers in the returns for the National Game Bag Census (Tapper 1992). Pesticide residues from agrichemicals and garden pesticides, especially molluscicides, potentially have an impact through the food chain, but no data are currently available on the pesticide levels present in hedgehogs, with still less available on their effects on the hedgehog population overall.

Finally, climatic changes could have a significant impact on hedgehog numbers. Hedgehogs have to reach a minimum weight of 450 g in order to survive a normal period of hibernation (Morris 1984). Hot dry summers reduce the availability of earthworms and other invertebrates, and this may have a significant impact on hedgehog numbers and/or the survival of young.

Mole *Talpa europaea*

Status: Native; common.

Distribution: Moles are found throughout mainland Britain wherever the soil is sufficiently deep for them to burrow. There are occasional records as high as 930 m in Scotland (Arnold 1993) and 1000 m in Wales (Milner & Ball 1970). Moles are absent from most islands except Anglesey, the Isle of Wight and a few of the Inner Hebrides.

Population data: Moles are present in most habitats. Originally they were inhabitants of deciduous woodland, but they have spread into agricultural habitats and thrive in pastures. In arable land colonisation from field boundaries occurs after ploughing. They are uncommon in coniferous forests, on moorland and in sand dune systems (Stone & Gorman 1991). There are very few density estimates available. In English pastures 8-16 per ha have been recorded in the summer (Larkin 1948), but in north-east Scotland densities in woodland and pasture remained similar throughout the year at 4-5 per ha (Stone 1986). Typical pre-breeding densities would be 1.3 per ha in poor habitats and 4.0 per ha in good habitats (M.L. Gorman pers. comm.). Thus population size was estimated by assuming a density of 1.3 per ha in coniferous plantations and woodlands, lowland heaths, arable habitats and lowland improved grasslands, and 4.0 per ha in all types of woodlands except coniferous plantations, parkland, scrub, bracken and lowland unimproved and semi-improved grasslands. Moles were assumed to be absent from all the other types of habitats, although they will occur in low densities in some of these, e.g. gardens on the edge of built-up areas.

Population estimates: A total pre-breeding population of about 31,000,000; 19,750,000 in England, 8,000,000 in Scotland and 3,250,000 in Wales. These are approximate figures, since there are very few density estimates for Britain, and these are limited to a small range of habitats. **Reliability of population estimate:** 3.

Historical changes: In eastern and northern Scotland the mole was common in the late 1800s, whereas it had been rare previous to 1860 (Millais 1904-1906). There are no other data on historical population changes.

Population trends: Unknown; the reduction in persecution may have led to an increase in numbers, whereas agricultural changes and high-intensity arable land-use may have led to population decreases. Deep ploughing is likely to be especially detrimental to mole populations.

Population threats: The current level of persecution by man is much less than in the past, and there are no known population threats. Agricultural operations such as

ploughing and re-seeding significantly reduce earthworm populations (Edwards & Lofty 1972), and the removal of hedgerows and areas of rough land eliminates the sanctuary areas from which moles could recolonise an area following cultivation. The impact of agricultural chemicals, particularly insecticides, on mole numbers is unknown.

Common shrew *Sorex araneus*

Status: Native; common.

Distribution: Found throughout mainland Britain at all altitudes, and on many islands except the Isles of Scilly, Orkney, Outer Hebrides, Shetland and some of the Inner Hebrides.

Population data: Common shrews are found almost everywhere where there is some low vegetation cover. They are most abundant in thick grass, bushy scrub, hedgerows and deciduous woodland. Occasionally they are found amongst heather and stable scree (Churchfield 1991a). Densities are very variable, but reach a summer peak of 42-69 per ha in deciduous woodland and grassland, and 7-21 per ha in dune scrub and scrub-grassland. In winter, densities in deciduous woodland and grassland are much lower (5-27 per ha) (Churchfield 1991a). Typical densities would be 6 per ha for grassland at Wytham, Oxfordshire (Pernetta 1977), 1.7-6.9 per ha (April and November) in Wytham Woods, Oxfordshire (Buckner 1969), 26 per ha in woodland near Exeter, Devon (Shillito 1960, 1963a), 4.9-13.5 per ha (July and November) in a larch plantation in south Wales (B.A.C. Don unpubl.), a mean density of 60 per ha over 16 months in grassland in Berkshire (Churchfield & Brown 1987) and 42 per ha in coarse herbage at Woodchester, Gloucestershire in July (Yalden 1974). Densities in arable areas are generally low, and in such habitats common shrews are largely confined to hedgerows (Tew 1994).

Since there are only a few density estimates for pre-breeding population densities, the population size was calculated using the following figures: a density of 10 per ha in low scrub, bracken, lowland unimproved grassland and sloping cliffs, 2·5 per ha in semi-natural broadleaved and semi-natural mixed woodlands, broadleaved and young plantations, parkland, tall scrub, lowland heaths, semi-improved and improved grasslands and arable land, 1 per ha in semi-natural coniferous woodlands, coniferous and mixed plantations, sand dunes, heather moorlands and upland unimproved grasslands, and 0·5 per ha for blanket and raised bogs, and in built-up areas.

Population estimates: A total pre-breeding population of about 41,700,000; 26,000,000 in England, 11,500,000 in Scotland and 4,200,000 in Wales. Comparing this with the estimated population size for the wood mouse *Apodemus sylvaticus* gives a ratio of 1·1 common shrews per wood mouse, which is in complete concordance with the overall ratio of common shrews to wood mice from a large variety of samples - see Tables 5-7, and the summary in Table 8. **Reliability of population estimate:** 3.

Historical changes: Unknown.

Population trends: Unknown; the loss of ancient grassland and meadows, plus the continuing widespread use of insecticides (MacGillivray 1994), have probably led to a population decrease, but numbers may have been locally increased by long-term set-aside (Brockless & Tapper 1993).

Population threats: The continued loss of prime habitats (see above) and use of agricultural insecticides may cause continued declines. Also, one study found that liming upland catchment areas to improve water quality reduced surface activity by common shrews for two to three months but, in contrast to pygmy shrews *Sorex minutus*, had no effect on common shrew numbers (Shore & Mackenzie 1993).

Pygmy shrew *Sorex minutus*

Status: Native; common.

Distribution: Found throughout mainland Britain at all altitudes. Pygmy shrews are absent from the Isles of Scilly and Shetland, but otherwise are widespread on small and large islands (Churchfield 1991b). Their presence on remoter islands (e.g. Barra, Lewis and Orkney) is almost certainly due to introductions. This is the only shrew present on Orkney and the Outer Hebrides.

Population data: Pygmy shrews are found in all types of terrestrial habitat, especially where there is plenty of ground cover; they show a preference for grassland over woodland. A maximum density of 12 per ha in summer but 5 per ha in winter was recorded in grassland in southern England (Pernetta 1977), and a mean density of 14 per ha over 16 months in grassland in Berkshire (Churchfield & Brown 1987). In lowland habitats they are generally less abundant than common shrews (Churchfield 1991b), e.g. one pygmy shrew per 4·3 common shrews in grassland in Berkshire (Churchfield & Brown 1987), but in moorland areas pygmy shrews outnumber common shrews, e.g. near Glossop, Derbyshire a ratio of 8·7 pygmy shrews per common shrew was found in pitfall traps (Yalden 1981). In the Peak District, pygmy shrews outnumbered common shrews by 2:1 on blanket bog, and were more numerous than common shrews above around 450 m (Yalden 1993). Based on 42 sites sampled over two years, the ratio of pygmy to common shrews in different moorland habitats were as follows: *Calluna* 8·2:1, *Calluna/Eriophorum* 7·1:1, *Eriophorum vaginatum* 19·0:1, *Juncus squarrosus* 6·7:1 and grasses 1·3:1 (Butterfield, Coulson & Wanless 1981).

Since there are so few data on densities but a lot more information is available on relative abundance, population size was estimated using the relative abundance of common:pygmy shrews in samples from a wide variety of sources and habitat types (Tables 5-8). From these a mean ratio was obtained of 5·4 common shrews per pygmy shrew in England, 5·0:1 for Scotland, and 2·8:1 for Wales. These data suggest that pygmy shrews are more common in Wales, yet in upland areas of Scotland pygmy shrews do not appear to be as common, relative to common shrews, as they are in upland areas of England. These ratios were used to calculate the size of the pygmy shrew population in each of the three countries.

Population estimates: A total pre-breeding population of about 8,600,000; 4,800,000 in England, 2,300,000 in Scotland and 1,500,000 in Wales. To improve this estimate, more information is needed on the population densities of pygmy shrews in a range of habitats. **Reliability of population estimate: 4.**

Historical changes: Unknown. At the turn of the century, pygmy shrews were thought to be generally, but sparsely, distributed (Millais 1904-1906). At that time, the distribution of pygmy shrews in Scotland was unclear, and there are no quantified data on which to assess any population changes.

Population trends: Unknown. The increasing use of insecticides and the loss of habitat have probably led to a population decrease, but numbers may have been increased locally by long-term set-aside (Brockless & Tapper 1993).

Population threats: Liming of watersheds is used to mitigate the effects of acidification on water quality, but one study found that this practice reduced the surface activity of pygmy shrews for up to 18 months, and this was associated with reduced food availability (Shore & Mackenzie 1993). Furthermore, liming also reduced the populations of pygmy shrews by 30-55%. This effect lasted from five months to over three years at different sites. Hence liming of upland catchment areas can have detrimental effects on pygmy shrew populations. Heavy grazing of moorlands by increased upland sheep and deer populations potentially also have removed much of the thick vegetation which pygmy shrews require.

Conversely, Environmentally Sensitive Area schemes and better grouse moor management should favour this species.

Water shrew *Neomys fodiens*

Status: Native; locally common.

Distribution: Widespread in mainland Britain but thought to be locally distributed in parts of northern Scotland. Present on Anglesey, the Isle of Arran, Bute, the Garvellachs, Islay, the Isle of Wight, Kerrera, Mull, Pabay (Skye), Raasay, Skye, South Shuna and possibly other islands (Churchfield 1991c). There are three records from Hoy (Orkney) from 1847-1964, but whether there are still water shrews on the island is unknown (Green & Green 1993).

Population data: Few water shrew density estimates are available. Peak numbers occur in the summer, and a maximum of 3·2 per ha was recorded in water-cress beds in southern England (Churchfield 1984). Whilst this may have been an under-estimate, water shrews were present at lower densities than common shrews even in this apparently optimal habitat. Other than this figure, there are no density estimates, and calculating numbers based on habitat availability is fraught with difficulties because there are no data on habitat preferences of water shrews. Whilst they are often associated with clear, fast-flowing, unpolluted rivers and streams, they are also found by ponds and drainage ditches, in north-west Scotland they occur amongst boulders on rocky beaches, and they are often found considerable distances from water in deciduous woodland (Shillito 1963b; Churchfield 1991c). However, Shillito (1963b) suggested that populations in woodland are transient and only present in the summer when there is an adequate food supply. Similarly, Tew (1994) recorded water shrews in hedgerows in arable areas, but noted that they were only transient, and suggested that linear features in farmland were important corridors for movement between preferred habitats. Even in apparently suitable habitats such as water-cress beds, Churchfield (1984) found that water shrews were intermittently nomadic, with frequent shifts of home range.

Since there is so little information on the population ecology of water shrews, population size was estimated using the relative abundance of common:water shrews in samples from a wide variety of sources and habitat types (Tables 5-8). From these a mean ratio was obtained of 22·1:1 for England, 31·7:1 for Scotland and 15·3:1 for Wales. These data suggest that water shrews are relatively more abundant in Wales, and relatively less common in Scotland.

Population estimates: A total pre-breeding population of about 1,900,000; 1,200,000 in England, 400,000 in Scotland and 300,000 in Wales. This estimate tends to agree with the relative paucity of records despite its very wide distribution - only 1228 records from 654 10 x 10 km squares (Arnold 1993). Information on water shrew population densities and behaviour in different habitat types is needed, both to improve this estimate and to understand how the species maintains such a wide distribution with a low population size. Even in an apparently favourable habitat, water shrews appear to be unable to compete with common shrews, and this may explain why populations seem to be more mobile than those of common shrews (Churchfield 1984). It may also explain why the species exists at low population densities. **Reliability of population estimate: 4.**

Historical changes: Unknown. At the turn of the century it was described as 'not by any means a rare animal, but would appear to be of local distribution' (Barrett-Hamilton & Hinton 1910-1921), and 'fairly common in England and Wales, as well as in Scotland' (Millais 1904-1906). Whether the current paucity of records indicates a population change is unknown.

Population trends: Unknown; there are no data on which to assess population changes. Water shrews may be declining, but since they are patchily distributed and populations are sometimes ephemeral, the problems of monitoring population changes are considerable.

Population threats: Although there is no firm evidence, it has been suggested that water shrews may be threatened in Britain by habitat destruction, particularly in southern England, and by disturbance and modification of waterside banks and vegetation (Churchfield 1991c). Water quality may also be a significant factor affecting water shrew populations, although the precise effect of water quality on water shrew populations is unknown (Churchfield 1991c). A survey of the quality of rivers, canals and estuaries in England and Wales in 1990 found that 89% of rivers, 90% of canals and 90% of estuaries were of either 'good' or 'fair' quality, as defined by the National Water Council, and 2%, 1% and 3% respectively were of 'bad' quality. These figures suggest that overall water quality in Britain is declining. Compared to a similar survey in 1985, about 15% of the total river length was downgraded, about 11% upgraded. Comparable changes for canals were 15% and 7%, and for estuaries 3% and 1% (National Rivers Authority 1991).

Lesser white-toothed shrew *Crocidura suaveolens*

Status: Introduced to the Isles of Scilly, probably in the Iron Age or earlier.

Distribution: Found on all but some of the smaller of the Isles of Scilly, with records from Bryher, Gugh, St. Agnes, St. Mary's, St. Martin's, Samson, Tean and Tresco. Lesser white-toothed shrews are also thought to occur on Annet (Spencer-Booth 1956).

Population data: They are commonly found in tall vegetation such as bracken, hedgebanks and woodlands, but are also found amongst boulders and vegetation on the shores. The peak density recorded is 1 per 30 m² (Pernetta 1973), but a more realistic average density is likely to be around 1 per 100 m². Spencer-Booth (1956, 1963) suggested that densities are higher at the top of the beaches than inland.

To estimate population size, a map of scale 1:10,560 was used to calculate the areas of suitable habitat on the main islands colonised by lesser white-toothed shrews. There were approximately 70 km of shoreline, 100 km of hedgerows and 500 ha of natural heathland-type vegetation. Densities of 1 per 10 m of shoreline, 1 per 50 m of hedgerow and 10 per ha of natural vegetation were used to estimate population size.

Population estimates: A total pre-breeding population of about 14,000, all in England. A great deal more information is needed on the habitat selection and population density of this species in different habitats to improve the population estimate. **Reliability of population estimate:** 4.

Historical changes: Unknown.

Population trends: Unknown.

Population threats: The species appears to be well-established, and there are no known population threats.

Order: Chiroptera

Because the population threats, population trends and methods of estimating population size were similar for many of the species of bat, a general section is included, and specific comments only made as they apply to individual species. In particular, producing population estimates for bats was especially difficult since there were few density estimates and little quantified data on bat numbers in relation to habitat associations and patterns of land use. Thus many of the population estimates were based on subjective estimates of relative abundance. Whilst such estimates may not be supported by quantitative data, those included here were based on the considerable amounts of field experience of the workers consulted, and since these

workers were in general agreement as to the size of the estimate, the figures are the best available. However, there is clearly scope to improve the quality of the data available on bat population sizes and population trends in Britain.

Population data: For greater and lesser horseshoe bats, population sizes are reasonably well documented from regular roost and/or hibernacula counts, but for most species of bat there are few data on population sizes. Therefore the population of pipistrelles *Pipistrellus pipistrellus* was estimated by Speakman (1991) by multiplying independent estimates of population densities of these bats in three areas (two in Scotland, one in Yorkshire) by their known current range. For those species for which there were no direct density or population estimates, Speakman (1991) calculated population sizes from the frequency of reports of roosts of those species relative to those for pipistrelles, using returns made to the Nature Conservancy Council. Details of the roost records he used are given in Mitchell-Jones *et al.* (1986). The figures were adjusted to take into account mean roost size relative to that for pipistrelles. Since most of the roost records he used refer to nursery roosts in houses, the same technique could not be used for Daubenton's bat *Myotis daubentonii* and the noctule *Nyctalus noctula*, which rarely use houses for their nursery roosts. Their populations were estimated from general reports of abundance relative to other species in surveys undertaken by local bat groups, and so their population estimates were likely to be the least accurate (Speakman 1991).

There are several problems with this approach. In particular, densities calculated for north-east Scotland by Speakman *et al.* (1991a) were minimum estimates, and the number of new bat roosts being found on their study area showed no signs of reaching an asymptote. What proportion of roosts had been found is unknown, and so how much influence this had on Speakman's (1991) estimate for the size of the pipistrelle population, and hence every species of bat scaled in abundance relative to pipistrelles, is unknown. Also, Speakman (1991) based his calculations on the mean size of pipistrelle roosts in north-east Scotland in the early summer, i.e. 117 (Speakman *et al.* 1991a), yet in recent years Scottish roosts have tended to be larger than those in England, and mean roost size for Britain as a whole, excluding records of only one or two bats, is 75·00 ± 1·82 (s.e.) (n = 2679) (A.J. Mitchell-Jones pers. comm.). This will have biased those of Speakman's (1991) estimates which included a measure of roost size relative to pipistrelles. There are other confounding effects, since colonies for some species (e.g. pipistrelle) are relatively mobile, whereas those for others, e.g. serotine *Eptesicus serotinus* are not, and for species such as the pipistrelle a number of roost reports may refer to one colony. Finally, Speakman's calculations were based on the area of the British Isles (308,700 km², i.e. including all of Ireland), whereas this review only covers Great Britain excluding the Channel Islands and the Isle of Man, a land area of 230,367 km²; thus for this review his figures have been adjusted accordingly for species that occur in Ireland. The population estimates obtained were for adult bats only at the start of the breeding season.

Independent estimates were also provided by A.M. Hutson, A.J. Mitchell-Jones and R.E. Stebbings, who all based their estimates on the calculations made by Speakman (1991) and the known distribution and relative abundance of each species of bat. Whilst this is a subjective approach, population size for some species (e.g. greater and lesser horseshoe bats) is reasonably well documented, and so there is a known basis from which to calculate relative population sizes. Thus, to determine whether the estimates for each species of bat were accurate at least to the right order of abundance, the relative proportions of each species in a variety of samples were compared (Table 9). Obviously each sample is biased. Those species that habitually roost in houses (Table 10) predominated in the enquiries made to the Nature Conservancy Council (and subsequently the country agencies). Yet even within house-roosting species there are biases.

For example, inspections of lofts revealed a higher proportion of brown long-eared bats *Plecotus auritus* relative to pipistrelles than did records of bats seen emerging from lofts. This is because pipistrelles leave their roost earlier than long-eared bats, and tend to occur in larger colonies (A.J. Mitchell-Jones pers. comm.). In contrast, Daubenton's bat was over-represented in records submitted to the Biological Records Centre because it is frequently recorded whilst seen hunting over water and at hibernation sites. Whilst the pipistrelle is the commonest bat, it was the species most likely to be under-reported to the Biological Records Centre, since recorders are more prone to report rare species or unusual records.

The least biased sample is probably the carcasses submitted for rabies examination, and when the relative proportion of each species in this sample is compared with the estimates of population size (Table 11), there is a good overall level of concordance. The exceptions to this are Daubenton's bat, whose riparian life style suggests that corpses are likely to be under-represented in the sample; brown long-eared bat, a species likely to be over-represented because it is prone to injury, such as by cats (A.M. Hutson pers. comm.); and the serotine, whose comparative over-representation may have been due to its large size and/or dependence on houses and as a result of the current research interest in this species (J.R. Speakman pers. comm.), so that carcasses were particularly likely to be submitted for examination. However, overall the agreement between the relative proportions in the sample submitted for rabies examination and the population sizes estimated here is remarkably close, and where the figures differ there are explanations to account for the disparity. Since the relative proportions for the two horseshoe bats, whose actual population sizes are reasonably well known, agree well, it suggests that the estimates for other species are also likely to be correct, at least to the right order of magnitude.

Population trends: These are particularly difficult to evaluate, since there is a paucity of historical data on bat population sizes, and so the following assessments are tentative. For the 14 species known to be breeding in Britain, only one (the lesser horseshoe) is considered to be increasing in some areas. The populations of two species (Natterer's bat *Myotis nattereri* and barbastelle *Barbastella barbastellus*) may be stable. Three species (greater horseshoe, noctule and brown long-eared) are believed to have declined this century or currently are believed to be declining, and for the rest current population trends are even less clear.

Counting bats emerging from roosts during the summer has been used to monitor population trends (R.E. Stebbings pers. comm.). These roosts are predominantly, but not exclusively, pipistrelle nursery roosts, and these counts provide a valuable long-term data set on population trends for the commonest species of bat (Table 12). However, care must be taken when interpreting these data. People tend to count large colonies as they are more obvious and impressive, and any such bias is most likely to exert an influence in the early days of the survey, when the number of roosts surveyed was small. With time, some roosts are abandoned, whereas others are either located for the first time or are genuinely new roosts. Whether the loss of a roost indicates a decline in bat numbers or a decline in the suitability of that particular roost site is usually unknown, as is whether new roosts indicate a change in location or an increase in bat numbers. Also, a mean decline in colony size could represent more small colonies rather than an actual decline in bat numbers, or else be due to a combination of the two factors. Finally, although a large number of roosts were involved in estimating the change from 1991 to 1992 (387), the number of colonies in 1979 was much lower, and for each of north England, Scotland and Wales was five or fewer. Thus changes are calculated against a very small baseline, and for Wales, mean colony size was particularly large, whereas for Scotland it was below average. Not surprisingly, against this baseline Wales

has subsequently shown the greatest decline and Scotland the greatest increase. If 1980 is taken as the baseline, when the total number of roosts counted exceeded 200, a similar but generally less extreme pattern is seen (Table 13). Using the current estimate of 2,000,000 pipistrelles, these figures on roost declines suggest that in 1980 the population was 3,500,000. If 1978 is used as the baseline, it suggests that there were then 7,500,000 pipistrelles. This figure does seem very high, and it is also difficult to see why 4,000,000 pipistrelles died in the two years 1978-1980. In the absence of any evidence to explain this dramatic change over two years, it seems more likely that the small samples in 1978 produced a skewed baseline figure.

Whilst it is not possible to use colony counts to produce an exact measure of bat population changes, especially since many of the yearly differences shown in Tables 12 and 13 were not statistically different, they do provide data on relative and regional trends. Thus the most significant changes occurred prior to the mid-1980s, and thereafter bat population changes have been much smaller. Also, the declines appear to have been greatest in south-east England, the midlands and Wales, whereas in Scotland mean roost size has increased (R.E. Stebbings & H.R. Arnold pers. comm.). In Scotland, pipistrelles appear to be found in fewer, larger roosts, and so roost size itself is not a measure of population density. However, whilst the declines have been greater in Wales, because mean colony size was originally largest in Wales (Table 12), mean colony size in 1992 (91, n = 32) was still larger than that for England (64, n = 324). In 1992 Scotland had a mean colony count of 279 (n = 31), and in fact although only 8% of the counts were from Scotland, over half the colonies that had in excess of 500 bats were recorded there (R.E. Stebbings & H.R. Arnold pers. comm.).

Population threats: These are numerous and have been discussed by Stebbings (1988). They generally fall into three main categories. Firstly, landscape changes can cause a significant reduction in foraging area due to loss of old pasture, deciduous woodland and the improvement and clearance of water courses. Woodland can be improved as a foraging habitat for bats by increasing the number of tree species and structural diversity (Mayle 1990). The removal of hedgerows and other linear features may lead to habitat fragmentation and the loss of foraging areas for the smaller species of bat, which are reluctant to cross open areas (Limpens *et al.* 1989). Furthermore, the removal of hollow trees, especially in hedgerows, is likely to have a serious impact on tree-roosting species, due to the loss of roost sites. A recent analysis indicated that in some landscapes in Britain there is a shortage of suitable foraging habitats, and this may be limiting bat numbers in these areas (Walsh, Harris & Hutson 1995). Secondly, the use of harmful pesticides, the insulation of cavity walls, the repointing of walls and the reroofing and the renovation of bridges and old buildings may be killing and/or excluding many species of bat that roost in buildings. In particular, the use of persistent insecticides such as lindane to protect timber in buildings from insects has been a serious threat (Mitchell-Jones *et al.* 1989). In the 1970s it was estimated that in Britain over 100,000 buildings underwent remedial timber treatment for wood-boring insects each year, and this posed a significant conservation problem for bats. However, following the discovery that timbers treated with lindane are potentially lethal for long periods (Racey & Swift 1986; Boyd, Myhill & Mitchell-Jones 1988), the number of timber-treatment products containing lindane or pentachlorophenol has declined from 72% to 10% from 1988 to 1992, and the lindane-based products should soon disappear from use (Mitchell-Jones, Hutson & Racey 1993). Bat population declines due to organochlorine insecticide poisoning may have been occurring for the last thirty years. Jefferies (1972) reported high levels of dieldrin and DDT in bats from the east midlands in the 1960s; it was thought that these pollutants were acquired from their insect prey. Laboratory tests showed that pipistrelles were particularly sensitive to DDT. Jefferies (1972) found that during 1968/1969, bats sampled from the east

midlands were carrying one third of the lethal level of organochlorine insecticides as 'background' residues, this rising to just under the lethal level after hibernation. D.J. Jefferies (pers. comm.) suggested that organochlorine insecticides were causing declines in bat populations from the late 1950s until at least 1975. The third main threat is disturbance; this is a particular threat for species that roost and/or hibernate underground. Disturbance of hibernating bats causes a significant decline in a bat's potential duration of hibernation due to a reduction in the fat stores associated with metabolic activity (Speakman, Webb & Racey 1991). Also, the large numbers of mines that have been solidly capped are lost both as hibernacula and as nursery sites for cave-dwelling species. Thus to help maintain bat populations, it is probable that roost sites, hibernation sites, foraging areas and corridors for movement must all be maintained. A conservation strategy that does not consider all these aspects is unlikely to be successful.

One other problem is that British bats are generally *K*-strategists (Gaisler 1989). They produce only one young annually, rarely twins, but compensate by living far longer than other small mammals, sometimes over 20 years. Features of their reproductive strategy such as low fecundity, delayed reproduction and a low intrinsic rate of population growth all mean that bats are slow to increase their population size following a decline, and so are vulnerable to further perturbations. Thus small population sizes are likely to put bats at greater risk than other groups of British mammals.

Greater horseshoe bat *Rhinolophus ferrumequinum*

Status: Native; very rare and endangered.

Distribution: Confined to south-west England and south Wales, south of the line Cardigan-Cheltenham-Southampton, including the Isle of Wight; vagrants are occasionally recorded elsewhere. Last century greater horseshoe bats were found in and around

London, including Hampstead Heath and Regents Park (Mickleburgh 1988; Stebbings 1989a).

Population data: There are a number of recent population estimates, and these are based on counts of summer roosts and hibernacula; there are now 35 known breeding and all-year roosts, and 369 hibernation sites (A.J. Mitchell-Jones pers. comm.). Recent increases in the number of known roosts has resulted in increased estimates of population size but these do not represent an actual population increase. Thus there were believed to be about 2200 greater horseshoe bats in 1983 (Stebbings & Griffith 1986), and 3500-3800 in the late 1980s (R.E. Stebbings pers. comm.). The minimum population size in 1992 was estimated by R.D. Ransome (pers. comm.) to be 2500, but that did not include counts from a new site discovered in Cornwall. Recently, R.E. Stebbings (pers. comm.) suggested the figure for the current population should be 4000, since two more traditional nurseries had been found since his last estimate. Hutson (1993) also estimated the population to number 4000. R.E. Stebbings (pers. comm.) estimated population size from the number of young born in all the nurseries and relating those figures to an average proportion of the number of adult bats in the nursery cluster compared with estimates of total population sizes for three colonies as determined by detailed capture-mark-recapture studies. This gave a total population estimate that was three to four times the size of the nurseries. A.J. Mitchell-Jones (pers. comm.) also suggested that, in the absence of better information, the total population was three times the number seen emerging from summer nursery roosts. Based on this technique, he estimated the maximum population size to be 6600. P. Chapman (pers. comm.) also suggested that 4000 is probably too low, and that 6600 is a more reasonable figure.

Population estimates: A total pre-breeding population of at least 4000, and possibly nearer 6600; in England 3650, in Scotland 0 and in Wales 350. Intensive searches for this species suggest that very few new colonies will be found, although a better understanding of the percentage of the population recorded at nursery roosts is likely to refine the estimate for total population size. **Reliability of population estimate:** 2.

Historical changes: Yalden (1992) argued that this large and characteristic inhabitant of caves ought to be prominent in sub-fossil and fossil cave faunas, and that its relative scarcity suggests that it was neither more widely distributed nor, perhaps, more abundant in former times. In more recent times, it was present in Kent until *circa* 1900 and at the turn of the century was considered to be fairly numerous on the Isle of Wight (Millais 1904-1906). It was also abundant in some parts of the south-west (Barrett-Hamilton & Hinton 1910-1921). This century there was a significant population decline and a loss of over half of its previous range (Stebbings 1988). It has been suggested that the population earlier this century may have numbered around 300,000 (Stebbings & Arnold 1989); this estimate was based on an estimated earlier distribution of about 6,000,000 ha and a known bat density for one particular colony of 0·05 per ha. Recently R.E. Stebbings (pers. comm.) has revised his estimate to about 330,000. Obviously, this estimate is based on a number of assumptions, many of which cannot be tested. In particular, the density at one colony may not be typical for the whole range. In optimum habitat the population density may have been considerably higher but there would also have been areas that were sparsely occupied (R.E. Stebbings pers. comm.).

Stebbings (1988) suggested that this decline in numbers occurred mostly during 1950-1980; of at least 58 nursery colonies that were known then, only 12 now produce more than five young per year. However, Ransome (1989) argued that the long-term studies in Devon from 1948 (Hooper & Hooper 1956; Hooper 1983) showed that this population did not number many thousands in the early 1950s, a view supported by J.H.D. Hooper (pers. comm.), because there is a shortage of suitable hibernacula over large areas of the range estimated by Stebbings (1988). J.H.D. Hooper (pers. comm.) suggested that, in the 1950s, up to 600 was a reasonable estimate for the population in south Devon, a long way short of the many thousands suggested by R.E. Stebbings (pers. comm.). Similarly, Ransome (1989) questioned the estimate of Stebbings & Arnold (1987) that the population in Dorset alone declined from 15,000 before 1953 to 90 in 1986; Ransome (1989) also argued that the British population before 1950 was probably considerably lower than 300,000. Ransome (1989), monitoring greater horseshoe bats around Bristol, found a significant decline from the winter of 1962/1963 until 1966/1967, followed by a temporary recovery and fall again between 1967/1968 and 1971/1972. This was followed by a slow recovery up to 1978/79, and relative stability until 1985/1986, with a further major reduction in 1986. The minimum number of bats alive in 1987/1988 was only 42% of the number alive in 1968/1969. J.H.D. Hooper (pers. comm.) estimated that the greater horseshoe bats in the Buckfastleigh/Chudleigh area in 1993 had increased to around 680, a very similar figure to when he started work in the late 1940s.

Population trends: Following a decline through the 1970s and 1980s, the population in Dorset is increasing following protection (R.E. Stebbings pers. comm.). The same applies in south Devon, where summer and winter surveys indicate that numbers have more than doubled in the last 20 years, although it is possible that this does not reflect a genuine increase but is due to immigration or to the adoption of improved monitoring techniques (P. Chapman pers. comm.). The south Wales population is believed to be stable or undergoing a small decline. The population in the Cotswold area is continuing to decline. Ransome (1989) has shown that population growth is limited by summer weather: poor summers lead to late births and, when followed by unfavourable weather and poor food supplies in late August and early September, lead to slow growth of juveniles, thereby reducing their chances of over-winter survival. Thus, at small population sizes, greater horseshoe bats seem to be particularly vulnerable to population declines as a result of a series of cold and wet summers.

Population threats: Populations benefited from mines for limestone, ochre and metal extraction falling into disuse early this century. More recently, many closures for safety reasons are thought to have seriously depressed numbers in Dorset and, to a lesser extent, in Avon, Gloucestershire, Somerset and Wiltshire (Ransome 1991a). Of 426 known hibernacula, 97 (23%) are SSSIs or proposed SSSIs, and these cover 72% of the known hibernating population of greater horseshoe bats (Mitchell-Jones, Hutson & Racey 1993). Although formerly roosting in caves in both summer and winter, this species now depends on buildings during the summer, since few cave sites provide sufficiently high temperatures for successful breeding (Arnold 1993). Large colonies are also known to have died following the use of pesticides (Stebbings 1988). The decline in numbers of large beetles (a major food source) following habitat changes, especially the loss of old pasture, potentially poses a major threat to the survival of greater horseshoe bats in many areas (Stebbings 1988).

Lesser horseshoe bat *Rhinolophus hipposideros*

Status: Native; rare and endangered.

Distribution: Widely distributed in south-west England and Wales, south and west of a line from Chester to Southampton. At the turn of the century lesser horseshoe bats were also found in Durham, the Peak District, North Yorkshire and Northumberland (Millais 1904-1906) and were still present in Surrey and Kent in the 1950s. Hibernating records from Yorkshire in the early 1980s have yet to be confirmed. Records elsewhere are of vagrants.

Population data: These were based on counts of known colonies. Heaver (1987) estimated a total population in 1985 of 4800

(1300 in south-west England, 1000 in the English border counties and 2500 in Wales), based on details of 261 hibernacula and 151 summer roosts known to have been in use since 1980. Stebbings (1988) suggested that the adult population was probably nearer 8000. More recently, as a result of intensive roost surveys, there are now 227 known breeding and all-year roosts, and 605 hibernation sites. Thus Hutson (1993), using estimates of known summer colonies plus estimates for colonies in areas where only hibernating populations were known, estimated that there were 7000 lesser horseshoe bats in Wales alone, with a comparable number in England, giving a total population of 14,000 (Hutson 1993). A.J. Mitchell-Jones (pers. comm.) provided a second estimate based on the maximum number of bats counted at each site since 1981 for 381 sites in England and 273 in Wales. The results were very similar to Hutson's (1993) estimate, i.e. 6947 in England and 6747 in Wales.

Population estimates: A total pre-breeding population of about 14,000; 7000 in England, none in Scotland and 7000 in Wales. Recent intensive searches for this species have improved the data on which the population estimate is based, and it is unlikely that further work will substantially increase this population estimate. **Reliability of population estimate: 2.**

Historical changes: Since this species seems to feed more in scrubby deciduous woodland and less over grassland than does the greater horseshoe bat, it may have been more abundant and/or widespread when woodland was more abundant (Yalden 1992). In the early 1900s, the lesser horseshoe bat was, as today, more widely distributed than the greater horseshoe bat (Kelsall 1887; Millais 1904-1906), and was found locally in some numbers, but was not common (Thorburn 1920). Since 1950 the lesser horseshoe bat has disappeared from much of the north of its European range, and colonies appear to be declining (often by up to 90%) over its European range (Stebbings 1988).

Population trends: Current population trends are less clear, since populations are highly localised and variable in size. The loss of abandoned mine sites probably depressed numbers and/or led to a range reduction, whereas densities in forested areas have increased recently (Ransome 1991b). Consequently this species has probably benefited from increased afforestation. The survey by Heaver (1987) suggested that there had been a range reduction, but with increased densities within the range. Based on roost counts, R.E. Stebbings (pers. comm.) estimated that, in the seven years up to 1992, there had been an overall size reduction of 12% in 36 roosts in England and Wales, but for the 24 roosts in Wales this reduction was 22%, although it is unlikely that this represented a real population decline. Certainly, there appears to have been a recent slight increase in range, with bats occurring further east in Dorset, although this may be due to increased recorder effort, and there has been an increase in population size in south Wiltshire (R.E Stebbings pers. comm.). Data from hibernacula in south-west England suggest that there has also been a population increase in this area (G. Jones pers. comm.). Overall, in the absence of hard winters for a number of years (see below), it seems that lesser horseshoe bats have been maintaining population levels and increasing in some areas (R.E. Stebbings pers. comm.).

Population threats: Reasons for the dramatic range reduction in much of northern Europe are unclear; in Britain the loss of mine sites has probably led to a range reduction. The loss of roosts is a continuing problem, and the lesser horseshoe bat is thought to be very vulnerable to severe winters since many colonies appear to lack suitable hibernacula to protect them from low temperatures (R.E. Stebbings pers. comm.). Of 909 known hibernacula, 161 (18%) are SSSIs or proposed SSSIs, including 53% of the known hibernating population of lesser horseshoe bats (Mitchell-Jones, Hutson & Racey 1993).

Whiskered bat *Myotis mystacinus*

Status: Native; locally distributed.

Distribution: Probably found throughout England and Wales. There are a few records from southern Scotland as far north as the Firth of Forth (Ayrshire, Borders, Dumfriesshire and Midlothian); it is probably absent from the highlands. Its status in Scotland is uncertain, although it is probably rare (Haddow, Herman & Hewitt 1989; J. Herman pers. comm.).

Population data: Speakman (1991) based his estimate on the ratio of the number of recorded whiskered/Brandt's roosts relative to pipistrelles, with the assumptions that whiskered bat roosts were on average the same size as pipistrelle roosts, that both species have an equal propensity to roost in buildings and that the roosts are equally mobile. Until 1970 whiskered and Brandt's bats were regarded as one species. They are difficult to tell apart, and most recent records still do not differentiate the two species. Speakman's (1991) estimate (adjusted for the area covered in this review) for the two species combined was 131,600. Of those records that do differentiate (n = 155), 69.4% were for whiskered bats (Arnold 1993). Assuming that this represents the true ratio of occurrence of the two species, the number of whiskered bats would be 90,000, based on Speakman's (1991) calculations. However, whiskered bat roosts are, on average, probably much smaller than the 117 (the mean for pipistrelle roosts) used by Speakman (1991) (A.M. Hutson pers. comm.). R.E. Stebbings (pers. comm.) suggested that whiskered bat colonies are approximately one third the size of pipistrelle colonies, and so estimated a population size of 30,000 to 40,000. A.J. Mitchell-Jones (pers. comm.) also estimated a population size of around 40,000, using the same arguments as R.E. Stebbings.

Population estimates: A total pre-breeding population of about 40,000; in England 30,500, in Scotland 1500 and in Wales 8000. At present there is only a limited amount of

information on this species, in particular on its abundance in different parts of Britain and its abundance relative to Brandt's bat. **Reliability of population estimate: 4.**

Historical changes: At the end of last century Harting (1888) suggested that whiskered/Brandt's bats were either overlooked or mistaken for pipistrelles. Thus the early status of this bat in Britain is unclear, partly because of confusion between whiskered/Brandt's bats and pipistrelles and partly because, until 1970, Brandt's bat was not recognised as a separate species in this country. However, in the late 1800s whiskered/Brandt's bats were considered to be generally distributed, and abundant in some counties such as Yorkshire, where they equalled brown long-eared bats and pipistrelles in abundance (Millais 1904-1906; Barrett-Hamilton & Hinton 1910-1921). Thorburn (1920) described them as numerous in various parts of the southern, western and midland counties, and not uncommon in Wales. In Scotland there were no confirmed records prior to 1987 (Haddow, Herman & Hewitt 1989).

Population trends: If this assessment of their relative abundance last century was correct, it would suggest there has been a significant decline in their relative abundance compared to pipistrelles, and hence a disproportionately large decline in the number of whiskered/Brandt's bats, although their range appears to be much as it was a century ago.

Brandt's bat *Myotis brandtii*

Status: Native; common in west and north England, rare or absent elsewhere.

Distribution: This is unclear because of confusion with whiskered bats, but Brandt's bats are believed to be widespread in England and Wales. The status of this species in Scotland is less clear. There is one record for 1874 from Rannoch, Perthshire (Haddow, Herman & Hewitt 1989), one recent record from England close to the Scottish border

(Arnold 1993), and several recent records in southern Scotland, particularly Dumfriesshire (R.E. Stebbings pers. comm.).

Population data: Speakman (1991) based his estimate on the ratio of the number of whiskered/Brandt's roosts relative to pipistrelles, and the assumption that the roosts of Brandt's bat were, on average, the same size as pipistrelle roosts. This assumption on roost size was unrealistic (see whiskered bat). This approach also assumed that both species have an equal propensity to roost in buildings and that the roosts are equally mobile. An estimate for the number of Brandt's bats was calculated from Speakman's (1991) adjusted estimate for whiskered/Brandt's bat, as described for whiskered bat; this suggested a population size of 40,000. However, Brandt's bat roosts probably contain, on average, far fewer bats than the 117 used by Speakman (1991) as the average size of pipistrelle roosts (A.M. Hutson pers. comm.). R.E. Stebbings (pers. comm.) suggested that Brandt's bat is only slightly rarer than whiskered bat, and so estimated that there are 30,000 Brandt's bats, based on his calculation of the number of whiskered bats. However, from hibernacula in Kent and Sussex, A.M. Hutson (pers. comm.) found that Brandt's outnumbered whiskered bats by about 1·5:1, and S. Bradley (pers. comm.) also thought that Brandt's predominated over whiskered bats in hibernacula in northern England. Clearly further work is needed to determine the relative abundance of Brandt's and whiskered bats.

Population estimates: A total pre-breeding population of about 30,000; 22,500 in England, 500 in Scotland and 7000 in Wales. Very little is known about this species in Britain, and it is not even clear whether Brandt's bat is more or less common than the whiskered bat. **Reliability of population estimate: 5.**

Historical changes: These are unknown due to early confusion with whiskered bats; see above for an account of whiskered/Brandt's bats.

Population trends: Unknown due to early confusion with whiskered bats; see above for an account of whiskered/Brandt's bats.

Natterer's bat *Myotis nattereri*

Status: Native; fairly common throughout much of Britain.

Distribution: Found throughout England and Wales; recent records have extended the known range of Natterer's bats in Scotland to all areas except the extreme north-west (Haddow 1992).

Population data: Speakman (1991) based his estimate on the ratio of the number of known Natterer's bat roosts relative to pipistrelle, and the assumptions that Natterer's bat roosts were, on average, the same size as pipistrelle roosts, that Natterer's bats have an equal propensity to roost in houses, and that the roosts are equally mobile. Correcting Speakman's (1991) estimate for the area covered by this review produced a population estimate of about 60,000. However, Natterer's bat maternity roosts are usually smaller than those for pipistrelles (A.M. Hutson pers. comm.), although Natterer's bat is a very widespread species, and R.E. Stebbings (pers. comm.) suggested that the population size is larger than that estimated by Speakman (1991). A.M. Hutson (pers. comm.) agreed, and he estimated 100,000 Natterer's bats, based on the belief that they are more common than whiskered and Brandt's bats combined.

Population estimates: A total pre-breeding population of about 100,000; 70,000 in England, 17,500 in Scotland and 12,500 in Wales. Since there is little information on this species, further data on its abundance relative to other species are needed in order to refine the population estimate. **Reliability of population estimate: 4.**

Historical changes: At the turn of the century, Natterer's bats were thought to be generally distributed but somewhat local

(Millais 1904-1906), and the known distribution (Harting 1889a; Millais 1904-1906) was very similar to that today, suggesting that there has been no significant change in distribution. Whether there has been any significant change in status is unknown.

Population trends: Currently unknown.

Bechstein's bat *Myotis bechsteinii*

Status: Native; very rare in central southern England.

Distribution: Most records are from south-west England and the Isle of Wight; there are some recent records from the south-west midlands (R.E. Stebbings pers. comm.), and one was found in Brecon in Wales in 1993 (J. Messenger pers. comm.).

Population data: All the records in Britain up to 1989 are detailed by Stebbings (1989b). There are no recent records of breeding colonies in Britain, the only accepted record of a nursery cluster being from Hampshire in 1886, and all the summer records are of single individuals. Since 1960, Bechstein's bat has only been recorded from 19 10 x 10 km squares (Arnold 1993). This is a truly woodland species which lives almost exclusively in hollow trees, and hence is difficult to find. In the absence of any firm information on this species, it is difficult to calculate the actual population size except on subjective criteria.

Speakman (1991) estimated the population to be *circa* 100 individuals, but assuming that this is a resident species that breeds in Britain, this is almost certainly far too low an estimate for a breeding population found over a relatively large area. A.M. Hutson and A.J. Mitchell-Jones (pers. comms) suggest that a population of at least 1000 would be needed to maintain a viable population over such a large area, and R.E. Stebbings (pers. comm.) suggests 1500-2000, although he argued that even this may be too low an estimate. This population estimate is based on the assumption that the species is resident and breeding. However, in the absence of known breeding colonies, and in view of the paucity of records, it could equally be argued that the species is only a vagrant in Britain (J.R. Speakman pers. comm.).

Population estimates: A total pre-breeding population of about 1500, all in England; whether there is an established population in Wales is currently unknown. **Reliability of population estimate: 4.**

Historical changes: There is some archaeological evidence that Bechstein's bat was much more abundant over 2000 years ago both in Britain and Poland, and being a 'foliage-gleaner', it appears to have been a major casualty of the post-Neolithic clearance of deciduous woodland (Yalden 1992). At the turn of the century records were few, and even then it was considered to be the rarest British bat (Barrett-Hamilton & Hinton 1910-1921); Millais (1904-1906) listed three known records, and fifteen years later this had only increased to six (Thorburn 1920).

Population trends: It may be that the species is, and in recent times always has been, rare throughout its range, and that populations are stable at low levels. If so, the current low numbers do not represent a recent decline. However, fragmentation of woodlands (see below) may have led to a population decline (R.E. Stebbings pers. comm.).

Population threats: If the population is as low as is currently believed, this species is one of Britain's rarest resident mammals and, in view of the low numbers, it must be very vulnerable to further population declines due to chance events. Also, it is thought to be characteristic of ancient deciduous woodland (Yalden 1992), and because it does not like flying in open areas, fragmentation of woodland is likely to pose a significant threat which may have led to population declines.

Greater mouse-eared bat *Myotis myotis*

Status: Records last century from southern England were discounted, but it is possible that this species occurred as an occasional vagrant, although there is no evidence that it was resident in Britain before the 1940s (Stebbings 1992). Colonies reported this century were probably never well established and are now extinct.

Distribution: All recent records are confined to south coast counties of England.

Population data: A small hibernating population was discovered in Dorset in 1956 and numbered at least 12 in December 1960. However, one of the nursery sites, discovered after the colony had effectively died out, suggested that the population was larger in the 1950s (Stebbings 1992). This colony was extinct by 1980. A stray migrant was recorded in Kent in the winter of 1985. The last known hibernating population was in Sussex; discovered in 1969 (Phillips & Blackmore 1970). The sex ratio of bats marked, and ringing returns, suggest that the colony probably numbered around 50 individuals (Stebbings 1992). However, it appears that the nursery colony was destroyed in 1974 (its whereabouts was unknown) (Stebbings & Griffith 1986), and only one male remained from 1985 to 1990. There have been no more recent records of this species (Stebbings & Hutson 1991).

Population estimates: Extinct. **Reliability of population estimate:** 1.

Historical changes: This species has probably never been other than an occasional resident in Britain, and at the turn of the century there were only a few occasional confirmed occurrences, although records were more widely distributed (Barrett-Hamilton & Hinton 1910-1921).

Population trends: Its largely south coast distribution in Britain suggests that colonies are periodically established, and it is possible that colonies will become established again.

However, at present, populations of greater mouse-eared bats are much reduced in the whole of north-west Europe, and the chances of recolonisation would appear to be remote until such time as populations generally have built up again (Stebbings 1992; Hutson 1993).

Population threats: It is probable that the Dorset colony was destroyed by excessive disturbance and popular interest. In addition it has been suggested that some were lost due to timber treatment of a roost, and that the nursery roost of the Sussex colony was destroyed by an unrecorded event (Stebbings 1992; R.E. Stebbings pers. comm.).

Daubenton's bat *Myotis daubentonii*

Status: Native; common throughout much of Britain.

Distribution: Widespread north at least to Inverness, and probably occurs throughout all of mainland Scotland, but only one roost is currently known north of the Great Glen (J.R. Speakman pers. comm.). The known distribution in Scotland is documented by Haddow (1992). A survey around Sheffield, South Yorkshire showed that Daubenton's bats are absent or rarely seen at altitudes greater than 200 m or in urban and industrial areas (Clarkson & Whiteley 1985).

Population data: Although a widespread species, it is to a large extent associated with riparian habitats and colony size tends to be small, i.e. 5-25 bats (R.E. Stebbings pers. comm.). Speakman (1991) based his adjusted estimate of 160,000 on the ratio of Daubenton's bats to other species in surveys organised by local Bat Groups. In Great Britain as a whole R.E. Stebbings (pers. comm.) estimated that Daubenton's bat is probably of similar abundance to Natterer's bat. Thus he suggested a population of 90,000-100,000. A.M. Hutson (pers. comm.) also argued that the very few known summer roosts, and the paucity of winter records from underground sites, gives a false impression of rarity. The species is widespread, associated with any area of open water, and he suggested that overall it is one and a half times as common as Natterer's bat. Thus he estimated a population size of 150,000. However, it is equally true that the concentration of this species around open water could give a false impression of its relative abundance, and so this could lead to an over-estimate of population size (A.M. Hutson pers. comm.).

Population estimates: A total pre-breeding population of about 150,000; 95,000 in England, 40,000 in Scotland and 15,000 in Wales. These estimates are based on its abundance relative to other species and the belief that the paucity of roost records gives a false impression of rarity. **Reliability of population estimate:** 4.

Historical changes: For a long time this was considered to be one of the rarer British bats, although even last century Harting (1889b) suggested that it had been overlooked or mistaken for other species. At the turn of the century Daubenton's bat was considered to be abundant in every part of England and Wales that afforded suitable combinations of water and woods (Barrett-Hamilton & Hinton 1910-1921), and in Scotland it was widespread but local with records as far north as Banffshire. However, this species is subsequently thought to have declined in the north. A survey in north-east Scotland suggested that at the start of the century Daubenton's bat may have been the commonest bat in the area but it is currently the rarest (Speakman *et al.* 1991b). Reasons for this perceived change are unknown, although different sampling methods may be partly responsible.

Population trends: There is no specific information on current population trends in Britain, but in Europe there have been significant increases in the numbers of Daubenton's bat (e.g. Daan 1980; Gaisler, Hanák & Horácek 1981). These increases may be because aquatic insects, which form the major source of food, have not declined in the same way that terrestrial insects have as a result of the use of insecticides (Daan 1980). In particular, eutrophication of fresh waters

may even have increased food availability for Daubenton's bats (Daan 1980). Changes in water quality in Britain (National Rivers Authority 1991) may lead to changes in the availability of suitable insect prey, and potentially affect the number of Daubenton's bats in the long term.

Serotine *Eptesicus serotinus*

Status: Native; widespread in southern Britain.

Distribution: Well established south-east of a line from Bristol to Great Yarmouth (including the Isle of Wight), with a few records from south-west England, central and south Wales, and one each from Nottinghamshire and Yorkshire (Arnold 1993). These latter records may be vagrants or evidence of a recent range extension.

Population data: Based on the ratio of the number of serotine roosts relative to pipistrelles, and a mean roost size for serotines of, on average, one tenth the size of pipistrelle roosts (C.M.C. Catto unpubl.), Speakman (1991) estimated the population size to be 15,000. R.E. Stebbings (pers. comm.) calculated the population size to be 10,000-12,000 by separating nursery from other roosts, and from the fact that serotine roosts are one quarter the size of pipistrelle roosts and not one tenth (mean $21 \cdot 4 \pm 1 \cdot 7$, n = 94; Stebbings & Robinson 1991). A.J. Mitchell-Jones (pers. comm.) agreed with this larger estimate of mean serotine roost size; his figure was $18 \cdot 4 \pm 2 \cdot 0$ (n = 66). He found that the number of nurseries was rather less than predicted from the number of casual records. A.M. Hutson (pers. comm.) suggested that whilst the species is not common, these figures could be a substantial under-estimate because there is no asymptote in the number of new roosts being found.

Population estimates: A total pre-breeding population of about 15,000; 14,750 in England, none in Scotland and 250 in Wales. However, this may be a significant under-estimate. J. Messenger (pers. comm.) believes that the species is under-recorded in Wales, and that the estimate for Wales in particular is too low. **Reliability of population estimate: 4.**

Historical changes: The known distribution and probable status at the turn of the century were much as today. Millais (1904-1906) described it as decidedly rare and local. There were only a few records from south-west England, and the serotine was regarded as rare north of the Thames (Barrett-Hamilton & Hinton 1910-1921) and rare except in a few districts in the south and south-east of England (Thorburn 1920). Thus it has always had a restricted range in Britain, but was considered to be numerous in some localities in the south-east in the mid-1800s.

Population trends: Some nursery colonies are known to have declined substantially since 1960 (Stebbings & Griffith 1986). R.E. Stebbings (pers. comm.) reported that a detailed study in East Anglia showed that the serotine population had declined by about 90% in ten years, with some colonies disappearing completely. Recent records from Nottinghamshire, Yorkshire and Wales may be indicative of a range expansion but are more likely to reflect the greater number of people recording bats; although a large bat, the serotine's crevice-dwelling habits and small colony size render it inconspicuous (Stebbings & Robinson 1991). Thus there is an absence of hard data on which to assess current population trends.

Noctule *Nyctalus noctula*

Status: Native; generally uncommon, but more numerous in well-wooded areas.

Distribution: Widespread over most of England and Wales. Vagrants were recorded in Orkney in 1976, 1978 and 1988 (Arnold 1993); there were records last century for Scotland (e.g. Millais 1904a) and there are some recent records from south-west Scotland, including a large colony near Newton Stewart (Haddow 1992). This is one of the few species of bat seen feeding over open moorland (Whiteley 1985). There have also been some recent records from North Sea oil rigs (J.R. Speakman pers. comm.).

Population data: Speakman (1991), basing his estimate on the ratio of the abundance of noctules relative to other species in surveys organised by local Bat Groups, suggested a population of about 40,000. R.E. Stebbings (pers. comm.) suggested a figure of 30,000-50,000, but had no firm data on which to base this estimate. A.M. Hutson (pers. comm.) produced an estimate of 50,000 based on their abundance relative to serotines.

Population estimates: A total pre-breeding population of about 50,000; 45,000 in England, 250 in Scotland and 4750 in Wales. The upper end of the suggested range seems a reasonable estimate, based on the relative abundance of noctules to other species of bat in the samples submitted for rabies testing. **Reliability of population estimate: 3.**

Historical changes: At the turn of the century the noctule was considered to be a common species, being described as plentiful in suitable localities in southern, eastern and midland counties, common throughout Yorkshire, abundant in Cheshire, and more or less plentiful in Lancashire (Millais 1904-1906). Further north it was rare, but there were a few records from as far north as Elgin in Scotland (Barrett-Hamilton & Hinton 1910-1921). Observations suggest a substantial and rapid decline both in range and numbers during this century, particularly after the 1940s, but there are no data with which to quantify this change (Stebbings & Griffith 1986).

Population trends: No quantitative information is available on current population trends. Although widespread, there are not many roosts in buildings and so there are few data on which to base an estimate of population trends. The loss of ancient woodlands and old hedgerows may have removed both foraging habitats and roost sites.

Leisler's bat *Nyctalus leisleri*

Status: Native; widespread but scarce in Britain.

Distribution: There are few records from Britain, and these are mostly from eastern and central England and the Welsh borders. The record from Holyhead, Gwynedd, in 1992 was probably of a vagrant (J. Messenger pers. comm.). R.E. Stebbings (pers. comm.) suggests that further work may show that the distribution covers the whole of Wales. There are two recent records from south-west Scotland (Haddow 1992), and one vagrant recorded from Shetland in 1968.

Population data: Colonies of up to 200 individuals have been recorded in a few buildings, but it is essentially a woodland species and is sometimes recorded from bat boxes in conifer plantations (Stebbings & Griffith 1986). Records from the area around Sheffield, South Yorkshire (19 in 1985) suggest that it is moderately widespread (Whiteley & Clarkson 1985). Speakman (1991) based his population estimate on the ratio of the number of Leisler's roosts relative to pipistrelle roosts, and the assumption that Leisler's roosts were on average half the size of pipistrelle roosts. This suggests that the population numbers about 4,000. However, R.E. Stebbings (pers. comm.) reported that whilst colony size can be up to 200 bats, the average is probably only a quarter that of pipistrelle roosts. Based on the distribution of the species and the number of records, R.E. Stebbings (pers. comm.) argued that Speakman's (1991) figure is far too low, and suggested that the population is around 15,000. A.M. Hutson & A.J. Mitchell-Jones (pers. comm.) based their estimate on the abundance and distribution of Leisler's bats relative to serotines. They suggested that the population is somewhere between 5000 and 15,000.

Population estimates: A total pre-breeding population of about 10,000; 9750 in England, 250 in Scotland and none currently known to occur in Wales. More information is needed to refine this estimate. **Reliability of population estimate:** 4.

Historical changes: At the turn of the century Leisler's bats appeared to be very local and were thought to be nowhere common (Millais 1904-1906), only being known from three districts viz. the Avon valley in Gloucestershire, Warwickshire and Worcestershire; Cheshire; and the West Riding of Yorkshire (Barrett-Hamilton & Hinton 1910-1921), and there is no evidence of a significant change in abundance in the last hundred years.

Population trends: Unknown, but it seems probable that this species has always had a restricted range and occurred at relatively low population levels in Britain. There has been a proportional increase in the number of recent Leisler's records, and the species may be increasing slightly (R.E. Stebbings pers. comm.).

Pipistrelle *Pipistrellus pipistrellus*

Status: Native; common in most areas. At present it is unclear whether this is a single species. Jones & van Parijs (1993) showed that the echo-location calls of pipistrelle bats fall into two distinct frequency bands, with frequencies containing most energy averaging 46 kHz and 55 kHz. The two phonic types also showed small differences in average morphometrics. Although both phonic types are found throughout Britain, they are reproductively isolated with separate maternity colonies. Thus *Pipistrellus pipistrellus* may actually consist of two cryptic sibling species, and further genetic work seems to support this view (G. Jones pers. comm.). Although the data are preliminary, there is some evidence that the low frequency type predominates on the south coast, whilst the high frequency type predominates in Scotland (G. Jones pers. comm.).

Distribution: Found throughout the British Isles and on many islands but probably not now resident in Orkney or Shetland, although pipistrelles were resident in Orkney in the 1970s (P.A. Racey pers. comm.). There were records from earlier this century from the Outer Hebrides (Millais 1904-1906; Barrett-Hamilton & Hinton 1910-1921; Thorburn 1920), and there is one recent Hebridean record, from Stornoway (R.E. Stebbings pers. comm.).

Population data: Speakman (1991) based his estimate of pipistrelle numbers on three early summer surveys of nursery roosts; these consist almost entirely of females. The estimated densities from the three studies were all similar. Walsh, Stebbings & Thompson (1987) found 0·05 females per ha in 500 km² around York, whilst J.S. Pritchard & F.M. Murphy (unpubl.) found 0·2 bats per ha in two glens in the centre of Scotland, which gave an overall estimated density of about 0·05 females per ha when the adjacent unsuitable moorland was included. Similarly, in an area of 3200 km² in north-east Scotland, Speakman et al. (1991a) found 0·18 bats per ha, which again was equivalent to about 0·05 bats per ha when surrounding areas of unsuitable habitat were included in the estimate. However, the number of new roosts found by Speakman et al. (1991a) never reached an asymptote, and so the density estimates (and hence total population figures) represent minimum numbers; what proportion of the total number of roosts was found is unknown. Thus these three independent estimates suggest a minimum of 0·05 breeding female pipistrelles per ha, at least in northern Britain.

To calculate population size, Speakman (1991) assumed that there are equal numbers of males and females in pipistrelle populations. However, the validity of this assumption is in doubt, since mist-netting samples caught at foraging sites contained fewer males than females (Speakman et al. 1991a), and a lower population of males might be anticipated from their lower survival rates (Lundberg 1989). Thus, using Speakman's (1991) adjusted figures, there would be 2,400,000 pipistrelles if the sex ratio is 1:1, but only 1,800,000 if the sex ratio is two females per male, as was found for a small sample of free-flying bats caught at a feeding site in Scotland (Speakman et al. 1991a). R.E. Stebbings (pers. comm.) calculated the population size from an estimated density of pipistrelle colonies in England. He extrapolated this density to comparable areas in Scotland and Wales, and used an average nursery cluster of 80 bats with a 40:60 sex ratio (because of higher male mortality). By this means he estimated 1,300,000-1,600,000 pipistrelles in Britain.

Population estimates: A total pre-breeding population of about 2,000,000; 1,250,000 in England, 550,000 in Scotland and 200,000 in Wales. To improve this estimate, more information is needed on the population structure of pipistrelles, and density estimates from areas in southern Britain. Also, since the density estimates used by Speakman (1991) in his calculations may have been some way below the actual density, this figure is likely to be an under- rather than over-estimate. **Reliability of population estimate: 3.**

Historical changes: At the turn of the century pipistrelles were probably numerous in every locality where bats could exist (Barrett-Hamilton & Hinton 1910-1921), and generally were the commonest species (e.g. Lilford 1887), although outnumbered by Daubenton's and long-eared bats in some parts of England and Scotland (Millais 1904-1906), or by whiskered, brown long-eared and noctule bats in parts of England (Barrett-Hamilton & Hinton 1910-1921). In Scotland pipistrelles were found in most if not all counties, but were less numerous in Sutherland and rare in Caithness. During the course of this century, the relative abundance of pipistrelles and other species of bats in north-east Scotland appears to have changed, and pipistrelles are now much more abundant than indicated in 19th century records (Speakman et al. 1991a). Why the population has increased in this part of Scotland is unclear, but the adaptability of pipistrelles and their ability to use modern buildings as nursery sites may be important factors.

Population trends: Overall, pipistrelles are thought to have undergone a substantial population decline since 1960; annual surveys of colonies in houses from 1978-1983 suggested declines of 55%, and average colony size fell from 119 to 53 (Stebbings & Griffith 1986). By 1987 population levels were only 38% of those in 1978 (Stebbings 1988), and there were few known colonies of more than 1000 individuals, although such large colonies were not unusual before 1960. Also, whilst there are regional differences in mean pipistrelle colony size (south-west England 56, mean of 44 colonies per year counted 1986-1992; south-east England 64, mean of 173 colonies per year counted 1986-1992; midlands 70, mean of 78 colonies per year counted 1986-1992; north England 85, mean of 122 colonies per year counted 1986-1992; Scotland 262, mean of 41 colonies per year counted 1989-1992; Wales 99, mean of 56 colonies per year counted 1986-1992) (R.E. Stebbings pers comm.), it is unclear whether these mean colony sizes represent different population densities. Although two studies in Scotland and one in Yorkshire found very similar population densities (Speakman 1991), mean colony size in Scotland was three times that in north England. Hence differences in mean colony size may not represent different population densities, and interpreting data on roost sizes is difficult. Thus, whilst it is likely that there have been declines in pipistrelle numbers, the magnitude of any decline is unclear.

Nathusius' pipistrelle *Pipistrellus nathusii*

Status: Currently thought to be a migrant winter visitor (Speakman *et al.* 1991b), although two young animals with barely fused epiphyses were caught outside a church near Peterborough, Cambridgeshire in 1992. Thus further surveys may show that this species is breeding in Britain (R.E. Stebbings pers.

comm.), although at present there are no British records during the breeding period. Rare.

Distribution: There are occasional records throughout Britain from Shetland to the south coast and the Channel Islands.

Population data: Most records are of single bats, except a possible occurrence of three together in Cornwall (Speakman *et al.* 1991b), and the two young animals from Peterborough. Up to the end of 1989, there had been 13 confirmed records from the area covered by this review (one in each of Cornwall, Dorset, Essex, Hertfordshire, London and Shetland, two from north-east Scotland and five from the North Sea). In addition, a 1940 record from Whalsey, Shetland, has now been documented (Herman 1992). By 1994 the total number of records, including the Channel Islands and North Sea, was well over 30 (J.R. Speakman pers. comm.).

Population estimates: Unknown; there are very few records, most of which are from May or September. This temporal distribution does not coincide with winds of a particular direction, and hence suggests that some bats migrate across the North Sea and English Channel to hibernate in Britain, returning to mainland Europe the following spring (Speakman *et al. 1*991b). However, R.E. Stebbings (pers. comm.) has suggested that the species may be breeding in Britain (see above), and their regular occurrence amongst the bats submitted for rabies testing (around 1% of bats submitted - Table 9) suggests that the species may be under-recorded (A.M. Hutson pers. comm.). However, this sample is biased by the inclusion of bats from North Sea oil rigs that are automatically sent for rabies testing (J.R. Speakman pers. comm.).

Historical changes: Unknown, since the species was first identified in Britain in 1969.

Population trends: Unknown. The recent spate of records may be due to a change of status and the species expanding westwards

(Stebbings 1988), but more critical recording by volunteer Bat Groups is likely to have been a significant factor contributing to the increased number of records (Speakman *et al.* 1991b).

Barbastelle *Barbastella barbastellus*

Status: Native; widespread but rare.

Distribution: Widely distributed throughout England and Wales, south of a line from the Mersey to the Tees (Arnold 1993), with early records as far north as Cumbria (Millais 1904-1906).

Population data: Since there are only 10-15 records each year (R.E. Stebbings pers. comm.), very little is known about this species and there are no known breeding colonies. Whilst the records are all of single animals, the number of records is increasing. In the absence of objective criteria on which to base a population estimate, Speakman (1991) suggested there are around 100 individuals. However, for such a widely distributed resident species, it is hard to believe that the population could be so low. A.M. Hutson and A.J. Mitchell-Jones (pers. comm.) suggested a population size of around 5000 would be needed to maintain the population over such a wide area, and R.E. Stebbings (pers. comm.) argued that it would need to be even higher, around 5000-10,000.

Population estimates: A total pre-breeding population of about 5000; 4500 in England, none in Scotland and 500 in Wales. Until we know more about the biology of this species, it is impossible to estimate population size more precisely. **Reliability of population estimate:** 5.

Historical changes: At the turn of the century the barbastelle was described as 'well-known, although not abundant' in Essex, Norfolk and Warwickshire, with definite colonies in Somerset, Worcestershire and Wales, and there were records from every county south of the Wash and east of the Dee (Barrett-Hamilton & Hinton 1910-1921). These authors concluded that it was widely distributed but in small numbers, a situation that is probably comparable to the current situation.

Population trends: Currently unknown. Arnold (1993) reported that despite the increase in records for most species of bat due to the recent increase in bat recording, the number of barbastelle records has declined after a peak in the 1950s and 1960s. He suggested that this might represent a population decline. An alternative explanation for the decline in the number of records is that barbastelles are known to respond to severe weather by entering caves, where they are more likely to be detected. Thus severe winters may have produced peaks of records that do not imply a subsequent real decrease. R.E. Stebbings (pers. comm.) questioned the reported decline in the number of records, and suggested that there has been an increase in records in the last decade in line with the increased activity of Bat Groups.

Brown long-eared bat *Plecotus auritus*

Status: Native; common.

Distribution: Occurs everywhere except in open uplands and perhaps in exposed regions of north-west Scotland and off-shore islands; there is one record of a specimen from North Uist, Outer Hebrides (Thorburn 1920).

Population data: Speakman (1991) calculated the population size using two estimates of brown long-eared bat population density from coniferous woodland in Norfolk (Boyd & Stebbings 1989) and from north-east Scotland (Speakman *et al.* 1991a). He suggested that brown long-eared bats occur at a density of about one tenth that of pipistrelles, i.e. 0·005 bats per ha. Since brown long-eared bats occupy about 80% of the range of pipistrelles, Speakman (1991) assumed that the population of brown long-eared bats is 8% that of pipistrelles. Since his figure for pipistrelles was 2,400,000 for

Britain, this produced an estimate of about 190,000 brown long-eared bats. He further suggested that an independent confirmation of this estimate comes from roost reports: 30·4% are for long-eared bats compared with 58·5% for pipistrelles (Mitchell-Jones et al. 1986), although A.J. Mitchell-Jones (pers. comm.) argued that the proportion of pipistrelle roosts is under-estimated because the majority of unidentified roosts were probably pipistrelles. Since brown long-eared bat roosts are about 14% as large as those of pipistrelle roosts, this also suggests that the population of brown long-eared bats is about 8% that of pipistrelles. R.E. Stebbings (pers. comm.) disagreed with the assumption that brown long-eared bats occupy about 80% of the range of pipistrelles because, whilst they are found throughout England, Scotland and Wales, they are restricted to woodland habitats. A direct comparison with pipistrelles is difficult, so he based his estimate on the relative abundance of the two species, and suggested a population size of the order of 150,000-200,000. A.M. Hutson (pers. comm.) also based his estimate on their abundance relative to pipistrelles. He suggested that the brown long-eared bat population was 10% that of pipistrelles, i.e. about 200,000.

Population estimates: A total pre-breeding population of about 200,000; 155,000 in England, 27,500 in Scotland and 17,500 in Wales. For the second most common bat in Britain, there is a surprising lack of information on which to base a more precise population estimate. **Reliability of population estimate: 4.**

Historical changes: At the turn of the century this was the most widely distributed bat and was also considered to be one of the most common, if not the commonest, species (Millais 1904-1906). Lilford (1887) recorded that it was 'exceedingly common' in most parts of England, although he also suggested that the pipistrelle was 'the' common bat in Britain. Brown long-eared bats were not known from Orkney and Shetland (Millais 1904-1906), but were recorded from the north of mainland Scotland, where they outnumbered all other

species, and were recorded from the Isle of Arran, Islay, Mull and North Uist (Barrett-Hamilton & Hinton 1910-1921). During this century brown long-eared bats have undergone a long-term decline in relative abundance, and also probably in their distribution. The reasons for this decline are unknown.

Population trends: These are currently unclear. Brown long-eared bats are very dependent on roof spaces and so, during the last 30 years, they have been at risk from timber treatment in buildings using organochlorine pesticides. Since this was coupled with the loss of deciduous woodland, a habitat of great importance to brown long-eared bats, R.E. Stebbings (pers. comm.) argues that the species has declined in recent decades and that this decline may have been substantial.

Grey long-eared bat *Plecotus austriacus*

Status: Native; very rare, and only a few small colonies are known.

Distribution: Found only in Devon, Dorset, Hampshire (including the Isle of Wight) and Somerset.

Population data: These are all subjective, based on the limited distribution and paucity of records. Speakman (1991), A.M. Hutson (pers. comm.) and A.J. Mitchell-Jones (pers. comm.) all suggested that the population is around 1000 individuals, and R.E. Stebbings (pers. comm.) suggested that the figure was in the range 500-1500.

Population estimates: A total pre-breeding population of about 1000, all in England. In view of the limited range and information on the species, this is the best available estimate. **Reliability of population estimate: 3.**

Historical changes: Unknown, but in view of its largely Mediterranean distribution, it has probably always been rare in Britain.

Population trends: Any long-term population trend is unknown. Grey long-eared bats are generally rare in north-west Europe, but common in southern areas, particularly around the Mediterranean. Thus they are vulnerable to harsh winters, and in the cold winter of 1962/1963 one colony in Dorset declined from 22 to 4 individuals (Stebbings & Griffith 1986). Three colonies in Dorset and one in north-west Devon have all declined to extinction in the last 20-30 years (R.E. Stebbings pers. comm.).

Order: Lagomorpha

Rabbit *Oryctolagus cuniculus*

Status: Introduced; in most areas numbers are expanding again following a dramatic decline after the introduction of myxomatosis.

Distribution: Rabbits are widespread throughout mainland Britain up to the treeline and on most small islands but absent from Rum and Tiree. Their distribution on islands is documented by Flux & Fullagar (1992).

Population data: The most suitable habitats are areas of short grasses, whether these are natural or agricultural. However, they are found in a wide variety of habitat types. Densities vary seasonally, with numbers relatively stable over winter (<1 to 15 per ha) followed by highly variable summer peaks (<1 to 40 per ha) (Tittensor 1981). Summer peaks are higher on sandy soils, and over-winter numbers are higher on sand and chalk than on clay soils (Cowan 1991). The following density estimates were available for over-wintering rabbit populations in specific habitat types: 8·4 per ha on chalk grassland, Oxfordshire, based on a capture/mark/recapture study averaged over six winters (Cowan 1984); 14-22 per ha on sand dunes, Holy Island, Northumberland, based on marking and population counts (MacDonald 1989); 2·1 per ha on sand dunes, East Lothian, using Leslie's trap out method (Kolb 1991a); 1·7 per ha on forestry/hill

grazing, Borders, using marking and Leslie's trap out method (Kolb 1991b); hill farm/open grazing, Borders, using Leslie's trap out method - (H.H. Kolb pers. comm.); 12·6 per ha on grassland/broom, Strathmore, Tayside, using Petersen/Bailey capture/mark/recapture calculations (H.H. Kolb pers. comm.).

These figures are for densities that are locally quite high, and if they were typical for all the areas of comparable habitat, they would suggest an over-winter rabbit population approaching 100,000,000. This would be comparable to the estimates of the rabbit population before the introduction of myxomatosis. Whilst the rabbit population is rapidly recovering, it has not reached pre-myxomatosis levels (see below). Thus, for the population estimate, the following density figures were used: 5 per ha for scrub, bracken, sand dunes and sloping coastal cliffs; 2·5 per ha for parkland, lowland heaths, lowland grasslands and arable land; 2 per ha in semi-natural broadleaved, semi-natural coniferous, semi-natural mixed and recently felled woodlands, and broadleaved, coniferous, mixed and young plantations; 0·5 per ha in upland unimproved grassland; and 0·1 per ha in heather moorlands.

Population estimates: A total pre-breeding population of about 37,500,000; 24,500,000 in England, 9,500,000 in Scotland and 3,500,000 in Wales. Compared to pre-myxomatosis days, there has been a very significant change in the relative abundance of rabbits in each of the three countries, with the change being most dramatic in Wales (see below). **Reliability of population estimate:** 3.

Historical changes: Rabbits were originally held in warrens, and there were only substantial increases in wild populations from the mid-18th century onwards, when changes in agricultural practice created favourable habitats and an increased interest in game led to intensive predator control (Thompson & Worden 1956). In Scotland, rabbits were for a long time mainly confined to a few islands and to coastal sand dunes. Early in the 19th century rabbits were rare north of the Tay and Clyde, and their range extension throughout Scotland was gradual (Millais 1904-1906). The natural spread of rabbit populations can be quite slow (Kolb 1994), and their spread in Scotland was largely due to 18th and 19th century introductions throughout the highlands and the north-west (Lever 1977). A similar pattern of events occurred in Wales. Until the early 19th century rabbits were mostly confined to large warrens on islands, but introductions to the mainland, coupled with agricultural changes and large-scale predator control, led to rapid increases in numbers (Lever 1977). At the turn of the century rabbit numbers were high, and average bag returns remained high until the onset of myxomatosis in 1953 (Tapper 1992). At that time the British rabbit population was estimated to be 60,000,000-100,000,000, with about 40,000,000 being culled each year for the meat and fur trade (Thompson & Worden 1956). Thompson & Worden (1956) believed that the upper limit was a conservative estimate, and that the spring and summer population was in excess of 100,000,000 rabbits. Myxomatosis destroyed over 99% of the British rabbit population (Thompson 1956). Assuming that the original estimate was reasonably accurate, this implies that fewer than 1,000,000 rabbits were left in Britain following the introduction of myxomatosis.

Population trends: For an *r*-selected species such as the rabbit, it is difficult to be precise about trends, because even several years of decline can be recouped remarkably quickly. However, its powers of recruitment are not as high as sometimes suggested by calculations based on counts of corpora lutea or of late term foetuses, since these ignore the rate of nestling mortality, which can be considerable (Bell & Webb 1991).

Since the advent of myxomatosis, bag records suggest that nationally the rabbit population has steadily recovered (Tapper 1992), although locally this may not be the case. On Forvie sand dunes, Grampian, rabbit numbers have declined from a peak in 1976, with

considerable and possibly regular fluctuations in abundance (I.J. Patterson pers. comm.). Long-term data from agricultural areas show that in 1953, before the onset of myxomatosis, 94% of farm holdings in England and Wales had rabbits on cultivable land. By 1970 this figure had only recovered to 59% (Lloyd 1970), and by 1986 rabbit numbers were still only around 20% of pre-myxomatosis levels (Cowan 1991). Assuming that the estimate of up to 100,000,000 rabbits pre-myxomatosis was correct, Cowan's (1991) estimate suggests that the rabbit population in the mid-1980s was around 20,000,000.

It is also clear that the rabbit population is still well below that recorded before myxomatosis. The National Game Bag Census data (Tapper 1992) suggest that rabbit numbers are currently between a third and a half of the pre-myxomatosis numbers, which is supported by the estimate presented here. In Scotland, 92.9% of farms had rabbits pre-1954. The corresponding figure was only 60.7% in 1970 and 80.7% in 1991. The number of farms with serious infestations fell from 54.9% pre-1954 to 0.4% in 1970, and recovered to 16.6% in 1991 (Kolb 1994). In addition to dramatic changes in rabbit numbers, there has also been a significant change in the distribution of rabbits. During the 1970s eastern and south-eastern regions consistently showed the highest rises in rabbit numbers, the south-west intermediate, and Wales and the north relatively low increases (Trout, Tapper & Harradine 1986; Kolb 1994). Pre-myxomatosis populations were high in the south-west and in Wales (Thompson & Worden 1956), whereas Wales now has one of the lowest rabbit populations. In Scotland, there have consistently been more farms with rabbit infestations in the east, Highlands and north-east. These areas also had more farms with serious infestations when compared with the rest of the country, both before and after myxomatosis (Kolb 1994). Trout *et al.* (1986) concluded that in many areas the carrying capacity for rabbits had still to be reached, and so further population increases are to be expected. All these observations agree well with the estimates for the size and distribution of the rabbit population presented here.

Population threats: Fresh outbreaks of myxomatosis cause local depletions, and rabbit control measures can suppress populations locally. Whilst myxomatosis is still prevalent in many areas, mortality during such out-breaks has fallen to 40-60% (compared with over 99% at the start of the epidemic) as a result of increasing levels of genetic resistance (Ross 1982; Ross & Sanders 1984). Also, from 1992 there have been reports of viral haemorrhagic disease in wild rabbits in Britain (Duff *et al.* 1994); whether this calicivirus will have a significant impact on British rabbit populations remains to be seen.

Annual changes in reproductive success, and particularly the onset of the breeding season, are affected by climatic factors, especially higher minimum ground temperatures and hours of daily sunshine in winter. Following mild winters, the first young of the year appear above ground about two months earlier (in February rather than April), and one study found that, over four years, annual average reproductive success per adult female ranged from 6·1 to 10·1 (Bell & Webb 1991). These data demonstrate the possible effects of predicted global warming on the productivity of rabbits, and hence the potential for an increase in rabbit numbers.

Brown hare *Lepus europaeus*

Status: Probably introduced to Britain by the Romans. There have been many subsequent introductions to islands. Common but has undergone a substantial decline this century.

Distribution: Widespread, and most common in agricultural areas. In Scotland brown hares are absent from the north-west and western Highlands, where they are replaced by mountain hares on heather moorland. Present on Anglesey and the Isle of Wight; they have been widely introduced to Scottish islands (Millais 1904-1906; Barrett-Hamilton & Hinton 1910-1921).

Population data: Three population estimates are available. The first was obtained by Tapper & Stoate (1992). Hares were counted on 12 areas between January and March 1988 and 1989, using spotlight counts as described by Barnes & Tapper (1985). These gave an absolute estimate of brown hare density within a given area; for each area the cropping pattern and presence or absence of a gamekeeper were recorded. From these an index of field size and habitat diversity was calculated. Habitat data from the Institute of Terrestrial Ecology's land classes were then used to calculate a relationship between an index of crop diversity and brown hare numbers, which in turn was used to estimate the number of brown hares that would be present both with and without the presence of gamekeepers to control the numbers of predators. By this means, Tapper & Stoate (1992) estimated that the number of brown hares in Britain in late winter lay between 1,250,000 and 1,911,000, the figures being, respectively, in the absence or presence of predator control. Whilst this approach gave a reasonable estimate of total population size using the data then available, it had its limitations. First, only a minority of land classes were surveyed for brown hares, and the results from 12 sample sites predominantly in southern and eastern England were extrapolated to produce a national estimate of hare numbers. Also, the 12 survey sites chosen were areas with known hare populations, and generally areas with reasonable population densities; no areas with few or no hares were included in their calculation of the relationship between hare numbers and habitat features. This is likely to produce an over-estimate. A second estimate was derived by the Game Conservancy from the National Game Bag Census, extrapolated to the whole country, based on the assumption that about 40% of hares are shot during winter hare shoots (Tapper & Stoate 1992). This suggested a population of about 1,000,000 hares before the main culling season.

A third estimate was produced by M. Hutchings & S. Harris (unpubl.), who organised a stratified national survey in which

734 randomly selected 1 x 1 km squares were surveyed for hares. This survey was undertaken in the winters of 1991/1992 and 1992/1993. A transect in each square (mean length 2950 m) was walked three times between mid-October and mid-January, and the position of each hare seen was recorded in relation to the transect line. The data were analysed using the program DISTANCE, an updated version of Burnham, Anderson & Laake's (1980) program TRANSECT. This program was used to calculate population densities in each of the four land class groups, based on a detection function. By this means, a mid-winter brown hare population of 817,500 ± 137,250 (95% confidence limits) was obtained. This figure is lower than the other two because a much wider range of habitats were sampled, including many 1 x 1 km squares with few or no hares. The relatively large 95% confidence limits are due to the very clumped distribution of the hare population, so that comparable habitats can have widely different hare numbers. This clumping is due to various anthropogenic factors, most notably the willingness of the land owner to tolerate the presence of hares. In many areas hare numbers are drastically reduced so that poachers are not attracted onto the land (M. Hutchings & S. Harris unpubl.).

Population estimates: A mid-winter population, at the start of the breeding season but before the onset of the main hare-culling season, of about 817,500; 572,250 in England, 187,250 in Scotland and 58,000 in Wales. Organised shoots at the end of the winter may lead to a 40% decline (Tapper & Stoate 1992). **Reliability of population estimate: 2.**

Historical changes: At the turn of the century brown hares were considered to be abundant throughout England, Scotland and Wales except on the higher parts of mountains, and in the 19th century were even found on open areas in London (Barrett-Hamilton & Hinton 1910-1921). Reports in the *Victoria Histories of the Counties of England* show that they were certainly much more abundant in the western parts of England than at present, but at the start of this century declines were already beginning in the south-west (M. Hutchings & S. Harris unpubl.). Prior to the Ground Game Act of 1880, the abundance of hares in some districts was described as 'quite extraordinary', but the Ground Game Act removed the protection that was enjoyed by brown hares and is thought to have led to a dramatic decline in numbers, followed perhaps by an increase around the turn of the century. Thorburn (1920) described brown hares as plentiful in cultivated areas, especially grasslands, when not driven away by persecution.

More recently, National Game Bag Census data (Tapper 1992) have shown that hare bags were highest in the early part of the century, and that after the late 1920s they declined until the latter half of the Second World War. Thereafter numbers increased until 1960 (but not to pre-1920 levels). This increase in the later half of the 1950s may have been aided by the decline in rabbit numbers, providing a niche into which the hares expanded (Rothschild 1963). This was followed by a further decline in hare numbers during the 1970s and 1980s. This decline occurred in virtually all regions (Tapper 1992). Tapper & Parsons (1984) concluded that it represented a real decrease in abundance, and that the hare bag was declining at a more or less steady rate when considered nationally. However, autumn counts from 1976-1992 in the Dane Valley, Cheshire, showed no evidence of any overall population change, although there were marked inter-annual variations (D.W. Yalden unpubl.).

Population trends: Many estates no longer hold as many large hare shoots as previously, which complicates the interpretation of the National Game Bag Census data. However, the available information suggests that overall hare numbers have remained constant for the last ten years (mean 2·80 shot per km^2 for the years 1983-1987, mean 2·95 per km^2 for the years 1988-1992), although there will be significant annual and seasonal fluctuations due to the effects of summer weather conditions on breeding success. Hunting records also suggest that, nationally, hare numbers have remained constant over the last few years (Stoate 1993). This index is based on the number of hares seen whilst out hunting with packs of beagles and is the average of all hunting trips for the entire season, and then averaged between packs. Thus the index is based on many data which are independent of the game returns. Neither source of data shows any change in hare numbers over the last ten years. This general pattern of population change over the last thirty years has occurred throughout much of Europe, and generally hare numbers appear to have stabilised at a relatively low level (S.C. Tapper pers. comm.). However, a recent national survey suggested that population declines may be continuing since hares are heavily culled in many areas in eastern England because they attract poachers. These declines would not be detected by the National Game Bag Census and hunting data, which are biased towards large keepered estates and hunting areas where hare populations receive a degree of protection. Also, it appears that hares may be continuing to decline in low density areas in the west, and again the National Game Bag Census and hunting data are not suitable for monitoring changes in such low density hare populations (M. Hutchings & S. Harris unpubl.).

Population threats: Numerous explanations have been advanced for the decline in brown hare numbers, but none is in itself totally satisfactory. Barnes & Tapper (1986) concluded that there was a boom in hare numbers in the late 1950s and early 1960s as a consequence of the myxomatosis epizootic in rabbits, which removed a potential competitor. However, the subsequent decline in hares could not be explained adequately either by the increase in rabbits or a series of poor breeding seasons for the hares. High hare numbers in bag returns are associated with mild springs (Barnes & Tapper 1986), and mild autumns appear to lengthen the breeding season, sometimes significantly (Hewson & Taylor 1975). Thus weather can have a dramatic impact on hare breeding success.

The most generally accepted cause of the decline of the brown hare is change in the agricultural ecosystem (Tapper & Barnes 1986; Tapper & Stoate 1994). This in itself does not explain the actual cause of the decline. We do not know the relative importance of habitat simplification, use of agrichemicals, changes in farming practice such as cutting silage instead of hay, increasing use of complex machinery, etc. All these factors are likely to have played a role in the decline of hares, and their relative impact will vary in different regions of the country. In addition, hare numbers have increased where fox *Vulpes vulpes* numbers have been reduced experimentally (Tapper, Potts & Brockless 1991), but whether predation has played a role in their general decline is currently unclear, as is whether hares are now more vulnerable to predation as a consequence of habitat simplification (Harris & Saunders 1993). Whilst the reasons for the decline in brown hare numbers are probably complex, and at present are poorly understood, it is clear that many factors are involved. Anecdotal observations suggest that the five-year set-aside scheme led to an increase in brown hare numbers in some areas.

Mass mortalities of brown hares are sometimes reported from parts of East Anglia, most often in the summer. A number of factors may be responsible: food shortage due to agricultural changes, such as the change from growing spring to winter cereals (G. McLaren & S. Harris unpubl.), grass sickness (Whitwell 1991; Griffiths & Whitwell 1993), or European brown hare syndrome (Duff *et al*. 1994), although this disease is most prevalent in the autumn (Gavier-Widén & Mörner 1991), whereas the mass mortalities occur earlier in the year. Their impact on brown hare populations is at present unknown.

In the Royal Museum of Scotland, Edinburgh, there are about 20 skins and skulls of specimens that appear to be brown hare/mountain hare hybrids, although whether they actually are hybrids has yet to be determined (Balharry *et al*. 1994). These came from Argyll, Ayrshire, Dumfriesshire and

Peeblesshire, i.e. those parts of Scotland where mountain hares were introduced in the middle of last century. Whether hybridisation is frequent in these areas needs to be determined (A.C. Kitchener pers. comm.). However, the current evidence suggests that wild hybrids occur only rarely, and so do not represent any real threat to the population (Balharry *et al.* 1994).

Mountain hare *Lepus timidus*

Status: Native but widely introduced outside its natural range; locally common in some upland areas.

Distribution: In the British Isles, mountain hares are indigenous only in the Highlands of Scotland; all the populations south of the Clyde and Forth are the result of introductions. Mountain hares are most numerous on grouse moors in north-east Scotland, and uncommon in west Scotland. They were present on Orkney in mediaeval times and died out; the modern population is the result of a recent introduction. Other introductions, mostly during the 19th century, were to Eigg (now extinct), Hoy, Islay (now extinct), Jura, Mull, Outer Hebrides, Raasay, Scalpay, Shetland and Skye. They were introduced into Ayrshire, Lanarkshire and Peeblesshire in the 1830s and 1840s, from where they dispersed widely (Barrett-Hamilton & Hinton 1910-1921), and to the Pennine area of South Yorkshire and Derbyshire about 1880. Introductions to the Cheviots and Lake District have not persisted. The population in North Wales, originating from introductions to the Vaynol estate near Bangor about 1885, is now extinct (Hewson 1991). No mountain hares have been reported in Wales for at least 15 years (R. Lovegrove pers. comm.).

Population data: Mountain hare populations are very localised; they reach the highest densities in north-east Scotland, and are particularly scarce in north and west Scotland (Watson & Hewson 1963). Population densities range from 3 to 46 per km², depending upon habitat type. The highest densities occur on heather moors overlying base-rich rocks, with the lowest densities where there are acidic rocks; locally densities may reach 300 per km² (Hewson 1991). In Scotland there are approximately 12,000 km² of heather moorland. Using a simple population estimate based on this area of heather moorland, and a mean density of 30 hares per km², the population in Scotland would be about 300,000. An alternative estimate was based on the following assumptions. Arnold (1993) recorded mountain hares in 363 10 x 10 km squares, including the Scottish islands and the Pennines. It was assumed that they were found in these squares but nowhere else, that they occurred at an average density of 2 per km² on the Scottish islands and north-west of the Great Glen (an area of about 5500 km²). Over the rest of Scotland a density of 20 per km² was assumed where they are present (an area of about 35,200 km²). However, hares are likely to be absent from large areas of this range which do not consist of heather moorland. Based on these two mean densities, and assuming that only half the range was suitable for hares, the population in Scotland would be about 360,000. In the Peak District, extensive surveys showed that the annual late winter density varied between 1·4 and 3·3 per km² (average 2·1 per km²) (Yalden 1984a). Since they occupy an area of 246 km², the late winter population for the Pennines is about 500 animals.

Population estimates: A total pre-breeding population of about 350,000 animals, split into several sub-populations; 500 in England, 350,000 in Scotland and none in Wales. **Reliability of population estimate: 3.**

Historical changes: Millais (1904-1906) described the distribution of mountain hares at the turn of the century. The National Game Bag Census records (Tapper 1992) show that high numbers were shot around the turn of the century, and even more after the First World War. They reached a peak around the early 1930s. Low numbers during the Second World War were followed by a recovery by

1950 to some 50% of those in the 1930s. There was then a decline which lasted from the mid-1970s to the early 1980s, since when the numbers shot have increased to equal the bag levels of the 1950s. At present the reasons for these population changes are unknown.

Population trends: Tapper (1987) showed that, whilst just over half of the populations he examined show irregular fluctuations in numbers, the rest showed a weak tendency towards regular population cycles with a periodicity of about 9.5 years. With species such as the mountain hare that fluctuate widely in number, it is difficult to detect long-term population changes.

Population threats: The main threat is probably population fragmentation. Populations in the Pennines, Mull, Orkney and Shetland are all relatively small and isolated. Furthermore, most recoveries of marked mountain hares are close to the point of capture; the maximum recovery distance in one study was 12 km (Hewson 1990a). Assuming that mountain hares will rarely cross more than 20 km of unsuitable habitat, the Scottish population is effectively fragmented into a number of sub-populations, particularly in the north and west (see map in Arnold 1993), and some of these could be quite small. The number of introduced populations that have died out shows the vulnerability of small mountain hare populations - see Millais (1904-1906). The Pennine population is also potentially vulnerable because of its small size, wide distribution, and the pressures placed upon it by high visitor use of the area.

It is possible that mountain hares are susceptible to climatic instability, and that adverse weather conditions affect juvenile mortality. Thus there is considerable variation in recruitment rate from place to place and possibly also from year to year (Flux 1970). Such chance events will enhance the vulnerability of small populations. Also, reduced management of heather moorland, and substantial reductions in the area of heather resulting from increased sheep-grazing, pose a threat to mountain hares

(Anderson & Yalden 1981; Hewson 1984a). However, current Common Agricultural Policy reforms may reduce grazing pressure in the uplands, as may some of the new Environmentally Sensitive Areas. The new Southern Uplands Environmentally Sensitive Area is specifically targeted at increasing the regeneration of heather moorland, and may thus benefit mountain hares (J. & R. Green pers. comm.).

In the Royal Museum of Scotland, Edinburgh, there are about 20 skins and skulls of specimens that appear to be brown hare/mountain hare hybrids. These come from Argyll, Ayrshire, Dumfriesshire and Peeblesshire, in those areas where the mountain hare population was established following introductions to Ayrshire in the middle of the last century (Hewson 1991). Whether hybridisation is frequent in these areas needs to be determined (A.C. Kitchener pers. comm.). However, the current evidence suggests that wild hybrids occur only rarely, and so they do not represent any real threat to the population (Balharry et al. 1994). Moreover, Irish hares were introduced to south-west Scotland in about 1923 (Hewson 1991), and J. & R. Green (pers. comm.) have suggested that the colour varieties seen in the hares in that part of Ayrshire may be the descendants of that introduction. Certainly, Irish hares have been introduced to a number of areas where mountain hares were present, e.g. Mull and Vaynol Park, and the two races remained distinct. The colony on Mull, for instance, was introduced around 1860, and the descendants were still identifiable fifty years later (Barrett-Hamilton & Hinton 1910-1921). Thus it is possible that Irish hares are still recognisable in Ayrshire 70 years after their introduction. These observations suggest that the two races may be reproductively isolated (Balharry et al. 1994).

Order: Rodentia

Red squirrel *Sciurus vulgaris*

Status: Native, but multiple introductions from continental Europe have produced a genetically mixed population. Red squirrels are vulnerable in England and Wales, and are already extinct in most parts of these two countries. They are locally common in Scotland.

Distribution: Isolated populations persist in southern England on three islands in Poole Harbour (Dorset), Cannock Chase (Staffordshire), the Isle of Wight and Thetford Forest (Norfolk). Introduced populations remain in north England, part of Wales and much of Scotland.

Population data: Red squirrels are found in small deciduous woods and copses, and also mature (older than 25 years) conifer forests, especially those larger than 100 ha. Densities over five years recorded in Scots pine *Pinus sylvestris* on Furzey Island (Dorset) ranged from 2·3 per ha pre-breeding to 7·5 per ha post-breeding (Kenward & Holm 1989); these densities are high, probably because the island provides a prime Scots pine habitat, with very large cone crops from mature, relatively uncrowded trees (R.E. Kenward pers. comm.). A mean density of 0·66 per ha recorded in January over two years in Cumbria (Tonkin 1983) probably reflects poor habitat quality (Kenward & Holm 1993). For coniferous woodlands, density estimates vary from 0·3-1·1 per ha (Shorten 1962; Tittensor 1977; Reynolds 1981; Moller 1986). Thus long term average densities of 0·5-1·5 per ha are normal for both coniferous and deciduous forest, but inter-annual fluctuations can be large and are affected by seed supplies and weather (Gurnell 1991a). Peak numbers occur in the autumn, with troughs in the spring before recruitment.

Red squirrel population size was estimated by J. Gurnell (pers. comm.) by taking the area of coniferous and broadleaved woodland in each of the three countries from a census in 1982, adjusting for the proportion of woodland greater than 15 years old, and calculating the proportion of woodland occupied by red squirrels. Assuming a minimum density of 0·1 per ha, a maximum density of 1·0 per ha and a median of 0·55 per ha, this gave median figures for England, Scotland and Wales of 30,000, 121,000 and 10,000 red squirrels respectively (with minimum and maximum figures of 6000 and 60,000 for England, 22,000 and 220,000 for Scotland, and 2000 and 20,000 for Wales).

Many of the English populations are fragmented, and most have very few red squirrels. Estimates of the size of the isolated populations in southern England were obtained as follows. In Poole Harbour there is a total pre-breeding population of 125 and 150-200 in the summer, as estimated by capture-mark-recapture studies (R.E. Kenward pers. comm.). In Cannock Chase and Thetford Forest the populations are too low to be estimated by conventional techniques, since red squirrels are seen only occasionally, but each population consists of fewer than 100 animals. On the Isle of Wight, the area of ancient woodland was 3695 ha (Spencer & Kirby 1992), and mean densities for the island were 0·3-1·6 per ha (Holm 1990), with a mean summer density for three sites over two years of 0·90 ± 0·17 per ha (Kenward & Holm 1993). Using the area of ancient woodland and the mean density figure gave a population for the Isle of Wight of 3330, but this does not include an estimate for the number of animals found in the coniferous plantations on the island. Densities on the island were dependent on the hazel nut crop, and numbers were lower when the hazel nut crop was poor (Holm 1990). For south Lancashire, between the Rivers Ribble and Mersey, red squirrels were present in 47 woods totalling 766 ha. The population estimate was based on an assumed density of 0·8 red squirrels per ha. This suggests a population of fewer than 600. However, this is probably an over-estimate since the habitats are mostly poor for red squirrels and because the 47 woods may include some transient sites

(P.W. Bright pers. comm.). The red squirrels at Formby were introduced from Europe about 60 years ago and now occupy 70 ha of mixed coastal forest, of which 40 ha are conifers (Gurnell & Pepper 1993). Due to supplementary feeding, densities are very high, up to ten times those found in natural habitats (Gurnell & Pepper 1993; Rice-Oxley 1993). Assuming a density of 10 red squirrels per ha of conifers gives a maximum population of 400 red squirrels at Formby. Thus the largest populations remaining in England are those in Cumbria, north Lancashire and Northumberland. These constitute about 85% of the red squirrel population in England.

Population estimates: A total pre-breeding population of about 161,000; 30,000 in England, 121,000 in Scotland and 10,000 in Wales. A more precise estimate needs up-to-date information on the current range of red squirrels, and more detailed studies of the densities of red squirrels in populations on the edge of their range. **Reliability of population estimate:** 3.

Historical changes: In Scotland, there appear to be no records to suggest that red squirrels are indigenous south of the Firths of Forth and Clyde (Harvie-Brown 1881a), but to the north of this area they were widespread and common. However, they became very rare due to widespread forest destruction during the 18th century, and persisted only in Rothiemurchus Forest in Inverness-shire. Populations were boosted by subsequent reintroductions from England (for details see Harvie-Brown 1881b), the increase in young woodlands, and possibly the control of predators (Millais 1904-1906). By the end of the 19th century, red squirrels were abundant in England and Scotland, and also in Wales according to Millais (1904-1906), although they were described as increasing in the newly wooded districts of Wales by Barrett-Hamilton & Hinton (1910-1921). However, there were further declines in the 1920s, with some, but not all, populations subsequently recovering. All these population changes occurred before grey squirrels were introduced to these areas.

Population trends: Following the spread of grey squirrels, the red squirrel has shown a steady decline in England and Wales in both range and numbers, although in Scotland red squirrels currently occupy more 10 x 10 km squares than they did 50 years ago due to increased afforestation (Gurnell & Pepper 1993). Using index numbers derived from the Forestry Commission's annual surveys over the period 1973-1988, Usher, Crawford & Banwell (1992) showed that there has been a dramatic decline in the distribution of the red squirrel in Wales, this being balanced by a modest expansion in Scotland. Compared to the 1988 situation, Usher, Crawford & Banwell (1992) predicted that the red squirrel would contract its range slightly, but none of the runs with their predictive model suggested that the red squirrel should become extinct in Britain or any of the three constituent countries.

However, when evaluating the status of individual populations, it is clear that the future of many is questionable. In England, the Isle of Wight population is probably secure, although it is possible that grey squirrels may become established on the island (Kenward & Holm 1989; Gurnell & Pepper 1993). Furthermore, the population is scattered and hence vulnerable. The populations in Poole Harbour are small and hence also vulnerable. The south Lancashire population is very vulnerable, especially since about half occurs in just one woodland complex, and the Welsh population is small, fragmented and vulnerable. Whether attempts to provide red squirrel sanctuaries in Cannock Chase and Thetford Forest will prove successful remains to be seen (Gurnell & Pepper 1993). Thus red squirrels appear vulnerable to extinction south of a line from Morecambe Bay to the Tees Estuary. Grey squirrels are already expanding into northern England, and the red squirrel populations there are threatened. A survey in 1991 showed that all but four reports of red squirrels in Wales were from state forests, and all but two 10 x 10 km squares with red squirrels also contained grey squirrels (Gurnell & Pepper 1993). The continued expansion of grey squirrels in eastern Scotland (Staines

1986) suggests that many Scottish populations are also threatened.

Population threats: The greatest single threat is competitive exclusion by grey squirrels (Kenward & Holm 1989) which, in deciduous woodland, live at higher densities. Modelling work has suggested that the rate of spread of grey squirrels was reduced due to competition with red squirrels (Okubo *et al. 1989*). Although the two species can co-exist for up to 20 years (Harris 1973/74; Reynolds 1985), red squirrels generally decline when grey squirrels colonise an area and are soon reduced to scattered 'island' populations that may persist for only a few years. In some parts of the Lothians red and grey squirrels appear to be currently co-existing (A.C. Kitchener pers. comm.); at what densities, and whether this is a stable situation, are unknown. Kenward & Holm (1993) showed that in oak-hazel woods, grey squirrel foraging, density and productivity were related to oak and acorn abundance, whereas red squirrels foraged where hazels were abundant, and their relatively low density and breeding success were related to the abundance of hazel nuts. In Scots pine, red squirrels can have densities and breeding success as high as grey squirrels in deciduous woodland.

Red squirrels cannot fully exploit acorn crops, and have a digestive efficiency for acorns of only 59%, apparently because they are much less able than greys to neutralise acorn polyphenols. Kenward & Holm (1993) developed a model to examine the competition for the autumn hazel crop, which was eaten by grey squirrels before the acorn crop, and showed that red squirrels are unlikely to persist with grey squirrels in woods with more than 14% oak canopy. They concluded that with oaks in most British deciduous woods giving grey squirrels a food refuge which red squirrels fail to exploit, replacement of red squirrels can be explained by feeding competition alone, exacerbated by the post-war decline in coppiced hazel. Furthermore, red squirrels increase their body weight in late autumn by about 10%, whereas grey squirrels increase their weight by about 20% (Kenward

& Tonkin 1986). This makes red squirrels more vulnerable to food shortages during the winter period. This is most likely to occur where the two species coexist and are competing for food resources (Gurnell & Pepper 1993). Since maintenance of body weight is important for reproduction, reduced reproductive success rather than reduced survival may explain why red squirrels have declined in conifer forests that also contain grey squirrels. This may also explain why red squirrels have managed to coexist with grey squirrels in Thetford Forest but continued to decline (Gurnell & Pepper 1993).

Red squirrels feed mainly in the tree canopy and spend about 70% of their time off the ground (Kenward & Tonkin 1986); thus they need continuous tree canopy, and habitat fragmentation is likely to pose a significant problem. The impact of habitat fragmentation was demonstrated by Bright (1993), who found that, in south Lancashire, those woods more than 5 km from a major red squirrel nucleus were unlikely to have red squirrels. Also, small areas of woodland are unlikely to provide adequate food resources in years of seed shortage.

Overall, the threats to red squirrel populations suggest that it is unlikely that large numbers will survive except perhaps in a few areas of extensive conifer woodland in Scotland, and in smaller numbers on islands such as the Isle of Wight, so long as they remain free of grey squirrels. A management strategy for conserving red squirrels is described by Gurnell & Pepper (1993). A further problem to consider is the status of British red squirrels; originally a distinct sub-species, introductions of European stock during the 18th and 19th century may mean that the endemic red squirrel in Britain is no longer validly distinct (Lowe & Gardiner 1983).

Grey squirrel *Sciurus carolinensis*

Status: Introduced in the 19th and early 20th centuries; common and increasing.

Distribution: Generally distributed in most of England and Wales, and patchily distributed in the central belt of Scotland and the east coast north to Aberdeen.

Population data: Found in areas of mature broadleaved forest, mixed forest, and mature conifers; also in suburban and urban areas. There are occasional records of grey squirrels from virtually every other habitat, but these rarely represent resident populations. Densities averaged over several years are usually greater than 2·0 per ha and often much greater e.g. a mean of 7·4 per ha in oak woodland in southern England (Gurnell 1983), although annual densities ranged from 5·2-9·8 per ha (Gurnell 1989). Summer densities for all types of British woodland are likely to be 1·5-4·0 per ha, with spring densities even lower (R.E. Kenward pers. comm.). For three oak-hazel woods in England, the mean pre-breeding density was 2·3 per ha for 14 site years and the summer density was 2·7 per ha (Kenward & Holm 1993). For 34 mixed woodland sites, all with some plantation, pre-breeding density was 1·6 per ha and summer density 2·1 per ha (Kenward & Parish 1986). Densities in broadleaved and mixed conifer/broadleaved woodland range from 2 to 8 per ha (Gurnell 1987), although occasionally higher densities (up to 16 per ha) can occur (Shorten & Courtier 1955). Since grey squirrels show reduced trapability in the autumn and winter, these data refer to spring and summer populations.

Long-term densities in pure coniferous woodland are not known. In Wareham Forest, Dorset, densities of 2·0 and 3·6 per ha were recorded in good Scots pines *Pinus sylvestris*, and 1·1 per ha pre-breeding and 1·6 per ha for summer in mature Corsican pine *Pinus nigra* (R.E. Kenward & S.S. Walls pers. comm.). However, both these were good conifer habitats, and most plantations will have fewer grey squirrels. Thus a study in Thetford Forest, Norfolk, suggested that there were considerably fewer than 1 per ha. In eight upland conifer sites in the Upper Derwent valley in the Peak District, pre-breeding density was 0·5 per ha, and post-breeding density 0·7 per ha (R.E. Kenward & C.A. Walls pers. comm.).

There are a number of problems when trying to estimate the number of grey squirrels in Britain. Populations show annual cycles, with peaks in the autumn before dispersal and troughs in the spring before recruitment. In addition there are annual variations in numbers depending on food availability (Gurnell 1991b), and densities are dependent on the tree species present. The problem is confounded by the absence of data from low density habitats (Gurnell 1991b). Also, grey squirrel numbers are particularly difficult to estimate for suburban and urban areas. Bird table feeding, litter-bin scavenging and direct feeding in gardens and parks means that these habitats probably support higher numbers than the highest rural woodland populations, and one poison-baiting exercise on the outskirts of London suggested a kill approaching 14 grey squirrels per ha (H.W. Pepper pers. comm.).

In 1986 B. Mayle and J. Rowe (pers. comm.) calculated the minimum and maximum numbers of grey squirrels, taking the area of colonised woodland to be 431,826 ha in England, 28,280 ha in Scotland and 3790 ha in Wales, and minimum and maximum densities of 2 per ha and 12 per ha in England and Wales but with a maximum density of 6 per ha for Scotland. They concluded that there were 865,000-5,180,000 grey squirrels in England, 57,000-170,000 in Scotland, and 7600-45,000 in Wales, i.e. a total population between just under 1,000,000 and 5,400,000. However, the density estimates used for this calculation were considerably higher than the typical densities detailed above. Therefore, to calculate the pre-breeding population of grey squirrels, the area of suitable habitat in those counties currently colonised by grey squirrels and the following pre-breeding densities were used: 2·5 per ha in semi-natural broadleaved and mixed woodlands; 1·5 per ha in broadleaved and mixed plantations, parkland and tall scrub; 0·5 per ha in semi-natural coniferous woodlands and coniferous plantations; and a mean of 0·1 per ha for all built-up habitats.

Population estimates: A total pre-breeding population of about 2,520,000; 2,000,000 in England, 200,000 in Scotland and 320,000 in Wales. **Reliability of population estimate:** 3.

Historical changes: The first record in Britain was from Denbighshire in 1828, and a number of records exist for Montgomeryshire prior to 1830. The earliest documented introduction was to Macclesfield, Cheshire, in 1876. From then until 1929 there were a number of introductions around the country. It became illegal in 1938 to import grey squirrels or to keep them in captivity (Lever 1977). The subsequent spread of grey squirrels is described by Middleton (1931), Shorten (1954) and Lloyd (1983), amongst others. The period of greatest range increase in England and Wales was 1930-1945, when the species became entrenched in the midlands and most of the south of England apart from Cornwall. East Anglia remained largely free of grey squirrels but animals were found as far north as Cheshire and north Wales in the west and north Yorkshire in the east. Thereafter the spread has continued more slowly (Gurnell 1991b), but in the decade following World War Two they increased in abundance in the north, parts of East Anglia, and parts of Wales. A bounty system in the 1950s failed to reduce grey squirrel numbers or prevent their spread (Thompson & Peace 1962). In England, by the early 1960s only parts of Cumberland, East Anglia, north Lancashire and Westmorland remained largely uncolonised. Williamson & Brown (1986) described the pattern of spread as random dispersal with occasional major advances. Okubo *et al.* (1989), using Reynold's (1985) data from East Anglia for the period 1965-1981, estimated a mean rate of spread of 7·7 km per year.

Population trends: The spread of grey squirrels is continuing, but changes since 1973 have been relatively small. Using Forestry Commission survey results, and calculating index numbers, Usher, Crawford & Banwell (1992) showed that in England and Wales grey squirrel distribution is nearly stable, but in Scotland there has been a steady increase

through the 1980s. However, grey squirrels continue to expand their range in north-west England; they are now more abundant than red squirrels in north Lancashire, and are well established in the Lake District as far north as Windermere and Ambleside (Lowe 1993). Predictive models suggest that the grey squirrel will continue to expand its range in Britain slightly, and should become more than twice as widespread as red squirrels (Usher, Crawford & Banwell 1992). Also, grey squirrels 'leap-frog' through unsuitable habitats (Reynolds 1985; Staines 1986), and in Scotland may spread (or possibly be spread) over hills to colonise river valleys (Staines 1986). Thus it is not clear what natural barriers will limit the spread of grey squirrels, nor what their final distribution or numbers will be. Their spread in Deeside has been slow; although they arrived in the early 1970s, they are still largely confined to estates or large gardens with mature deciduous trees and are very much restricted in range and density (B. Staines pers. comm.). However, a survey in 1991 found grey squirrels were present only 25 km south of Huntly in Aberdeenshire, and so the northern limit to their spread has not yet been established (Gurnell & Pepper 1993). The numbers killed nationally show no clear long-term trend, and overall have remained roughly constant from 1960-1990, although there are considerable annual variations, probably due to fluctuations in seed crops (Tapper 1992).

Population threats: None.

Bank vole *Clethrionomys glareolus*

Status: Native; very common.

Distribution: Found throughout mainland Britain and on Anglesey, Bute, Handa, the Isle of Wight, Mull, Raasay and Ramsey; the subspecies on the island of Skomer is dealt with separately below. Bank voles were found between 1966 and 1970 in the Brodick Castle area of the Isle of Arran, probably the result of an unrecorded recent introduction (Gibson 1973).

Population data: Bank voles prefer areas of mature mixed deciduous woodland with a thick shrub or field layer, but in Britain they are also found in grassland habitats, young deciduous plantations, conifer plantations and hedgerows (Alibhai & Gipps 1991). Populations in Britain are non-cyclic and do not attain very high densities. Numbers reach a peak in the autumn followed by a decline over winter and spring, and in some years numbers tend to increase from winter to summer after winter breeding. Numbers may fluctuate dramatically, and are significantly greater in the summer following a good seed crop than after a poor one (Mallorie & Flowerdew 1994). Thus densities can vary from 5 to (exceptionally) 130 per ha depending upon season and habitat. Good densities for bank voles in woodland would be 23 per ha in winter and 66 per ha in summer (H.C. Mallorie & J.R. Flowerdew pers. comm.). In linear features in arable areas, a density of 60 per km of hedgerow would be typical for hedgerows of reasonable quality; the actual density does not change significantly during the year, although during the summer bank voles will move from the hedgerows into the crops (Tew & Macdonald 1993; Tew 1994).

Samples from pellets (Table 5), bottles (Table 6) and traps (Table 7) all show that bank voles are rarer than wood mice, and overall the ratio of wood mice to bank voles is 1·7:1 (Table 8). This is in part due to the fact that wood mice colonise a greater range of habitats than bank voles, which are more dependent on cover. The following data were used to calculate pre-breeding population size: for linear features an average of 40 per km of all types of hedgerow in arable areas, 10 per km in pastoral areas and 5 per km in marginal upland areas; a mean of 10 per ha for semi-natural broadleaved woodlands; 5 per ha in semi-natural mixed woodlands and scrub, 2·5 per ha in broadleaved and mixed plantations and semi-natural coniferous woodlands, and 1 per ha in coniferous and mixed plantations and bracken.

Population estimates: A total pre-breeding population of about 23,000,000; 17,750,000

in England, 3,500,000 in Scotland and 1,750,000 in Wales. A high proportion of the population is in England because this is where the majority of the hedgerows in arable landscapes are found; hedgerows in arable landscapes in England alone contain over a third of the British pre-breeding bank vole population. This estimate for the total bank vole population also suggests a ratio of 1·7 wood mice per bank vole, which is the same ratio as in the samples summarised in Table 8. **Reliability of population estimate: 3.**

Historical changes: Bank voles were not recognised until 1832, but were subsequently found to inhabit a wide area in Great Britain, although for many years bank voles were considered to be rather uncommon in places where they were found to be plentiful later that century (Harting 1887). It is unlikely that this observation reflects anything except a lack of recording (Millais 1904-1906), although at the turn of the century they were still thought to be scarce in northern Scotland.

Synchronous countrywide reductions in woodland rodent populations were indicated by Southern's (1970) analysis of tawny owl *Strix aluco* breeding success. In particular, bank vole (and wood mouse) numbers were low in the springs of 1955 and 1958, leading to low nesting activity and breeding success of the tawny owls in those two years. To look for evidence of, and reasons for, synchronous population fluctuations in woodland rodents, the Mammal Society initiated a long-term woodland rodent trapping survey, which involved trapping every May/June and November/December; the preliminary results for 17 sites for up to six years each during the mid-1980s are presented by Mallorie & Flowerdew (1994). This study confirmed the synchronous dynamics of bank vole populations over wide geographical areas, with tree seed crops having a strong influence on numbers the following summer and a weaker one on numbers in the winter following the seed crop. In addition there is evidence of density dependence in both summer-autumn and winter-spring periods, possibly regulated by the curtailment of the breeding season at high densities (Alibhai & Gipps 1985). Thus bank vole numbers were low in the summer of 1982, following the very cold winter of 1981-1982 and the failed seed crop the previous year (Tubbs 1986; J.R. Flowerdew pers. comm.).

Population trends: Unknown. In general, bank vole numbers are probably as great now as they have ever been. Future fluctuations in numbers will depend on the seed crop of woodland trees and to some extent the severity of winter weather (J.R. Flowerdew pers. comm.). Also, in view of the large proportion of the population found in arable landscapes, this species may benefit substantially from changes such as hedgerow planting, farm woodland schemes, and long-term set-aside. However, large-scale hedgerow losses (Barr *et al.* 1993) probably led to significant population declines.

Population threats: None known.

Skomer vole *Clethrionomys glareolus skomerensis*

Status: Native; locally common.

Distribution: Confined to the island of Skomer, south-west Wales.

Population data: They are closely associated with dense cover of bracken and bluebells, where peak densities can reach 475 per ha (T.D. Healing pers. comm.). Population estimates were made during surveys of small mammals on the island in 1960, 1981 and 1992 (Fullagar *et al.* 1963; Healing *et al.* 1983; T.D. Healing pers. comm.), combining live-trapping data from seven trap lines and two grids to produce a total population estimate. By this means, the population was estimated to be 21,536 in 1960 (Fullagar *et al.* 1963), 21,161 in 1981 (Healing *et al.* 1983) and 19,859 in 1992 (T.D. Healing pers. comm.). These were all late summer populations; assuming the winter population is roughly 35% that of the summer population

suggests a pre-breeding population of 7000 voles.

Population estimates: A total pre-breeding population of about 7000 voles on an island of 290 ha, all in Wales. **Reliability of population estimate: 1.**

Historical changes: Unknown.

Population trends: The results of the surveys quoted above suggest that the population is stable, although interpreting data from such widely spaced surveys is difficult. About 70% of the voles on Skomer are found in dense bracken and bluebells. This habitat occupies about 15% of the surface area of the island, a proportion which has varied little in the last 30 years (Fullagar *et al.* 1963; Healing *et al.* 1983; T.D. Healing pers. comm.). Thus it is probable that the population of voles has also remained relatively stable. However, trapping on one grid in August from 1977 to 1981 inclusive revealed densities of 224, 145, 122, 218 and 318 voles per ha in each year; whether these fluctuations follow a regular cycle over the years is unknown (Healing *et al.* 1983).

Population threats: None known. The 1992 population survey found a significant increase in the number of wood mice on the island. Whether this will be detrimental to the vole population is unknown.

Field vole: *Microtus agrestis*

Status: Native; locally common.

Distribution: Widespread on the British mainland. Field voles occur on most of the Hebridean islands, but are absent from Barra, Lewis and some of the Inner Hebrides (Colonsay, Pabay, Raasay, Rum, Soay and South Rona). Field voles are also absent from the Isles of Scilly, Lundy, Orkney and Shetland.

Population data: Mainly found in rough, ungrazed grassland, including young forestry plantations with a lush growth of grass. Low population densities occur in marginal habitats such as woodlands, hedgerows, blanket bog, sand dunes, scree and open moorland; field voles have been recorded at over 1300 m in the Cairngorms (Gipps & Alibhai 1991).

There are both cyclic and annual changes in abundance. Richards (1985) reviewed the field vole studies carried out at the Wytham estate, Oxfordshire, from 1949 to 1978. He concluded that these populations showed annual, rather than cyclic, fluctuations, and he attributed this to the patchy nature of the habitat available to the field voles in Wytham. It seems likely that habitat type influences field vole population dynamics, and that vole cycles occur where there are extensive areas of habitat, such as upland forestry plantations, rather than in small patches of habitat. In Scotland and north England, there seems little doubt that field vole populations cycle (Snow 1968; Marchant *et al.* 1990). In southern England the situation is less clear; studies in Sussex farmland suggest cyclical fluctuations (Tapper 1979), whereas in Cambridgeshire and Leicestershire Village & Myhill (1990) found fluctuations in numbers that could be considered cyclic in arable land but not so much in mixed farmland. These cyclical changes make estimating population sizes difficult.

Estimating field vole numbers is also complicated by populations being very patchily distributed at the landscape level. This clumped distribution means that they are easily missed by trapping (D.J. Jefferies pers. comm.), and so density estimates for such a patchily-distributed species are largely meaningless. Although the species is both widespread and abundant, there are few estimates of population density, and most density estimates are from isolated fragments of suitable habitat, and so are probably atypical. Tapper (1979) calculated a density of 100 per ha for spring populations in suitable grasslands in southern England, with peak densities of 300 per ha. Ferns (1979) recorded 97 per ha in spring in a young larch plantation, reaching a peak of 128 per ha in early winter.

Whilst field voles occur in the grassy banks of arable hedgerows, densities are low (Tew 1994). Densities vary from 1 to 15 per ha in mixed farmland in Morayshire (M.L. Gorman pers. comm.). There are no recent data on densities from upland areas, especially for Scotland and Wales, yet these habitats probably contain the great majority of the field vole population. The final problem when trying to estimate field vole numbers is calculating how much habitat is available to support such high densities.

Since there are few density estimates, and the availability of suitable habitats is unknown, the only basis on which to estimate the size of the field vole population is from their relative abundance in a wide range of samples (Table 8). This showed that, nationally, field voles were 1·9 times as common as wood mice and 1·8 times as common as common shrews. This suggests a pre-breeding population of 75,000,000 field voles. Estimating the distribution by country was more problematic, since there are relatively few samples from upland and other habitats from Scotland and Wales (see Tables 5-7). The figure for each country was obtained by deriving approximate ratios to common shrews and wood mice in arable, pastoral, marginal upland and upland habitats in Scotland and Wales, and using the availability of these habitat groupings and the estimated numbers of common shrews and wood mice in these habitat groups.

Population estimates: A total pre-breeding population of about 75,000,000; 17,500,000 in England, 41,000,000 in Scotland and 16,500,000 in Wales. The skewed distribution of field voles between the three countries (England: 56·6% of the land area and 23·3% of the field vole population; Scotland: 34·4% of the land area and 54·7% of the field vole population; and Wales: 9·0% of the land area and 22·0% of the field vole population) is because field voles now appear to be strongly biased in their distribution towards upland areas. In lowland areas this species is now very clumped in its distribution. It should be remembered that, in the absence of many density estimates, these figures are based on relative abundance to other species of small mammal, and that for many habitats, e.g. upland areas of Scotland, there are very few samples on which to base this analysis. **Reliability of population estimate: 4.**

Historical changes: At the turn of the century field voles were abundant throughout Great Britain wherever there was sufficient grassland (Thorburn 1920). Since then, field vole populations have almost certainly declined substantially due to the loss of rough grassland by both natural and anthropogenic changes, the removal of linear features and the general tidying-up of the rural landscape. This reduction in field vole numbers has led to a cessation of the vole plagues that were frequent until early this century (Ritchie 1920; Elton 1942). Whilst such vole plagues were comparatively rare in Britain, when they did occur, the numbers of voles were compared to swarms of locusts, devastating agricultural crops and barking young trees. In 1891-1893, for instance, there was a great increase in the vole numbers in the area of the Scottish border, and 370-470 km² were infested with voles, with parts of this area rendered useless (Millais 1904-1906).

The field vole is a major food item for a number of predators. Snow (1968) concluded that the number of fledgling kestrels *Falco tinnunculus* ringed showed a strong relationship with field vole numbers. Using ringing records for 1926-1966 from lowland Scotland, north England and north Wales, he concluded that peaks in vole numbers occurred in 1926, 1930, 1932/1933, 1937/1938, 1957, 1961 and 1964. The data in Marchant *et al.* (1990) suggest further peaks in 1968 and 1972/1973, and are then difficult to interpret until further peaks occurred in 1981 and 1984. A large-scale sampling programme in Cambridgeshire and Leicestershire (Village & Myhill 1990) also suggests that field vole numbers in arable farmland reached a peak in 1981 and 1984, and possibly in 1987. These peaks also coincided with the peaks in abundance of field voles in south-west Scotland (Taylor *et al.* 1988). Records from the early 1940s showed

that in southern England cyclical fluctuations in kestrel numbers were barely detectable (Snow 1968; Marchant *et al.* 1990), possibly because of the lack of synchrony of local vole populations or a lack of cycles (J.R. Flowerdew pers. comm.).

After myxomatosis, vole populations benefited from the increased grass growth, and their habitats expanded greatly (Sumption & Flowerdew 1985). This is corroborated by studies of the numbers of weasels taken by gamekeepers; after myxomatosis the numbers of weasels killed increased markedly until the early 1970s in both Suffolk and Sussex (Tapper 1982; King 1989), suggesting higher levels of prey availability, at least until the early 1970s. In addition, peaks in the number of weasels killed and vole peaks are probably correlated (with a slight delay); thus in Suffolk the number of weasels killed peaked in 1953, 1956, 1960, 1964, 1967, 1970 and 1973, probably as a direct result of field vole peaks (Tapper 1979), but thereafter the recovery of rabbits and stoats confuses the picture. Some at least of these peaks in vole numbers appear to be widespread. There was a vole plague in the Carron Valley, Stirlingshire, in 1953/1954 (Lockie 1956), and in 1956/1957 vole numbers throughout Wales reached plague levels, and this was more widespread than any previous vole plague in living memory. During this plague, damage to forestry was extensive (Cadman 1957), as used to occur earlier this century (Elton 1942). Thus it seems likely that there was a general increase in field vole numbers, and in distribution on a local scale, in the mid-1950s to early 1970s, which subsequently fell from the mid-1970s as rabbit numbers increased and suitable habitats consequently declined.

Population trends: Numbers have been declining since the mid-1970s, when habitats were lost due to an increase in grazing pressure following the increase in rabbit numbers and intensive agriculture, especially in the south. Field voles also like 'marginal land', exactly the sort of habitat that has positively attracted development in the south-east, so that much suitable habitat has been lost to roads, houses and out-of-town industrial and trading estates. There has also been a significant loss of habitat because grassland is a transitional type of vegetation, and it is lost by scrub encroachment if not managed. Managing grassland in a way that maintains its suitability for field voles is not cost-effective in the lowlands. This reduction in field vole numbers, and perhaps also a reduction in their accessibility to aerial predators, seems to have contributed to the decline in the numbers of barn owls *Tyto alba* (Shawyer 1987). An increase in permanent (but not rotational) set-aside (Brockless & Tapper 1993), woodland planting schemes and other landscape management practices that increase the area of rough grassland should increase the amount of available habitat, and hence field vole numbers. However, the increase in rabbit numbers will further increase grazing pressure and thereby help limit field vole numbers, and so if there is any overall population increase due to changes in agricultural policy, it is unlikely to be as large as that which occurred in the mid-1950s.

Population threats: Continuing loss of habitat may lead to a further decline in numbers, especially in the south, and this problem is likely to be exacerbated by the increasing number of rabbits, although this may be partially off-set by the increase in long-term set-aside.

Orkney vole *Microtus arvalis orcadensis*

Status: Introduced to Orkney, probably by Neolithic settlers before 3500 BC. The skull characteristics of Orkney voles suggest that their affinities are more with populations in south Europe than elsewhere, and that they probably came with early settlers from the eastern Mediterranean (Berry & Rose 1975). It is common where it occurs.

Distribution: Confined to six of the Orkney islands: Mainland, Rousay, Sanday, South Ronaldsay, Stronsay and Westray. There is a pellet record from Eday in 1965, and two recorded introductions to the same island

involving a few voles in 1987 and 1988 (Arnold 1993).

Population data: Within the intensively managed agricultural landscapes that now dominate Orkney, the voles are largely confined to linear features which maintain very high population densities and also serve to connect otherwise fragmented pieces of natural habitat (Gorman & Reynolds 1993). Voles used to be present in agricultural habitats in Orkney e.g. in rich grass and clover fields (Millais 1904b) and in both pasture and arable fields in the 1940s (Hewson 1951). The current marked absence of voles from agricultural areas in Orkney, may be due to the particularly intensive nature of current land management on the islands, especially the high stocking rates and the extensive areas devoted to silage (Gorman & Reynolds 1993).

To calculate total population size, density estimates were made for a variety of habitat types on Mainland in July-August by snap trapping and Longworth trapping over a three-year period and averages calculated. These gave densities of: damp heath 273 per ha, heather moorland 102 per ha, marsh 57 per ha, coniferous plantation with grass understorey 129 per ha and pasture 0 per ha (Gorman 1991). Land cover estimates for those Orkney islands which have voles were based on the Macaulay Land Use Research Institute's land classification system. Combining these figures produced an estimated annual low in April of 1,000,000 voles, and an annual high in September of 4,000,000 voles (M.L. Gorman pers. comm.).

Population estimates: A total pre-breeding population of about 1,000,000, all in Scotland. **Reliability of population estimate:** 1.

Historical changes: Only recognised as a member of the British fauna at the turn of the century (Millais 1904b); at that time it was widespread (but probably locally distributed) in Orkney in both natural and man-made habitats. However, Orkney voles have disappeared from agricultural areas in the last fifty years, and it is likely, therefore, that there has been a very substantial decrease in vole populations since the Second World War (Gorman & Reynolds 1993).

Population trends: Numbers have been declining, probably substantially, through agricultural pressures, especially the loss of heath and moorland. On Orkney Mainland alone it is likely that habitat that could support over 100,000 voles has been lost from what was once moorland (Gorman & Reynolds 1993). However, this decline may have halted, since the rate of loss of habitat to agriculture has decreased (M.L. Gorman pers. comm.).

Population threats: Since 1936 the area of Orkney used for agriculture has increased from 37% to 81% at the expense of natural habitats. This has led to a very substantial reduction in vole populations, and population fragmentation and isolation has increased (Gorman & Reynolds 1993).

Water vole *Arvicola terrestris*

Status: Native, and probably still moderately common, although declining.

Distribution: Found throughout mainland Britain but mainly confined to lowland areas near water. Water voles are very locally distributed in north and north-west Scotland and absent from most islands, but present on Anglesey, Bute, the Isle of Wight, and a few small islands. In Scotland they are found in headstreams up to 660 m altitude, but most populations occur at altitudes of less than 50 m (D.J. Jefferies pers. comm.). They are more numerous in upland and peatland habitats than formerly thought (Green & Green 1993).

Population data: Estimating population size is difficult because, on some river systems at least, water voles are patchily distributed around 'core sites', and their distribution is discontinuous because some sites are unsuitable or are too remote from existing populations (Lawton & Woodroffe 1991). Of 2970 sites surveyed in Britain in 1989-1990, 47.7% were positive for water voles (Strachan

& Jefferies 1993). For each water authority region in England, the percentage of sites positive for water voles and the number of water voles per km of bank (in brackets) were: Anglian 63.2% (42.5); North West 34.5% (29.3); Northumbria 52.6% (32.7); Severn Trent 34.9% (32.7); South West 8.1% (17.2); Southern 68.5% (42.6); Thames 70.8% (41.5); Wessex 34.5% (28.6); Yorkshire 35.7% (29.6); and in mainland Scotland 26.5% (32.1) and Wales 15.0% (28.0) (Strachan & Jefferies 1993). The actual number of animals per km was calculated from the number of latrines found, using the formula described by Woodroffe, Lawton & Davidson (1990a). Based on the lengths of aquatic habitats given in Table 4, this gave a total population size of 3,895,000 water voles, with 2,506,000 in England (Anglian region 768,000, North West region 137,000, Northumbria region 221,000, Severn Trent region 315,000, South West region 20,000, Southern region 380,000, Thames region 379,000, Wessex region 103,000 and Yorkshire region 183,000), 1,254,000 water voles in mainland Scotland and 135,000 water voles in Wales. For this calculation it was assumed that for rivers and canals both banks are used by the same water voles. For wider waterways this will not be true, and for these the length of bank should theoretically be doubled, thus increasing the population estimate slightly. Also, these figures are for the summer, and the winter population is likely to be only 30% of this (Woodroffe 1988) i.e. 1,168,500.

Population estimates: A total pre-breeding population of about 1,169,000; in England 752,000, in Scotland 376,000 and in Wales 41,000. **Reliability of population estimate: 3.**

Historical changes: At the turn of the century water voles were abundant in all suitable localities in England, were found in all low-lying districts of Scotland except Argyll, and were common in the streams of Anglesey and North Wales, but were comparatively scarce in south Wales (Millais 1904-1906). Subsequently there has been a long-term decline (Jefferies, Morris & Mulleneux 1989; Strachan & Jefferies 1993). Jefferies, Morris & Mulleneux (1989) showed a statistically significant decline in the use of words such as 'common' to describe water voles in local mammal reports, although such information could not be used to quantify the magnitude of the decline. A recent field survey (Strachan & Jefferies 1993) showed that there has been a steady long-term decline this century, with two periods of accelerated site loss, the first in the 1940s/1950s, and the second within the last two decades. The first decline was most marked in northern and western Britain and may correlate with increased afforestation and subsequent acidification of waterways (Harriman & Morrison 1982; Nature Conservancy Council 1986). The second period of loss, most marked in the 1980s, is correlated with the spread of mink (Strachan & Jefferies 1993). Prior to, and in addition to, the escape of mink from farms, habitat destruction by riparian engineering works causing fragmentation and isolation of colonies, coupled with water pollution, acted as cumulative factors which also contributed to this decline. Since 1900, 68% of occupied water vole sites have been lost, and this could be as high as 77% (Strachan & Jefferies 1993). Also, the number of voles at each site is believed to decline with the percentage of occupied sites, and so the reduction in water vole numbers has been even greater (D.J. Jefferies pers. comm.).

Population trends: Continuing to decline. Calculating the rate of decline this century, Strachan & Jefferies (1993) estimate that by the end of this century 94% of formerly occupied sites may be lost, with an even greater reduction in water vole numbers, making this the most dramatic population decline of any British mammal this century .

Population threats: There is no conclusive evidence as to what has led to the decline; predation by mink *Mustela vison*, habitat destruction, human disturbance, pollution (especially by organochlorine insecticides in the 1950s and 1960s), increasing numbers of cattle grazing river banks and thereby

reducing the available cover, and climatic changes have all been mooted as causal factors. Nationally, the relative contribution of any or all of these is at present unknown (Jefferies, Morris & Mulleneux 1989). A study in the North Yorkshire Moors National Park showed that gaps occur in the distribution of water voles because some habitats are unsuitable (approximately 45% of sites examined), and of sites with suitable habitat, about 30% lack water voles because they are too isolated, thereby reducing colonisation rates, and/or suffer very high levels of mink predation (Lawton & Woodroffe 1991). Other studies have shown that mink predation can have a significant impact, at least locally (Woodroffe, Lawton & Davidson 1990b), and a survey in 1989-1990 showed that water voles had declined in numbers, particularly where mink were present (Strachan & Jefferies 1993). The questionnaire survey by Jefferies, Morris & Mulleneux (1989) also identified the presence of mink as being an important factor leading to the decline of water voles. However, there is good evidence that the population decline had begun well before mink became widespread, probably due to pollution and habitat degradation, and so a number of, probably inter-acting, factors have played a role in the decline of water voles.

It appears that the effects of predation are exacerbated by the water vole's specialised habitat requirements, and the loss of populations in marginal habitats due to predation can lead to increasing fragmentation of populations in prime habitats, thereby increasing the potential for population losses due to chance events. The interactions of predation, isolation, fragmentation and habitat quality are presently unknown (Lawton & Woodroffe 1991). However, Howes (1979) presented some interesting data from Yorkshire comparing fox and barn owl predation on water voles in adjacent areas where the vegetation had or had not been removed. Water voles occurred in 24·5% and 8·1% of fox scats and represented 13·2% and 1·6% of barn owl prey items respectively from sites without and with bankside vegetation. Clearly, vegetation loss renders water voles susceptible to a wide variety of predators and not just mink. The relative impact of different types of predators on water vole populations has yet to be determined. The results from a questionnaire survey suggest that disturbance, particularly dredging operations, also have a significant impact on water vole populations (Jefferies, Morris & Mulleneux 1989).

Wood mouse *Apodemus sylvaticus*

Status: Native; widespread and very common.

Distribution: Found throughout mainland Britain, although absent from many small islands, e.g. the Isle of May, Lundy, North Rona and from the Isles of Scilly other than Tresco and St Mary's (Flowerdew 1991). Many island populations are the result of accidental introductions (Berry 1969).

Population data: Wood mice are highly adaptable and inhabit most habitats if they are not too wet, including woodland, arable land, ungrazed grassland, heather, blanket bog, sand dunes, rocky mountain summits and vegetated parts of urban areas (Flowerdew 1991). Densities vary seasonally, with autumn/early winter peaks and spring/summer troughs; densities of 1-40 per ha are usual in mixed deciduous woodland, but after a good seed crop densities of 130-200 per ha have been recorded, although such high densities are very rare. Montgomery (1989) suggested that the average April-June density for wood mice in mixed deciduous woodland is about 7 per ha. This would also be the typical spring density for coniferous woodland, although densities vary a little depending on the age of the trees and extent of ground cover (W.I. Montgomery pers. comm.). In arable and pastoral landscapes, the length and nature of the field boundary per unit area may be more important than land use in determining absolute density (W.I. Montgomery pers. comm.). In arable areas of Britain, seasonal variation in density is from 0·5 per ha in the summer to 17·5 per ha in winter, with winter peaks as low as 8·4 per ha (Green 1979; Wolton 1985; Attuquayefio, Gorman &

Wolton 1986; Wilson, Montgomery & Elwood 1993; Tew & Macdonald 1993; Tew 1994). In mixed farmland on the Moray coast, Grampian, wood mouse numbers varied from 2 to 30 per ha (M.L. Gorman pers. comm.). These low spring densities in arable fields may simply reflect the large size of fields.

There are no data on wood mouse populations in pastoral areas of northern and western England, Scotland or Wales. A study in Northern Ireland in a very similar habitat, where there were 1·9 farms and 9·2 km of field boundaries per km^2, found a density of 3·0 per ha in summer and 2·5 per ha in winter, with 99% of these in field boundaries and only 1% in buildings (Montgomery & Dowie 1993). A study on sand dunes in Scotland suggested that densities range from less than 0·5 per ha in spring to around 12 per ha in the autumn (Gorman & Zubaid 1993). In urban areas, densities can be very high in isolated habitat patches due to restricted dispersal (Dickman & Doncaster 1987), although suitable habitat patches are scattered and overall densities in urban areas are much lower. Marginal habitats for wood mice, such as moorland, grasslands and sand dunes, do not show as marked a seasonal cycle as woodland populations.

Median figures for spring populations were used to calculate the population size. These were: 7 per ha in all types of woodland and scrub; 2·5 per ha in bracken, unimproved grassland and marshy areas; 1 per ha in arable land; and 0·5 per ha in sand dunes, moorlands, improved and semi-improved grasslands, urban areas and other marginal habitats. To calculate the autumn population size, spring densities were multiplied by three (W.I. Montgomery pers. comm.).

Population estimates: A total pre-breeding population of about 38,000,000; 19,500,000 in England, 15,000,000 in Scotland and 3,500,000 in Wales. The autumn population would be about 114,000,000. **Reliability of population estimate:** 3.

Historical changes: As for bank voles, synchronous countrywide reductions in woodland rodent populations were indicated by Southern's (1970) analysis of tawny owl breeding success. In particular, the numbers of both species were low in the springs of 1955 and 1958. The preliminary results for 17 sites monitored for up to six years during the mid-1980s as part of the Mammal Society's survey (Mallorie & Flowerdew 1994) confirmed the synchrony between the dynamics of wood mouse populations over wide geographical areas. During this period, wood mouse numbers were lowest in the summer of 1982, following a poor seed crop the previous autumn and the very cold winter of 1981/1982. The survey showed that wood mouse densities were significantly greater in the winter and the summer following a good seed crop, and that population highs and lows tended to coincide at different sites. This is due to widespread heavy tree seed crops, although at each site different species of tree may be involved. Mallorie & Flowerdew (1994) suggested that weather synchronised the seed crop between species: frosts in spring will destroy newly fertilised tree seeds and fruits, flowers and early seed may be lost during high winds and heavy rain or hail in May/June, and cool wet weather in summer may prevent ripening.

Population trends: Assumed to be stable.

Population threats: There are a number of threats to populations on arable land. Laboratory and field studies have shown that wood mice are susceptible to poisoning by insecticidal seed treatments, herbicidal sprays and methiocarb molluscicide pellets (Tarrant & Westlake 1988; Tarrant *et al.* 1990). They are particularly susceptible to seed treatments because of the attractiveness of seeds as food. Johnson, Flowerdew & Hare (1991) showed that the surface application of molluscicide pellets drastically reduced field populations of wood mice, although applications over several years on the study site failed to produce any long-term depression of wood mouse numbers. This was possibly due to the small size of the study fields, and the presence of

hedgerows and nearby woods which supported reservoir populations. The problem would possibly be more significant on larger fields with fewer hedgerows and few nearby wood mouse populations to recolonise the treated fields. Johnson, Flowerdew & Hare (1991) also showed that drilling molluscicide pellets substantially reduced wood mouse mortality.

In addition, harvest has a dramatic affect on recruitment and population density in arable areas. Whilst harvesting itself leads to little mortality, 60% of the wood mice in one study disappeared within ten days of the harvest, and increased predation risks were a major factor (Tew 1992). Further mortality occurred due to stubble burning, although sufficient wood mice survived to overwinter and sustain the following year's population (Tew & Macdonald 1993). A reduction in the use of herbicides, e.g. to produce 'conservation headlands' around the edges of arable fields, leads to an increase in the abundance of both floral and invertebrate food supplies and hence to increased populations of wood mice (Tew, Macdonald & Rands 1992).

Yellow-necked mouse *Apodemus flavicollis*

Status: Native; locally common.

Distribution: Mainly eastern and south-eastern England, the English/Welsh border and southern Wales. There are occasional records outside this range in south-west England and further north to Northumberland.

Population data: This species is largely confined to mature deciduous woodland, and there is some evidence of an association between the distribution of yellow-necked mice and areas of ancient woodland (Montgomery 1978). Marginal habitats include hedges, rural gardens and buildings (Montgomery 1991), and yellow-necked mice enter houses more frequently than wood mice, generally in the autumn (Arnold 1993). An association between the distribution of yellow-necked mice and arable fields has been reported in Essex (Corke 1977), but there is no evidence for this being more widespread (Montgomery 1978).

Yellow-necked mouse numbers reach a peak in late autumn/early winter, and decrease throughout winter and spring. Although a long-term study in Gloucestershire found a marked seasonal cycle (Montgomery 1985), it is likely that this was more extreme than that seen in many populations, and overall autumn populations are around three times higher than spring ones (W.I. Montgomery pers. comm.). There are also variations in peak abundance between years which are positively correlated with mast production. Patterns of woodland management, in particular increasing amounts of conifer planting and the concomitant loss of seed-producing trees, reduce yellow-necked mouse numbers (Yalden & Shore 1991).

Whilst densities can reach 50 per ha in good habitats in the late autumn, long term trapping in an area of ancient woodland in Gloucestershire suggested that good sites would have 10 per ha in the spring and average sites 2 per ha (Montgomery 1980; D.W. Yalden unpubl.). Studies in Kent suggested similar figures, i.e. 3-12 per ha (D. Roberts pers. comm.). Population size was therefore estimated as follows. Based on the figures in Spencer & Kirby (1992), there are approximately 230,000 ha of ancient woodland within the main yellow-necked mouse range (Avon, Berkshire, Dorset, Essex, Gloucestershire, Gwent, Hampshire, Herefordshire, Hertfordshire, Kent, Shropshire, Surrey, Sussex, Wiltshire and Worcestershire). It was assumed that yellow-necked mice are found in all the ancient woodland in these counties, since the documented distribution almost certainly represents under-recording. This is primarily because it is not easy to differentiate the skulls of wood mice and yellow-necked mice (Fielding 1966), and so there are very few records from bottles (Morris 1970) or owl-pellets (Glue 1974). Thus the spring population, at an average density of 2 per ha of ancient woodland, would be around 450,000. This calculation takes no account of

yellow-necked mouse populations in habitats other than ancient woodland, and there are also a number of isolated populations outside the contiguous range (Arnold 1993). However, in many areas of apparently suitable habitat the species is transient (J. Gurnell pers. comm.), and coppicing (M. Hicks pers. comm.) and other woodland management practices (Yalden & Shore 1991) adversely affect yellow-necked mouse numbers. Thus, even allowing for these other populations, the total population is unlikely to exceed 750,000. The separate numbers for England and Wales were calculated from the areas of ancient woodland (Spencer & Kirby 1992) and the relative distribution of records (Arnold 1993).

Population estimates: A total pre-breeding population of about 750,000; 662,500 in England, none in Scotland and 87,500 in Wales. **Reliability of population estimate:** 4.

Historical changes: Records from Neolithic and Roman sites indicate that the range was formerly more extensive (Yalden 1984b), and the current distribution suggests that this is a relict of a formerly widespread woodland species (Montgomery 1978; Yalden 1992). It was only recognised as a separate species in 1894 when de Winton (1894) described it as very local, and even at the turn of the century yellow-necked mice were thought to be sporadic in their distribution (Barrett-Hamilton & Hinton 1910-1921).

Population trends: In recent years yellow-necked mice are believed to have been declining, probably both in range and abundance, although the rate and magnitude of any population change is unknown.

Population threats: Being a species that is probably closely associated with ancient woodland, it is very vulnerable to the effects of habitat loss and fragmentation (Harris & Woollard 1990). In addition, a long term study at one site in Gloucestershire has shown that relatively small changes in habitat management can have a significant impact on yellow-necked mouse numbers (Yalden & Shore 1991). In this site, the replacement of deciduous woodland with conifers, and the loss of elms (*Ulmus* spp.) and some yew trees (*Taxus baccata*), caused a significant decline in yellow-necked mouse numbers (Montgomery 1985), probably because they depend on seeds more than other rodents (Hansson 1985). As this one example shows, the combined effects of exacting habitat requirements and habitat fragmentation can have a significant effect on yellow-necked mouse numbers.

Harvest mouse *Micromys minutus*

Status: Probably a post-glacial introduction (Sutcliffe & Kowalski 1976); limited in distribution but locally can occur in large numbers.

Distribution: England south and east of central Yorkshire, plus parts of the coastal belt of Wales; scattered colonies outside this area probably represent long-standing introductions, possibly from last century (Harris 1979a). In particular, most, if not all, the Scottish records represent isolated colonies established as the result of accidental introductions. The only recent record from Scotland was of a colony to the south of Edinburgh that was first reported in the nineteenth century (Harris 1979a). This site has now been destroyed by a housing estate (S. Pritchard pers. comm.). However, searches of suitable habitat in the south and east of Scotland may reveal other colonies.

Population data: Harvest mice are found in areas of dense monocotyledonous vegetation. Most records collected during a survey in the 1970s (Harris 1979a) were from linear features such as hedgerows, ditches, field edges and roadside verges; nowadays they are rarely found in cereal fields. Harvest mice are often the most abundant small mammal in wetlands (M.R. Perrow & A. Jowitt pers. comm.). There are few density estimates because there are particular difficulties in calculating densities for this species. Harvest mice may be patchily distributed, both spatially and temporally. Accurate population

estimates in tall vegetation require above-ground sampling, and although the proportion of catches on the ground increases in winter, it is still often less than 10% of the total catch (M.R. Perrow & A. Jowitt pers. comm.). Occasionally, densities can be very high (>200 per ha), but such high numbers are very localised, and peak densities are often followed by several years of low numbers (Trout 1978; Harris & Trout 1991). Mean density estimates between July and October for the following habitats were supplied by M.R. Perrow & A. Jowitt (pers. comm.): 0·05 per ha in barley; 0·4 per ha in wheat; 2·5-5·0 per ha in rough and damp meadows; 20 per ha in reedbeds, although numbers in reedbeds built up to a peak later in the year. Also, the over-winter mortality of harvest mice (from a peak in November) can be greater than 95%, and this is matched by an equally rapid population increase in late summer/early autumn.

In view of the paucity of density data, especially pre-breeding densities, the fragmented nature of the habitats used by over-wintering populations of harvest mice, and the very clumped, and often ephemeral, nature of harvest mouse populations (Harris 1979a), it was impossible to calculate population size from the available density data. Instead the ratio of harvest mice to wood mice in a variety of samples was used. This suggested that there were 26·6 wood mice per harvest mouse (Table 8) i.e. a pre-breeding population of 1,425,000 harvest mice. The distribution of harvest mice in Wales is very patchy, and they seem to be most frequently recorded in *Molinia* grassland on bogs. However, there are no data on which to accurately estimate population size, and so the population in Wales was estimated as follows: pre-breeding density was assumed to be 0·1 per ha of blanket bogs and marginal inundations, and 2 per km of hedgerow in arable areas.

Population estimates: A total pre-breeding population of about 1,425,000; 1,415,000 in England, no colonies currently known in Scotland and about 10,000 in Wales. We need to know a great deal more about population ecology of this species before this estimate can be improved. **Reliability of population estimate:** 5.

Historical changes: Harvest mice are believed to have been accidentally introduced in Neolithic times (Sutcliffe & Kowalski 1976; Harris 1979a; Yalden 1992), and their spread was largely dependent on the clearance of woodlands. How much of this spread was due to natural colonisation as opposed to further accidental translocations is unknown. Many of the isolated populations on the edge of the range are almost certainly due to accidental transport in hay and cereals (Harris 1979a). The species is predominantly eastern in its distribution, and whilst it spread naturally into eastern Europe in post-glacial times, it only became common in Poland in Neolithic times (Nadachowski 1989). It would appear that their subsequent spread into western Europe generally is probably due to accidental Neolithic translocations, and that the current abundance of harvest mice in much of Europe is therefore a comparatively recent event.

This species is easily overlooked (Harris 1979a) and even Thorburn, a competent naturalist living in the centre of its range, recorded that 'I have never succeeded in finding the nest' (Thorburn 1920). Millais (1904-1906) described it as a scarce and local resident in all the counties in which it was found. Thus the paucity of harvest mouse records, other than when specific surveys have been undertaken, means that there are no data on which to assess any long term population changes. A survey in the 1970s recorded harvest mice in 23 Watsonian vice-counties for which there had been no previous records (Harris 1979a), and there is no evidence that there has been a decline in range this century, although some isolated populations that were the result of introductions are known or believed to have disappeared. However, widespread changes in agricultural practice during the course of this century have removed large areas of suitable habitat in which harvest mice appeared to be abundant (Harris 1979b), and numbers must have

declined substantially. Even at the turn of the century writers were reporting that harvest mice were much less common than in the middle of the 19th century (Barrett-Hamilton & Hinton 1910-1921), and this decline was attributed to the advent of close-cutting reaping machines. Hardy (1933) even called for the reintroduction of the harvest mouse, arguing that the species was in imminent danger of extinction in Britain. Yet as late as the 1950s, large numbers of harvest mice were still being recorded in cereal ricks, e.g. Rowe & Taylor (1964). However, this habitat disappeared soon afterwards. There are other changes in agriculture which have probably caused declines in harvest mouse numbers since the 1950s. The sowing of winter cereals promotes earlier harvests, before the peak of the harvest mouse breeding season (Harris 1979c), and the shorter-stemmed cereals now grown are less suitable for nest building (Harris 1979a).

Population trends: Since a substantial proportion of the population may now be living in linear features in agricultural landscapes, further agricultural improvements leading to the loss of linear features are likely to lead to further population declines. However, set-aside will rapidly supply additional habitat adjacent to existing populations, and so should benefit this species.

Population threats: As a species living in marginal habitats and wetland areas, populations are vulnerable to habitat changes. A survey in the mid-1970s found that each year 12% of known sites were destroyed (Harris 1979a). In addition, mean litter sizes have declined from 6.75 ± 0.40 pre-1917 to 5.40 ± 0.16 in the 1970s; why this decline occurred is unknown (Harris 1979c). Harvest mice seem to favour dry continental climates, and it has been suggested that their distribution in Britain is limited by summer rainfall (Adams 1913). Heavy rain can lead to high juvenile mortality (S. Harris unpubl.), and cold and wet are important climatic factors that terminate the breeding season (Harris 1979c). Thus climate changes could have a significant impact on numbers. Although there are no quantitative data on the diet of harvest mice in Britain, they are known to have a mixed insectivorous and granivorous diet, and so the increasing use of insecticides (O'Connor & Shrubb 1986) could also have contributed to a decline in numbers.

House mouse *Mus domesticus*

Status: Introduced; present in Britain from at least the Iron Age. Locally abundant.

Distribution: Widespread but very patchily distributed throughout mainland Britain and most inhabited off-shore islands. The St Kilda race became extinct following the evacuation of the human population in 1930, apparently due to an inability to compete successfully with wood mice (Berry & Tricker 1969).

Population data: It is particularly difficult to provide a total population estimate, since the reproductive behaviour of house mice is 'boom and bust': very large populations may build up quickly in favourable, often temporary, habitats, and then disappear even more quickly (R.J. Berry pers. comm.). The classic example of this is in the cereal, particularly wheat, ricks that used to be built in the early autumn and then broken down for threshing the following spring. Southern & Laurie (1946) found that almost all ricks were infested with house mice, with some populations exceeding 2000 in a single rick, and with a population doubling time of around two months. However, at threshing these rick populations underwent a very high mortality, even if the statutory barriers around the rick were not used (R.J. Berry pers. comm.). Thus, whilst the national rick population of house mice could be extremely large, it was temporary, but did serve to maintain a constantly-replenished field population. However, threshing is now confined to a few farms (mainly in Somerset and Devon) where long-stalk wheat is grown for thatching, and some of the Scottish islands (R.J. Berry pers. comm.). The main concentrations of house mice in Britain today are probably in hen houses (R.J. Berry pers. comm.).

Although a highly successful commensal species, house mice can live completely independently of man provided that potential competitors are absent (Berry, Cuthbert & Peters 1982). Thus house mice have successfully colonized many islands, where high populations may be attained e.g. up to 500 on the 250 ha island of Faray, Orkney (Berry *et al.* 1992), 450-3250 on the 57 ha Isle of May (Triggs 1991) and 150-5000 on the 100 ha island of Skokholm, with densities of 60 per ha recorded in rock outcrops and grassland (Berry & Jakobson 1975). However, their distribution on the mainland is limited by competition with other small mammals, particularly wood mice (Berry 1991). Hence house mice are rare in British woodlands, and avoid open fields with little cover, although in the late 1950s they were as common as wood mice in agricultural habitats in north-west Scotland and the Hebrides (Delany 1961).

Infestations in farm buildings range from 7 to 362 (mean 70, n = 44), based on trap-outs, with mean population size being lowest in ancillary stores (22) and highest in dairy units (109), with granaries (80) and mixed-food stores (87) being intermediate (Rowe, Swinney & Quy 1983). A survey of 14 different types of agricultural premises in 1974 showed that, in decreasing order of priority, pigs and poultry holdings, general crop holdings, cereal holdings, dairy holdings, mixed holdings, specialist dairy holdings and mainly poultry holdings were most likely to be infested with house mice, all with over 60% levels of infestation. The least likely to be infested were mainly vegetable and mainly fruit holdings, both with less than 25% levels of infestation (Ministry of Agriculture, Fisheries and Food unpubl.). Highest densities have been recorded in buildings with an abundance of food and an absence of common rats (*Rattus norvegicus*): house mouse numbers in buildings seem to be severely restricted by the presence of rats (R.J. Quy pers. comm.). Thus the highest numbers occur in isolated buildings that are rat proof. In Britain 130-300 per ha have been recorded in piggeries (Tattersall 1992), 70,000 per ha in a

Texas hen house (Berry 1991) and even higher densities in commensal situations elsewhere. However, unlike some other parts of their range, British house mouse populations do not exhibit population explosions leading to mouse plagues.

Whilst there is little information on house mouse populations in arable landscapes, there is even less information on house mouse populations in pastoral landscapes. In Northern Ireland, Montgomery & Dowie (1993), in an area with 1·9 farms and 9·2 km of field boundary per km², found a mean density of 6·7 and 35·9 per km² in winter and summer respectively. In winter they were all confined to buildings, but in summer 89% were in field boundaries. However, the numbers indoors in winter varied five-fold between years, from 4 to 20 per km².

In urban areas, house mice are probably more numerous than common rats, and are generally rare away from buildings (Yalden 1980). Thus in London it was estimated that in 1972 9% of buildings were infested with house mice (Rennison & Shenker 1976), although locally higher levels of infestation can occur e.g. nearly 50% in an area of central London (Meyer & Drummond 1980). Anecdotal evidence suggests that urban infestations average 4-5 house mice (R.J. Quy pers. comm.). A survey of house mouse (and common rat) infestations in non-agricultural premises in England and Wales from 1976 to 1979 inclusive showed that house mice were significantly less prevalent in either large towns, i.e. more than 20,000 inhabitants (3·8%), or small towns, i.e. 3000-20,000 inhabitants (3·8%), than they were in rural areas, i.e. those including a village or town up to 3000 inhabitants (5·6%). Infestations showed a regular seasonal pattern, with winter peaks and summer troughs. Also, over the four years of the survey, in all areas the level of prevalence was declining (Rennison & Drummond 1984). In Britain, non-commensal populations increase approximately eight-fold during the breeding season (Berry 1968), but in farm buildings and other situations breeding occurs throughout the year when there is a

year-round food supply (Rowe, Swinney & Quy 1983).

Estimating population size is very difficult, because local infestations are erratic in occurrence but may attain many hundreds in number. However, to provide a guide-line on population size, for arable landscapes a pre-breeding density of 20 per km², and for pastoral landscapes a density of 10 per km², were assumed, based on the data from Montgomery & Dowie (1993) and the fact that infestations in farm buildings in Britain (Rowe, Swinney & Quy 1983) generally seemed higher than those recorded in Ireland. This gave a population of 1,540,000 in rural areas in England, 335,000 in Scotland and 23,000 in Wales. To estimate the number of house mice in domestic premises, details of the number of urban and rural households recorded in the 1981 census were obtained from Office of Population Censuses and Surveys (1984). Based on the survey of Rennison & Drummond (1984), it was assumed that 3·8% of urban and 5·6% of rural premises were infested, with a mean of 4·5 house mice per infestation. This gave a total of 2,600,000 house mice in urban, and 395,000 in rural, domestic premises in England; 275,000 in urban, and 47,000 in rural, domestic premises in Scotland; and 140,000 in urban, and 43,000 in rural, domestic premises in Wales.

Population estimates: A total pre-breeding population of about 5,192,000; 4,535,000 in England, 657,000 in Scotland and 206,000 in Wales. These estimates must be considered as minimum figures, since there are no data on the frequency of high-density populations in farms and other premises, and no information on the numbers of house mice in buildings other than domestic premises. **Reliability of population estimate:** 5.

Historical changes: House mice used to be the third most common small mammal (after wood mice and bank voles) in arable land in southern England, forming about a fifth of the small mammals trapped on farmland in the Oxford area (Southern & Laurie 1946).

However, with the advent of combine harvesters and the decline of cereal ricks, house mouse numbers in agricultural land have declined (Southern & Laurie 1946; Davis 1955), probably considerably (R.J. Berry pers. comm.). More recently, Rowe, Taylor & Chudley (1959) only caught house mice on arable land in the late summer/early winter, and several studies in hedgerows on cereal land in East Anglia caught few or no house mice (Pollard & Relton 1970; Eldridge 1971; Jefferies, Stainsby & French 1973). The paucity of house mice in owl-pellets (Table 5), bottles (Table 6) and traps (Table 7) also suggests that house mice are now rare in agricultural landscapes. The presence of common rats around farm buildings seems to reduce the number of house mice (R.J. Quy pers. comm.).

Population trends: It would appear that there has been a dramatic decline in house mouse numbers during this century (see above), although numbers may now be stable, at least in non-rural habitats. During 1993 the Ministry of Agriculture, Fisheries and Food organised a new national rodent survey. The preliminary results show that since the late 1970s there has been no significant change in the overall levels of infestation in non-agricultural premises. Within this broad trend, there has been a significant reduction in the levels of infestation of properties used for business purposes, but there has been a significant rise (from 3·7% to 5·9%) in infestation levels in domestic premises in rural areas. There has been no significant change in infestation levels in domestic properties in urban areas (A. Mayer & A. Shankster pers. comm.)

Population threats: Competition limits the numbers of house mice in non-commensal situations (Tattersall 1992). In commensal situations, pest control measures have substantially reduced house mouse numbers over the last fifty years. However, field and laboratory trials have shown that the toxic effects of agrichemicals such as paraquat and carbofuran on population size and structure may be ameliorated through behavioural

mechanisms such as feed aversion and toxicant avoidance (Linder & Richmond 1990). Richards (1989) suggested that a decline in urban infestations in the late 1970s may have been due to the introduction of more effective mouse toxicants.

Common rat *Rattus norvegicus*

Status: Introduced in the first half of the 18th century; common.

Distribution: Found throughout Great Britain except in the most exposed mountain regions and on some of the small off-shore islands (Taylor, Fenn & Macdonald 1991). There are few records from the Outer Hebrides and Shetland (Arnold 1993), but whether this reflects the true status of the common rat there is unclear.

Population data: Common rats are generally limited to habitats where competing species are few or absent or where food supplies are augmented by humans. Very dense populations can occur in favourable habitats. Typically they are associated with farms, refuse tips, sewers, urban waterways and warehouses, and the number of common rats in and around farm buildings increases in October and November as rats move in from the surrounding area (Clark & Summers 1980), although the presence of resident common rat populations may prevent field populations becoming established in farm buildings in the autumn (Taylor 1978). They occur in hedgerows around cereal crops, principally in summer and autumn; in winter around cover crops such as maize and kale planted for game birds; and in root crops, particularly sugar beet, all year round. Certain features nearly always guarantee the presence of common rats away from farm buildings. They are hedgerows, copses and ditches bordering fields of wheat, oats, barley, maize, kale, stubble, turnips and sugar beet, but not oil-seed rape and linseed. Rat numbers are further boosted by game-rearing practices, since wide hedgerows, shelter belts and supplementary feeding of birds provide all that rats need (R.J. Quy pers. comm.). Common rats also occur in areas with dense ground cover close to water, occupying grassland as well as all types of coastline (Taylor, Fenn & Macdonald 1991). Populations independent of man occur in many coastal habitats, and on many islands (e.g. Lundy and Rum).

Populations tend to be high in the autumn and early winter and low in the spring. However, estimating population density is particularly difficult for this species, and a study on three rural rubbish tips showed that estimates based on capture-mark-recapture data and on the rate of bait uptake under-estimated population size by factors ranging from 1·3-7·0 (Taylor, Quy & Gurnell 1981). In 1987, 53% of farm grain stores were infested with rats, and, based on trap-outs, the mean size of infestations on farms on the English/Welsh border (n = 50) was 52; in Hampshire (n = 16) 155; and in Surrey/Sussex (n = 24) 89. Since it is likely that those caught formed about 90% of the rat populations (Quy, Cowan & Swinney 1993), the mean population sizes were 58, 172 and 99 respectively. These variations reflect differences in the area covered by farm buildings, the dominant agricultural activity of the area (the border farms are mainly livestock, the Hampshire farms mainly cereals, and the Surrey/Sussex farms mixed arable crops with livestock rearing) and the ability to control rats (rats on arable farms are more difficult to control than on livestock farms, and Hampshire contains rats that are resistant to many poisons, whilst most rats in Surrey/Sussex are susceptible) (R.J. Quy pers. comm.). This pattern of common rat distribution on farms is also reflected in the pattern of rodenticide usage. A survey in 1990 of 706 farms growing arable crops showed that 54% by weight of all the rodenticide used was in the eastern region, 20% in the northern region and 11% in the south-western region (Olney & Garthwaite 1990).

In the absence of more detailed data on the size of rural rat populations, it was assumed that the pre-breeding population was associated with farm buildings and that there were none in field situations. Data from a survey in 1970 detailed below (Ministry of Agriculture, Fisheries and Food unpubl.) were used to estimate that a mean of 45% of all agricultural premises over 2 ha in England and 34% in Wales were infested with common rats. There were no data for Scotland, but a figure of 40% was selected, which was slightly lower than that for agricultural holdings in the north of England. Data on the number of holdings in 1986 in each of the three countries was obtained from the Government Statistical Service (1988). It was assumed that an average pre-breeding infestation was 60 common rats. Using these figures suggested a rural common rat population of 3,860,000 in England, 870,000 in Scotland and 680,000 in Wales. These must be minimum figures, since there are no data on pre-breeding rat populations in canal banks and other non-agricultural rural habitats.

In urban areas rat populations are smaller, but small and distinct colonies on the surface may be linked to a large population in the sewers. During the 1960s and 1970s, Drummond, Taylor & Bond (1977) trapped out surface infestations in Folkestone, Kent. None were found in open areas such as rough ground, parks or allotments, and at any one time only 0·16% of Folkestone's rateable properties were infested, with an average of 2·2 common rats each. A more extensive survey in England and Wales found that the average level of infestation in rural areas was 7·8% of premises and in urban areas 3·8% of premises in towns of less than 20,000 inhabitants and 2·7% in larger towns (Rennison & Drummond 1984).

To estimate the size of the common rat populations in domestic premises, data for the number of households in rural and urban areas in each country were obtained from the 1981 census (Office of Population Censuses and Surveys 1984). It was then assumed that there was a mean of 7·8% of rural, and 3·25% of urban, domestic premises infested with common rats, with a mean of 2·2 rats per infestation. This gave a common rat population of 270,000 in rural, and 1,110,000 in urban, domestic premises in England,

30,000 and 120,000 respectively in Scotland and 30,000 and 60,000 respectively in Wales. These must also be minimum estimates, since there are no data on which to calculate the size of urban rat populations in buildings other than domestic premises, or in sewers and rubbish tips.

Population estimates: A minimum pre-breeding population of about 6,790,000; 5,240,000 in England, 870,000 in Scotland and 680,000 in Wales. These are minimum estimates because there are no data from a number of habitats permanently occupied by common rats. **Reliability of population estimate:** 4.

Historical changes: The common rat reached England around 1728 and its subsequent spread was rapid. It first appeared in Scotland between 1764 and 1774, but its spread appears to have been slower, and in some remote areas was described as 'recently introduced' as late as 1855 (Matheson 1962). Whilst there was no reliable estimate of the size of the common rat population at the start of the century, it was clearly considered to be a major economic pest, and there were a number of publications on how to exterminate rats, e.g. Ministry of Agriculture and Fisheries (1932). A widely quoted figure for the number of common rats was that of Boelter (1909) who, after a long series of enquiries, assumed that there was not less than one rat to each cultivated acre, or alternatively one rat per human; this gave a minimum population of 40,000,000 common rats. The figure of one common rat per person in Britain is still widely quoted today. However, Hinton (1920) reported that, even when this estimate was produced, it was generally viewed as a significant under-estimate.

In view of the current estimated population size, there must have been a dramatic decline in common rat numbers since the early part of this century. However, there are no accurate data on recent changes in the size of the common rat population in Britain. A survey in 1970 of the distribution and percentage of farms infested with rats in England and Wales found that 20.6% of agricultural holdings over 2.025 ha (5 acres) in size in south-east England had field infestations, whereas 38.3% had infestations in farm buildings. Comparable figures for south-west England were 11.8% and 47.8%, for the east midlands 30.2% and 56.0%, for the west midlands 13.4% and 37.9%, for east England 64.1% and 55.7%, for north England 9.9% and 43.5%, and Wales 7.7% and 34.1%. Rat infestations were more numerous on farmland in east and south-east England and the east midlands than in the remaining four regions, and were most numerous in east England. Infestations in farm buildings were most numerous in east England and the east midlands. The highest infestation rates occurred in the regions with the most arable land, and there was a significant relationship between the incidence of farmland infestations and the percentage of agricultural land under cereals and under root, fodder and vegetable crops and also between the incidence of farm building infestations and the percentage of land under cereals. A survey of 14 different types of agricultural premises in 1974 showed that, in decreasing order of priority, pigs and poultry holdings, cereal holdings and mixed holdings were the most likely to be infested with rats, all with over 60% levels of infestation. The least likely to be infested, in decreasing order, were sheep rearing, mainly vegetable and mainly fruit holdings, all with less than 35% levels of infestation. This second survey also suggested that since the 1970 survey there had been an increase in the number of premises infested (Ministry of Agriculture, Fisheries and Food unpubl.).

A survey of common rat (and house mouse) infestations in non-agricultural premises in England and Wales from 1976-1979 inclusive showed that common rats were associated with 3.6% of the 62,055 premises inspected. Of these, 73.8% were confined to the gardens or other outdoor areas, and only 10.1% were wholly within buildings; of the remaining 16.1%, rats were present both indoors and outside. The situation in towns was significantly different to that in rural areas. In towns, 77.3% of the infestations were wholly external, 12·6% wholly internal and 10·0% mixed. In rural areas the figures were 70·6%, 7·9% and 21·5% respectively. The situation in domestic premises was also significantly different from non-domestic premises. In the former, 84·6% of infestations were wholly external, 7·2% wholly internal, and 8·2% mixed. For non-domestic premises, the figures were 59·0%, 12·8% and 28·2% respectively. Rat-infested premises were most prevalent in rural areas (7·8%), and also significantly more prevalent in small towns, i.e. less than 20,000 inhabitants (3·8%), than in larger towns (2·7%). The percentage of rat-infested premises fell each spring to a low summer value, and then rose each autumn to a winter peak (Rennison & Drummond 1984).

Population trends: The National Game Bag Census data show that the number of common rats killed by gamekeepers has decreased; since this has been coupled with an improvement in control techniques, it is probable that this reflects a real decline in rural rat populations (Tapper 1992). Other factors, such as the loss of habitat, will also have contributed to this decline. These changes include the removal of hedgerows, ditches, etc. to make larger fields and the loss of cereal ricks where, in inter-war years, populations would build up during the winter to reach very high numbers (Venables & Leslie 1942; Matheson 1962). Thus since 1945 the numbers killed in rural areas have been only a small proportion of those recorded earlier (Tapper 1992).

Whilst there has been a dramatic decline in numbers over the last fifty to a hundred years due to the control of rick and urban populations, and the loss of farmland populations, this trend may now have been reversed. During 1993 the Ministry of Agriculture, Fisheries and Food organised a new national rodent survey (for house mice and common rats) in both urban and rural areas. The preliminary results show a significant rise in common rat infestation levels of non-agricultural premises from 4·4% to 4·8%. This rise was most marked in domestic premises in both urban and rural

areas, where the rise was from 3·3% to 4·6% (A. Meyer & A. Shankster pers. comm.). One possible factor contributing to this increase is higher crop yields over at least the last 20 years. As a result, there is more food available, and improvements in storage facilities have not kept pace with the increased production, so that more food is stored where it is accessible to rats (R.J. Quy pers. comm.).

Population threats: Populations are locally controlled where numbers become noticeable. However, the spread of resistance to currently available rodenticides is likely to hinder attempts at population control, especially in southern England (R.J. Quy pers. comm.). The general improvements in urban hygiene may have led to population declines in urban areas. In the countryside, however, there has been no such general improvement, and old farm buildings, untidy yards, agricultural dumps, 'fly-tipping' and landfill rubbish tips all contribute to a greater availability of habitats suitable for rats. This will have been offset by the loss of hedgerows and ditches to make larger fields; such changes will have led to population declines (R.J. Quy pers. comm.). Populations used to be extensive in drift mines (Twigg 1961), and the size of the infestation increased with the size of the installation. Furthermore, urban mines had more rats than rural mines, and those in farmland more than those in moorland areas; this agreed well with the distribution of common rats generally (Twigg 1975). However, common rat infestations of drift mines were particularly high around stables, but now that pit ponies are no longer used, these populations of rats have also declined (Twigg 1975). Common rats have never been a problem in shaft mines.

Unlike urban house mouse populations, it is possible to largely eliminate common rats from urban areas, and the concept of 'rat-free towns' has been popular in Europe for some years (Drummond 1985). This involves an active campaign to eliminate existing populations, followed by a substantial improvement in environmental hygiene (Richards 1989). At present only the control of rat populations in sewers is routine in British urban areas.

Ship rat *Rattus rattus*

Status: Introduced at least as early as the 3rd century, with further introductions from ships, which continue to the present day. Since the 1950s, there has been a continued contraction in distribution and most mainland populations appear transient (Twigg 1992).

Distribution: Except for populations on Lundy, Devon, and Carnach Mhor on Garbh Eilean, the main island of the Shiants, Inner Hebrides, records are largely (but not exclusively) confined to port areas. In the period 1985-1989, a questionnaire survey showed that there was an increase in the number of mainland localities (Twigg 1992).

Population data: The following estimates by G.I. Twigg (pers. comm.) were based on the 1989 distribution and how many ship rats were likely to be present at a mainland site, based on a subjective estimate of abundance. At four localities, where control of black rats was needed or was being carried out, it was estimated that an average of 50 rats were present. At those sites where rats were seen occasionally, a mean of 15 rats was assumed. The presence of up to five rats was assumed for temporary occurrences, e.g. the loading bays of multistores and other rapidly changing and unpredictable environments where numbers cannot build up. There were also seven occurrences of isolated animals, in which no more were seen once one animal had been killed, for example at food importers. These estimates suggest 200-300 ship rats were to be found in Britain in 1989 excluding the populations on Lundy and Garbh Eilean (G.I. Twigg pers. comm.).

For Lundy, it is not possible to estimate the total population size. Ship rats persist despite a poisoning campaign in the early 1990s against rats in general, but only four were caught during a survey in 1991 (Smith *et al.* 1993). Whilst a survey in 1992 suggested that the population was very high and occurred all over the island (P. Smith pers. comm.), the pre-breeding population is unlikely to exceed 500 animals, and is likely to be substantially fewer. On Garbh Eilean, there is similarly no estimate of the total number present, but it is believed to be in the low hundreds (D. Bullock pers. comm.), and so we have assumed that this population also numbers no more than 500.

Population estimates: A total pre-breeding population of at most 1300 animals; fewer than 750 in England, about 550 in Scotland and none currently known to occur in Wales. Since there are no data on which to estimate the size of the two major populations, it is impossible to be more precise. For this estimate, we have assumed that each numbers no more than a few hundred animals, and there may well be fewer on each island. **Reliability of population estimate:** 2.

Historical changes: From Roman times, the ship rat was widespread and common, but following the introduction of common rats in the early 18th century, its numbers rapidly declined. However, in 1780 it was still the prevailing species in London, although it had been replaced by common rats in many of the shires (Batten, n.d.). Ship rats were still common in parts of Scotland well into the 19th century. They still infested Benbecula in the Outer Hebrides until the 1880s and Shetland as late as 1904 (Millais 1904-1906; Lever 1977). In Orkney, they declined during the 18th century, but persisted until the 1930s in South Ronaldsay and possibly the 1940s in Kirkwall (Booth & Booth 1994). However, in 1939 a German grain ship went aground on Westray, Orkney, and ship rats became established on the island, where they were locally a pest; the last definite record was in 1968, and they are now presumed extinct (Booth & Booth 1994).

In mainland Britain, ship rats were more or less extinct by 1890, although they were still fairly common in parts of Cheshire and north Wales. However, Millais (1904-1906) reported that in 1905 ship rats were very numerous in Yarmouth. During the Second World War in those ports where ship rats abounded, they were more abundant than common rats, and in London there were roughly four ship rats to every common rat in the port (Twigg 1975). By 1956 ship rats were restricted to a few sea ports and major cities, and some small islands (Bentley 1959). A survey in the 1960s showed a further loss of ground due to improved methods of rodent control, better buildings, disinfection of ships, etc., and extinction seemed likely (Bentley 1964). However, populations persist, although most are impermanent, and ship rats were reported from only 23 mainland sites between 1981 and 1989 (Twigg 1992).

Although there are no quantitative data on the size of the ship rat population on Lundy, it seems to have undergone substantial changes in size in recent years. The population probably arose from survivors of ship wrecks several hundred years ago (Smith *et al.* 1993). A survey in 1962 showed that ship rats were more widely distributed on the island and in greater numbers than common rats (Anon. 1963), a situation that was reversed by 1983 (Smith 1985). In the second half of the 1980s, there was a significant decline in common rat numbers following a poisoning campaign, and in 1991 ship rats were probably restricted to the south-east part of the island (Smith *et al.* 1993). It was concluded that their future looked bleak. Yet a survey in 1992 showed that ship rats were widespread throughout the island, and greatly outnumbered common rats (P.A. Smith pers. comm.). Whether this increase was due to a reduction in competition with common rats is at present unclear (P.A. Smith pers. comm.). Nothing is known about the history of the ship rat population on Garbh Eilean, but it is believed to be long established (D. Bullock pers. comm.).

Population trends: Current trends are unclear. Future ship-borne entry of large numbers seems unlikely because of effective inspection systems, but lorry-borne entry does occur and is more difficult to prevent, and increased vehicular traffic through the Channel Tunnel may increase the number of ship rats

entering the country. The potential effects of climate change are also unknown (Twigg 1992).

Population threats: Ship rats are generally controlled whenever populations or individuals are located. The populations on Lundy and Garbh Eilean are of particular interest. Whilst there is much speculation as to their possible impacts on the sea bird colonies on these two islands, based on experiences elsewhere, proof of any impact in Britain is currently lacking.

Common dormouse *Muscardinus avellanarius*

Status: Native; localised and declining.

Distribution: Widespread but patchily distributed. Dormice are most common in England in Avon, Buckinghamshire, Devon, Dorset, Gloucestershire, Hampshire (including the Isle of Wight), Kent, Somerset, Surrey and Sussex, and in Wales in Gwent (P.W. Bright pers. comm.). Elsewhere in England this species is sparsely distributed, although isolated populations occur as far north as Cumbria and Northumberland. Dormice are probably under-recorded in east Wales along the English border and also in south Wales (P.W. Bright pers. comm.). A recent survey in south-east Dyfed produced 27 records, and the species is believed to be widespread, if sparsely distributed, in the area (A. Lucas pers. comm.).

Population data: The principal habitat for dormice is ancient woodland (Bright, Mitchell & Morris 1994), although they may be absent from isolated fragments due to chance events or historical patterns of management (Bright & Morris 1990, 1992). In addition, an unknown proportion of the population lives in secondary woodland, and in hedgerows, perhaps particularly in south Wales. Therefore, to calculate the population size, the total area of semi-natural ancient woodland in the eleven counties in which dormice are most common (approximately 168,000 ha) was obtained from Spencer & Kirby (1992). Dormice live at very low densities, only attaining 8-10 per ha even in prime habitat (Bright & Morris 1992), and a typical density would be nearer 5 per ha (P.W. Bright pers. comm.). At such a density, the total population of dormice would be 840,000. Allowing for scattered populations in other counties would suggest a total population figure of around 1,000,000. However, dormice are unlikely to persist in woods with an area of less than 20 ha, or isolated by more than 1 km (Bright, Mitchell & Morris 1994). Moreover, they are often absent from areas of ancient woodland altogether, perhaps as a consequence of past management. Thus the total could be substantially lower due to populations being lost as a consequence of long periods of isolation from larger populations (Bright, Mitchell & Morris 1994). Whilst the extent of these past losses is unknown, we have assumed that dormice are absent from about half of the available suitable habitat.

Population estimates: A total pre-breeding population of about 500,000; 465,000 in England, none in Scotland and 35,000 in Wales. More information on the local distribution of, and the effects of past patterns of woodland management on the survival of, common dormouse populations is needed in order to improve this estimate. **Reliability of population estimate: 3**.

Historical changes: Dormice occurred much more widely last century, although even where they were common they were still patchily distributed (Thorburn 1920). Their distribution and status at the end of last century was summarised by Rope (1885). In England they were more widely distributed in the north than now, although they were rare in the midlands and absent from some eastern areas. In Wales dormice were found in all counties, including Anglesey, and were more frequent in the north and west of Wales (Barrett-Hamilton & Hinton 1910-1921). A recent survey in Dyfed revealed that dormice were still widespread in the area, and it is possible that this species has still to be

'rediscovered' in many other parts of Wales. However, in the absence of records, dormice are generally perceived to have declined in both range and abundance during this century, although there are no data on the rate or pattern of decline. A survey from 1975 to 1979 (Hurrell & McIntosh 1984) provided widespread evidence of a decline, including no recent records from seven counties where dormice had been reported a century earlier by Rope (1885). The frequency of common dormouse records in local mammal reports declined by approximately 50% from the 1930s to the 1970s (Morris 1993b).

Population trends: Being on the edge of its range, the distribution of common dormice in Britain has always been very patchy. Thus whilst an absence of records does not prove that the species is absent (the recent confirmation of sites in Cumbria and Northumberland shows how easy it is to miss fringe populations), it is likely that local extinctions have already occurred and continue to occur in many areas of England. The common dormouse population that is likely to be viable in the long term can be estimated by excluding those areas of semi-natural ancient woodland below 20 ha in size. These comprised 83% of the woods, using the size class distribution given by Spencer & Kirby (1992). This would suggest a viable population of only 150,000. However, in Dyfed common dormice were frequently recorded in woodlands of less than 20 ha, occupying small pieces of ancient woodland, hazel-rich hedgerows, and the scrub at the edges of conifer plantations. Thus in some areas fragmented habitats can still sustain dormice.

Population threats: Dormice are threatened by absolute loss of habitat, especially the removal of ancient woodland or its substitution by plantations (especially softwoods), and the incidence of dormice is higher in ancient semi-natural woodland than in ancient replanted woodland (Bright, Mitchell & Morris 1994). Dormice are also threatened by the management of woodland in ways that are inappropriate to their requirements, including clear-felling, short coppice rotations or neglect (Bright & Morris 1989). The problems are exacerbated by the fact that the dormouse raises few young per year, but compensates by breeding for more than one year. It is thus a relative *k*-strategist (compared to the wood mouse or bank vole, which are more prolific breeders). This strategy is poorly suited to an animal on the fringe of its distributional range, where climatic uncertainties may reduce successful breeding for several years in succession. Dormice are specialist feeders that require a succession of fruiting trees and shrubs to maintain a regular food supply; thus they are confined to woodland with a high diversity of tree types, and those with a species-rich understorey that is not heavily shaded by taller trees (Bright & Morris 1990, 1993). Poor woodland management that leads to heavy shading and loss of the shrub layer leads to extinction even if the woodland itself persists. Their reluctance to cross open areas at ground level also means that they require aerial pathways to interconnect feeding sites and so proper habitat management is crucial for their survival (Bright & Morris 1989).

Poor summers, leading to a late start to the breeding season, may reduce survival of offspring, particularly if they do not reach a minimum weight of 15 g before the onset of winter (P.W. Bright & P.A. Morris unpubl.). A succession of poor summers could therefore lead to local extinctions. The problems that dormice face are exacerbated by low breeding rates and low population densities. In Dyfed, the main threat to populations is open-cast mining, which destroys and fragments the woodlands in which the dormice are found (A. Lucas pers. comm.).

Fat dormouse *Glis glis*

Status: Introduced to Tring Park, Hertfordshire, in 1902. Locally common, but fat dormice have spread slowly from their point of release. Both numbers and range are still increasing.

Distribution: Found in conifer plantations, mixed and deciduous woodland, orchards, gardens and houses in Buckinghamshire and Hertfordshire. A survey in 1980-1988 showed that fat dormice were present in 70 1 x 1 km squares, with records as far west as the Bledlow Ridge, east at least to Potters Bar and south to High Wycombe (L.M. Jones-Walters unpubl.). There is an outlying record from Sandy, Bedfordshire, in 1974, and earlier records from Shropshire, Warwickshire, Wiltshire and Worcestershire, with unconfirmed records in Berkshire, Gloucestershire, Hampshire, Northamptonshire, Oxfordshire and Surrey. These scattered records suggest that there were other introductions that did not persist (Lever 1977; Arnold 1993).

Population data: In Europe densities fluctuate from 1-30 per ha, and 1-5 per ha is normal (Storch 1978). Whether such high densities are achieved in Britain is unknown, but a small pilot study in the Chilterns recorded densities of 1 per ha in suitable woodland (Hoodless & Morris 1993). No other British data are available, although very high numbers have been recorded inside single houses (P.A. Morris unpubl.). Assuming that half of the 70 1 x 1 km squares constitute suitable habitat for fat dormice, at densities of 1 per ha the total population size would be 3500 animals, and at densities of 5 per ha the population would be 17,500. The actual population probably lies around the mid-point i.e. approximately 10,000 animals. Since there are about 15,000 ha of woodland in the Chilterns as a whole, not all of which is suitable for fat dormice, this suggests that the estimate of 10,000 is reasonable.

Population estimates: A total pre-breeding population of about 10,000, all in England.
Reliability of population estimate: 3.

Historical changes: Following their introduction to Tring Park in 1902, fat dormice multiplied very quickly and caused considerable damage to thatch and to corn and other crops. As a result a campaign was conducted which was thought to have exterminated them. However, between 1925 and 1927 a number were seen in Tring Park and in the surrounding countryside. Subsequent early records are detailed by Lever (1977). The spread has been slow, and in the first 85 years the average rate of spread from Tring Park was about 380 m per year (Jones-Walters & Corbet 1991), with most records still within 25 km of the release site.

Population trends: It is increasing both in range and numbers, albeit slowly. Most spread has been to the south and east, and this is assumed to be due to an absence of suitable habitat to the north and west. However, translocations are known to have occurred, with at least one of them leap-frogging a major barrier to natural dispersal. This was of a fat dormouse caught in Wytham Wood, Oxfordshire, on the other side of the treeless Vale of Aylesbury. Should fat dormice become established in areas beyond the natural barriers that have so far limited their spread, there is every reason to expect that they will become far more widely distributed. This seems almost inevitable, since people who trap fat dormice in their house are often reluctant to kill them, and so release them in a piece of woodland, sometimes some distance away.

Population threats: None known, but control measures in houses may have some effect on local populations.

Coypu *Myocastor coypus*

Status: Introduced. There have been no sightings since December 1989, when one was trapped in the Fens, Cambridgeshire, and this species is now believed to be extinct in Britain.

Distribution: Coypu were first brought to Great Britain for their fur in 1929, with most of the early farms in Hampshire, Surrey and Sussex. Most escapes occurred between 1932 and 1939, mainly in these three counties but with some in East Anglia, Scotland and Wales. However, from about 1940 feral coypu colonies from the south largely disappeared

(Lever 1977), with only those in East Anglia persisting. All the fur farms had closed down by 1945 (Gosling & Baker 1991). Feral populations only became established near Slough, Berkshire, and in the valley of the River Yare in Norfolk, whence they spread throughout much of East Anglia. By 1965 they extended north to Lincolnshire, west to Huntingdon and Peterborough, and south to Essex and Hertfordshire (Gosling & Baker 1991).

Coypu were very destructive to crops. They also damaged natural aquatic macrophyte communities of conservation importance and which were vital to the stability of river banks in the face of wash from passing boats. Also, their large burrows were a threat to the integrity of the flood defences in a part of England where much valuable farmland and property lies below river level. In view of these threats a major trapping campaign was instigated, and this led to the eradication of the species (Norris 1967).

Population data: During the eradication campaign, population size was estimated using a retrospective census technique based on trapping results (Gosling, Watt & Baker 1981). This was possible because most adult animals were eventually killed by trapping (Gosling & Baker 1989).

Population estimates: Extinct. **Reliability of population estimate:** 1.

Historical changes: The size of the Slough population is unknown, although it was believed to be small, and disappeared about 1954 (Norris 1967). The Norfolk population had spread throughout much of East Anglia by the late 1950s, when the population, based on capture returns, was believed to number about 200,000 (Norris 1967), although this figure may have been an over-estimate (Gosling & Baker 1989). Thereafter numbers declined, but increased from 2000 in mid-1970 to nearly 19,000 in late 1975 because of mild winters and low trapping intensity (Gosling, Watt & Baker 1981). However, in the late 1970s more trapping and colder winters kept the population below 14,000 and the population declined to fewer than 6000 following the cold winter of 1978/1979. From 1981, a coypu eradication policy was introduced, with the aim of exterminating coypu within ten years. The population declined from around 6,000 adults in 1981 to 15 in 1987, 3 in 1988 and 1 in 1989; the success of the trapping campaign was enhanced by an above-average number of cold winters (Gosling & Baker 1989). No coypu have been recorded since 1989, and this species is now extinct in Britain.

Population trends: The Coypu (Prohibition of Keeping) Order 1987 prohibits the keeping of coypu in Britain and so this species should not become established again, since only small numbers are now kept in secure conditions in a number of zoos.

Order: Carnivora

Red fox *Vulpes vulpes*

Status: Native. Animals were introduced from Europe last century to reinforce populations for hunting (Vesey-Fitzgerald 1965). Increasing in range and probably in numbers.

Distribution: Foxes are found throughout mainland Britain. They are present on the Isle of Wight. They were absent from Anglesey until 1962 when they were introduced, and until recently they were absent from all the Scottish islands except Skye (Harris & Lloyd 1991). However, foxes appear to have been recently introduced to Harris in the Outer Hebrides (A.C. Kitchener pers. comm.).

Population data: A population estimate was produced by Macdonald, Bunce & Bacon (1981) by selecting 256 1 x 1 km squares, eight from each of the 32 land classes, and subjectively estimating fox densities for each square. By this means they estimated a spring population of approximately 252,000 resident adult foxes, noting that these figures could double by late summer by the inclusion of juveniles and itinerant adults. What proportion

of this increase would be due to itinerant adults is unclear, but presumably they would also have to be added to the spring estimate of adult population size.

When Macdonald, Bunce & Bacon (1981) produced their population estimate, only a small proportion of the 1 x 1 km squares in Britain had been assigned to a land class, and the subjective estimates of fox density were interpolated for unclassified regions by averaging values of the surrounding classified squares. This estimate took no account of a number of variables such as non-resident adult foxes and regional variations in fox social group size. For many areas of Scotland, this approach seemed to over-estimate fox densities significantly (Hewson 1986). Also it ignored fox densities in urban areas.

In view of these problems, density estimates for rural areas were obtained for a number of habitats in England (Insley 1977; J.C. Reynolds pers. comm.), Scotland (Hewson 1986, 1990b) and Wales (Lloyd 1980). These were assigned to land classes, and mean densities were estimated as the number of social groups per km². Those land classes for which there were no density estimates were graded on a sliding scale based on subjective estimates of habitat suitability and ranked between land classes for which there were density estimates. Thus densities of one fox social group per km² were used for land classes 1, 2, 5, 6 and 7; one per 2·5 km² for land classes 3, 4, 8, 9, 10, 11, 12, 13, 14, 15 and 16; one per 5·0 km² for land classes 19, 20, 26 and 27; one per 7·5 km² for land classes 17, 18, 25 and 28; one per 10 km² for land classes 21, 22, 29 and 31; and one per 25 km² for land classes 23, 24, 30 and 32. This gave a total British fox population of around 75,500 social groups: 60,000 in England, 7500 in Scotland and 8000 in Wales. However, it should be remembered that for many land classes there were no density estimates at all, and virtually none with more than one estimate.

There are few data on the demography of rural fox populations. To estimate how many foxes there are per social group, data from Kolb & Hewson (1980) and Lloyd (1980) were used. Thus it was assumed that each rural fox family group had an adult male and a breeding female. In addition the data from Lloyd (1980) suggested that in Britain on average about 25% of vixens are barren. Thus, in addition to the 75,500 breeding vixens, there would be a further 19,000 barren vixens. There are no data on the ratio of itinerant:resident foxes, and so it was assumed that there were a further 0.5 itinerants per family group. This gives a mean social group size significantly below that recorded in urban areas, and reflects the higher levels of persecution of rural fox populations.

For urban areas, much more precise data are available, and population size was estimated as follows. Detailed population surveys were undertaken in nine English towns (Harris 1981; Harris & Rayner 1986a), and the results of these surveys were used to develop a predictive model to estimate fox numbers in other urban areas (Harris & Rayner 1986b). The distribution of foxes in urban areas of Britain is given by Harris & Rayner (1986c). Mean population estimates for all these urban areas were obtained by Harris & Smith (1987a) using a simplified version of the predictive model of Harris & Rayner (1986b), and total fox population sizes were estimated for every urban area with a population of more than 50,000 people in 1951. These density estimates were calculated as social groups per km², and these were converted to actual fox numbers using the demography data for Bristol (Harris & Smith 1987b). The demography data for Bristol were applied to all urban areas, since few urban fox populations are now controlled. This also applied to London, where fox control was much less than when the data for London given by Harris & Smith (1987b) were collected. The Bristol data showed that at the start of the breeding season an average urban fox family group consisted of 3.4 adults; thus to obtain the adult urban fox population, the estimated number of family groups was multiplied by 3.4.

This technique provided a detailed estimate of the number of foxes in all the major urban areas in Britain. It did not include small towns and villages, since many of these have only low numbers of resident foxes, and a high proportion of those seen in settlements at night are likely to be foraging animals that are normally resident in the surrounding rural area (Harris & Smith 1987a).

Population estimates: A total pre-breeding population of about 240,000; 195,000 in England, 23,000 in Scotland and 22,000 in Wales. Of these, the urban fox population was as follows: total 33,000, England 30,000, Scotland 2,900 and Wales 100. In addition, assuming a mean litter size of five, around 425,000 cubs are born each spring. The paucity of population data for this species in rural habitats meant that it was particularly difficult to produce a population estimate. **Reliability of population estimate: 4.**

Historical changes: At the turn of the century, the fox was common in many parts of Britain, and this was attributed to its status as a beast of the chase; otherwise, foxes would have disappeared from many areas as a result of the activities of gamekeepers (Millais 1904-1906). Although then perceived to be common, foxes have increased their range in Britain this century, particularly in parts of Norfolk and coastal areas in eastern Scotland, where until recently they were absent or uncommon (Harris & Lloyd 1991). In Scotland, changes in fox numbers and distribution have been described by Hewson & Kolb (1973), Kolb & Hewson (1980) and Hewson (1984b). They showed that there were large changes in demography and the number of foxes killed in relation to food abundance. With the onset of myxomatosis, the abundance of diseased rabbits led to an increase in the number of foxes killed. Later poor reproductive success and cub survival coincided with the period of reduced rabbit numbers. However, the massive reduction in the numbers of rabbits led to an increase in vegetation cover, which in turn promoted an increase in the numbers of field voles and an improved food supply for the foxes. With an increase in the number of adult foxes killed, there was a decrease in the cub:adult ratio, probably due to a decrease in the proportion of breeding vixens as population density rose. Changes in over-winter mortality, which were associated with food supply, appeared to be the main cause of the fluctuation of numbers.

Records of the numbers killed by gamekeepers show a steady increase in the mean number of foxes killed per km^2 since 1960 for all regions of mainland Britain (Tapper 1992), with four times as many killed per km^2 in 1990 as in 1960. The increase has been greatest in south-east England (seven fold) and East Anglia, and lowest in Scotland (two fold). Although these data suggest an increasing fox population, it is impossible to quantify the scale of any increase from such data. In East Anglia and the east midlands, the fox population in 1960 was probably very low, since foxes are very sensitive to dieldrin poisoning, and large numbers were found dead after having consumed poisoned wood pigeons *Columba palumbus* (Taylor & Blackmore 1961). Lloyd (1980) reported 1,300 dead foxes being found by huntsmen, and there was evidence of a substantial reduction in fox numbers (Rothschild 1963; Lloyd 1980). Also, a gamekeeper will kill not only resident territorial foxes but also itinerants immigrating from other areas, so that the number killed locally can sometimes far exceed the pre- or post-breeding density. Thus the trend towards larger numbers killed may result from increasing productivity, increasing breeding density, less effective control by man, or most likely a combination of all these factors. The increasing number killed per unit area certainly reflects a real increase in population density in East Anglia and coastal areas of eastern Scotland, where foxes were absent or rare prior to 1960 (Harris & Lloyd 1991; Tapper 1992). Whether it reflects a real increase in other parts of the country is unclear.

Control by man may have become less effective for two reasons. First, the number of gamekeepers roughly halved during the 30 years after 1960 (Tapper 1992), so that each shooting estate was more likely to be adjoined by unkeepered land, leading to increased immigration. Secondly, there has been a shift from spring and summer control using snares, cyanide gas and (formerly) gin-traps, to night shooting using a rifle and spotlight, a method which is easiest in late autumn, winter and early spring when cover is short and visibility therefore good. Since this is the main dispersal period (Trewhella & Harris 1988), shot foxes are likely to be quickly replaced, thereby allowing large numbers to be shot per unit area and thus giving the impression of an actual population increase.

Changes in food resources must also have influenced fox breeding density and/or productivity. Whilst a four-fold increase in productivity of a fox population is theoretically possible in response to changes in food availability (see review by Lloyd 1980), this would be extreme, and it seems unlikely that increased productivity and/or increased cub survival alone have contributed to the increase in the number killed by gamekeepers. Thus it seems likely that there has also been an increase in fox breeding density. Evidence from at least some estates and from other studies (Hewson & Kolb 1973; Lloyd 1980) suggests that fox numbers were very low in 1960, perhaps as a result of myxomatosis in rabbits. However, myxomatosis was introduced in 1953, and the number of foxes killed per km^2 in 1990 was four times the number killed pre-myxomatosis in 1946 on the same estates (Tapper 1992). Thus the increase in fox numbers cannot be explained solely by increasing rabbit numbers. The presence of large numbers of foxes in urban areas in southern England is unlikely to be responsible for the increase in the number of rural foxes killed since a study in Bristol showed that the urban fox population was self-regulating, with little net emigration (Harris & Smith 1987b).

Population trends: It appears that fox numbers may be increasing, although this assessment is based on the numbers killed by gamekeepers rather than any measure of changes in actual population densities. Thus the magnitude of any change is unclear. The reasons for any population increase are unknown, but an increased rabbit population and other food supplies, such as the very large increase in the number of reared pheasants (Reynolds & Tapper 1994), the presence of sheep carrion in upland areas, the exploitation of urban food resources, and the relaxation of control by man, are all likely to be contributory factors.

Population threats: Very high mortality rates, e.g. up to 100,000 per year killed in the late 1970s for their skins (Harris & Lloyd 1991), had no discernible effect on overall fox numbers in Britain, although a decline was reported in Ireland due to the numbers killed for the skin trade (Wilson 1982). At present the very low price for wild British fox skins means that this trade is negligible. Foxes are extensively culled by gamekeepers, and this can locally reduce numbers. Foxes are also the most common wild mammalian victims of deliberate poisoning incidents in England and Wales but these are unlikely to pose a significant population threat except locally. The most frequent reasons for such abuse of pesticides were game and sheep/lamb protection (Greig-Smith 1988).

Pine marten *Martes martes*

Status: Native. Locally common in parts of Scotland, very rare in England and Wales.

Distribution: In England found in Cumbria, Durham, Northumberland and North and West Yorkshire; in Wales found in Clwyd, Dyfed, Gwynedd and Powys, with a 1994 sighting on Anglesey (D.J. Jefferies pers. comm.); and in Scotland found in Dumfries & Galloway, Grampian, Highland, Strathclyde and Tayside. In 1980-1981 12 animals were released in Dumfries by the Forestry Commission (Shaw & Livingstone 1992). Some survived and are now breeding (Velander 1991; G. Shaw pers. comm.).

Population data: Field surveys in England and Wales were undertaken in 1987-1988 by surveying transects 2 km long in suitable habitats. Even where martens were present,

evidence was sparse, rarely exceeding ten droppings per 2 km compared to up to 30 scats for similar tracks 2 km long in Scotland. This suggests that pine martens in England and Wales survive only at a low density. Most signs were found in coniferous plantations or at sites adjacent to crag outcrops or scree slopes (R. Strachan pers. comm.). Population sizes in England and Wales were estimated subjectively from these field signs. This approach suggested that in the late 1980s in England there were fewer than 100 individuals: fewer than 50 in the Kielder Forest region, Northumberland, fewer than 30 in the Lake District, and fewer than 20 in North Yorkshire. Records in the area between North Yorkshire and the Kielder Forest populations may only represent wanderers. In north Wales it was estimated that there were fewer than 50 pine martens.

An analysis of the records from the 1987-1988 survey and historical data showed that only the Northumberland/Durham population was possibly spreading. The populations in Cumbria, North Yorkshire and West Yorkshire appeared to be contracting, and that in Wales was static (D.J. Jefferies pers. comm.). Surveys in the Lake District in 1993 and north Wales in 1994 suggested that there had been further significant declines in numbers (P.W. Bright, S. Harris & R. McDonald unpubl.), and that these populations were probably no longer viable. In the absence of a corpse or reliable sighting, despite appeals for records, D. Brown and S. Parr (pers. comms) were pessimistic about the status of the pine marten in north Wales. Morgan (1992/93) has summarised the information on the distribution and status of the pine marten in mid and south Wales. Based on the frequency of records, his survey suggested that pine martens could be established, albeit in very small numbers, in the upland areas of mid and south-west Wales. At this stage it is impossible to estimate the number of animals involved, but they are unlikely to push the total population for England and Wales above the maximum estimate of 150 individuals calculated by R. Strachan (pers. comm.), who believes that the total number is probably much smaller, with a minimum number of around 40.

In Scotland, Balharry (1993) estimated densities of 1 per 4 km² to 1 per 10 km² depending on the area of woodland within the territory. Woodland habitats were found to be selected in preference to open vegetation types, and regardless of territory size, there were no significant differences in the area of woodland (126 ha per individual) contained within marten territories. Also, territorial structure was intrasexual. Thus population size was estimated by Balharry (1993) as follows. The average area of woodland in each pine marten territory 126 ± 40 ha (s.d.) and there is 273,240 ha of woodland in the Highland region, all of which was assumed to be spatially orientated such that it was available to pine martens. This suggested a total population of around 2200 (range 1650-3150) individuals in the Highlands. For the other regions of Scotland (Dumfries & Galloway, Grampian, Strathclyde and Tayside), it was assumed that there was a 50% occupancy of woodland, thus giving a total maximum population of 3500-6800. D. Balharry (pers. comm.) suggested that the population lies at the lower end of this range.

Population estimates: A total pre-breeding population of about 3650; <100 in England, about 3500 in Scotland and <50 in Wales.
Reliability of population estimate: 2.

Historical changes: Until the 19th century, pine martens were widespread throughout mainland Britain, the Isle of Wight, Jura and Lewis. In the middle of the 19th century a rapid decline of the pine marten took place. Millais (1904-1906) documented the last records for each English county, and its decline in the latter part of that century has been described by Langley & Yalden (1977). Persecution by gamekeepers had led to its extinction in some English counties by 1800, and it was rare in many others. During the 19th century most of the remaining English populations became extinct, as did many in Scotland and Wales. In the late 1930s pine martens remained only as a relict population in

north-west Scotland, but by the 1940s there were a few signs of recovery. By 1959, the main population was still north and west of Loch Ness but with animals reported in the Grampian region (Lockie 1964). By 1982 the range extended further south and east, although there was little evidence of animals in the far north (Velander 1983). By 1987, pine martens were again being seen in the northern areas as far east as Bettyhill, Highland (Velander 1991), and in the mid-1980s they were more widespread in the southern Highlands than reported by Velander (1991). In 1985 they colonised the area south-west of Loch Tay, Tayside, and have subsequently moved south into Strathyre and Loch Lomond-side, Strathclyde. Also in 1985 a pine marten was killed on the road near Dunfermline, Fife, well beyond the established range (J. & R. Green pers. comm.). Of the two release sites chosen in the Galloway Forest Park, Dumfriesshire, only one led to the establishment of a breeding population, and this population seems to be consolidating in a radius of 12 km south and west of Glen Trool (Shaw & Livingstone 1992).

Population trends: Their spread southwards from the Highlands and in south-west Scotland seems to be continuing, although whether they would have recolonised the south-west without the help of an introduction in the 1980s is unclear. However, in the 1960s, an animal was killed on an estate in south-west Scotland (J. & R. Green pers. comm.). This may have been a vagrant, suggesting perhaps that natural colonisation would have occurred with time. Alternatively, this animal may have resulted from an undocumented translocation. There continued to be records from the area in the 1970s (Shaw & Livingstone 1992). Total colonisation of north-east and south-east Scotland may be prevented by factors such as natural barriers, interspecific competition and conflict with man (Balharry 1993). Based on the total area of woodland in Scotland, the maximum potential population could be 6800-13,100 individuals, i.e. double the present population (Balharry 1993).

Population threats: Pine martens breed relatively slowly (1-5 young per year when over three years old), and live at very low densities. Isolated populations are therefore likely to be susceptible to population perturbations, local persecution or high levels of, for example, road mortality, and the death of relatively few pine martens may result in the removal of the breeding population from a wide area (Balharry 1993). Thus their continued persistence at such low population levels is probably unlikely. In Scotland unselective methods of predator control are still widespread, and this is probably limiting further spread (D. Balharry pers. comm.). It is not known whether pine martens will spread naturally through large areas of unsuitable habitat to colonise new areas. Also, it is possible that the presence of wildcats or feral cats may limit the distribution and density of pine martens or *vice versa*. Slight differences in food supply or habitat may allow one to gain the competitive edge and exclude the other, or both could co-exist at sub-optimal densities (Balharry 1993).

Stoat *Mustela erminea*

Status: Native. Common and possibly declining.

Distribution: Found throughout mainland Britain at all altitudes, and on many islands, including Anglesey, Islay, Jura, Mull, Skye and the Isle of Wight. Introduced to both Orkney and Shetland, stoats became extinct in Orkney but persist on Mainland Shetland.

Population data: Stoats are found in a wide variety of habitats, including any type of woodland cover, farmland, moors, marshes and in linear features in open areas. The National Game Bag Census data show that there is no large variation in the regional distribution of stoats killed per unit area by gamekeepers, although slightly more are killed in East Anglia and some southern counties than in counties with large areas of upland grouse moor (Tapper 1992).

Density and distribution are more closely related to prey availability than to habitat *per se*, and there are marked variations in density both within seasons and between years - stoat numbers may follow cycles in prey abundance. There are no density estimates for Britain, although autumn densities in Europe and Canada probably average 3-10 stoats per km² (King 1991a). However, mean body size in those populations is much smaller (King 1989), and so extrapolation of those densities to Britain is questionable (C.M. King pers. comm.). Much higher densities were recorded in some areas before myxomatosis (Jefferies & Pendlebury 1968), but these were based on the numbers killed by gamekeepers in a comparatively small area, and this is not a reliable basis for estimating population density. To obtain a population estimate for Britain, we assumed a density of 6 per km² for all types of woodland, parkland, scrub, bracken and coastal sloping cliffs; 2 per km² for coastal sand dunes, lowland heaths, heather moorlands, bogs, upland and lowland unimproved grassland and arable land; and 1 per km² for semi-improved and improved grasslands.

Population estimates: A total pre-breeding population of about 462,000; 245,000 in England, 180,000 in Scotland and 37,000 in Wales. Obviously this is only an approximate estimate, since there are no density estimates for British habitats, and there is little information on variations in density both between years and between habitats. However, Tapper's (1992) figure for the number of stoats killed by gamekeepers each year (average of about 1·5 per km²) suggests that this estimate for the pre-breeding population (approximately 2·0 per km² for Britain as a whole) is reasonable. **Reliability of population estimate:** 4.

Historical changes: At the turn of the century stoats were still abundant despite relentless persecution (Millais 1904-1906). However, populations were severely reduced for 15 to 20 years following the outbreak of myxomatosis. On one Suffolk estate, there was a ten-fold reduction in the number of stoats killed in 1960 compared to 1950. From 1960 to 1976 the number of stoats killed, as recorded in the National Game Bag Census, doubled, but the number killed in northern areas declined again after 1965. This was probably because the increase in rabbits had been less in northern areas (Trout, Tapper & Harradine 1986). However, since the mid 1970s, the number of stoats killed by gamekeepers throughout Britain has declined again. Reasons for this decline are unclear; since the number of rabbits killed nationally has continued to increase (Tapper 1992), a further rise in the stoat population might be anticipated. However, any rise in fox numbers may be a contributory factor to the failure of the stoat population to increase in response to rising rabbit numbers, since increasing fox numbers can lead to a decline, or even local extinction, of stoat populations (Mulder 1990). The impact of fox predation on stoat numbers may be further enhanced by habitat simplification, particularly the loss of linear features in the countryside (Harris & Saunders 1993).

Population trends: Continuing to decline.

Population threats: Unknown. The reasons for the apparent recent decline are not clear, but it may at least in part be due to reductions in the numbers of farmland birds and larger mammalian prey such as common rats, which are important prey items in areas where rabbits are not readily available, and possibly to increased competition with foxes. Also, stoats may be at risk from secondary poisoning in arable areas by consuming rodents contaminated with insecticides and/or molluscicides.

Weasel *Mustela nivalis*

Status: Native, common.

Distribution: Found throughout mainland Britain and on some islands, including Anglesey, Sheppey (Kent), Skye and the Isle of Wight, but not found on smaller islands or those without native stoat populations.

Population data: Weasels are found in a wide range of habitats, although most are killed in arable farming counties (Tapper 1992). The correlation between the local density and distribution of weasels and small rodents is well-established (King 1991b). Being closely related to fluctuations in rodent numbers means that weasel populations are very unstable, varying over a wider range of densities than do stoats. For instance, in Wytham Woods, Oxfordshire, weasel densities in different years varied from 4·5 per ha to less than 1 per ha, depending on small mammal abundance (King 1989). Moors (1974) recorded an average density of one weasel per 7·7 ha on farmland in north-east Scotland. Lockie (1966) recorded peak densities of 10 males and 3 females on 32 ha in the Carron Valley, Stirlingshire, but this was when field vole numbers were high, and the weasels resident with stable territories; after the first year the system broke down, and weasel numbers were much lower. Also, weasels show cyclic fluctuations in numbers with a 3-4 year quasi-cycle that correlates with cycles in field vole numbers. However, not all weasel populations are cyclic, and this may be because in woodland habitats they feed on other rodents such as bank voles, which are less cyclic than field voles (Tapper 1992), and because field voles are only cyclic in certain habitats (see field vole account).

Estimating a typical density of weasels for particular habitat types is very difficult, and there are few density estimates for British habitats. Whilst home range sizes suggest that weasels could attain densities of 30 per km², i.e. three times the density of stoats (see figures in King 1991b), this density figure is unrealistic since home ranges are invariably measured in favourable patches of habitat much less than 100 ha in size, and extrapolation to larger areas is invalid (C.M. King pers. comm.). Thus densities cannot be calculated from home range estimates. In the absence of data from a range of habitat types, weasel numbers were calculated based on their abundance relative to the number of stoats. The ratio of stoats to weasels probably depends on the proportion of prey of different sizes; where small rodents are common, weasels outnumber stoats, and *vice versa* where small rodents are less common. Whilst weasel densities probably vary more on a regional basis than stoat densities (Tapper 1992), kills by gamekeepers suggest that, overall weasels probably equal stoats in abundance (C.M. King pers. comm.). The relative abundance of weasels in each of the three countries was determined from the distribution of records in Arnold (1993) and the relative numbers killed per km² recorded by Tapper (1992).

Population estimates: A total pre-breeding population of about 450,000; 308,000 in England, 106,000 in Scotland and 36,000 in Wales. **Reliability of population estimate: 4.**

Historical changes: At the turn of the century weasels were exceedingly common in England, Scotland and Wales (Millais 1904-1906). The outbreak of myxomatosis in the early 1950s led to a flush of vegetation and a great abundance of small rodents in 1957-1958; this led to a record catch of weasels on game estates (Sumption & Flowerdew 1985). The National Game Bag Census shows that there has been a progressive decline in the number of weasels killed since 1961; this is most marked in East Anglia and the east midlands but barely apparent in the south-west and Scotland (Tapper 1992). The gradual recovery of the stoat from the early 1960s to the mid-1970s was accompanied by a substantial decline in the number of weasels, perhaps due to interference competition. However, since the mid-1970s the number of stoats killed by gamekeepers has declined again, but there has been no apparent increase in the number of weasels killed.

Population trends: Continuing to decline, although weasels have not yet declined to the pre-myxomatosis ratio of 2-3 stoats per weasel (King 1991b).

Population threats: Unknown. As for stoats, recent declines may, at least in part, be due to scarcity of prey or to secondary poisoning but it is doubtful whether these provide a full explanation. Nor is it clear why weasel numbers have not responded to declining stoat populations. If stoat numbers are being reduced by increased levels of fox predation, this would also act to reduce weasel numbers (King 1989), although for both stoats and weasels, population density is more likely to be controlled by productivity rather than mortality (C.M. King pers. comm.).

Polecat *Mustela putorius*

Status: Native. Locally common and increasing.

Distribution: Found throughout Wales except Anglesey, and in England in 12 to 15 counties from Cheshire south to Avon and apparently as far east as Leicestershire and Northamptonshire (J.D.S. Birks pers. comm.). There have been introductions into Cumbria (two), in the Oban area of Argyll (two) and on Speyside in the 1970s and 1980s, but both the purity of the stock used for the releases and their subsequent fate are currently unknown (A.C. Kitchener pers. comm.).

Population data: Densities apparently are not great, and studies in mid-Wales found a mean territory size of 101 ha, with territories clumped for no obvious reason (Blandford 1987; Blandford & Walton 1991). However, polecats are generally regarded as a lowland species, so Blandford's data from hill areas of mid-Wales may not be typical. Also, cull data in Tapper (1992) suggest that population densities in the English midlands are currently lower than in parts of Wales closer to the historical stronghold of the species. Whether this is part of the recolonisation process or a function of habitat quality is currently unknown (J.D.S. Birks pers. comm.).

Weber (1987) estimated polecat population density in Switzerland to be 0·1 per km² in the areas with fewest polecats and 0·5-1·0 per km² in areas with the highest polecat densities. K.C. Walton (pers. comm.) calculated British polecat population estimates by applying these Swiss density figures to the area of each county colonised by polecats (including upland areas, but making allowance for areas populated by humans). Thus, if the British range supported polecats at the lowest Swiss density, 0·1 per km², the British population would be 2143; and at the highest Swiss density, 1·0 per km², the British population would be 21,429 polecats. A second estimate was provided by N. Teall (pers. comm.), using figures from Tapper (1992) of <0·015 to >1·5 polecats killed per km². The current distribution is approximately 235 10 x 10 km squares (Arnold 1993), of which half were thought to have a density of 1·5 polecats per km² and half no more than 0·15 polecats per km². By this means N. Teall (pers. comm.) estimated around 19,000 polecats. Recently, preliminary results of live-trapping in Herefordshire farmland by J.D.S. Birks (pers. comm.) has suggested a density of 0.5-1.0 animals per km², so the population estimates used by Teall for his calculations are likely to be minimum figures. Also, the distribution of records from estates in Wales is biased, and there appear to be no records from the former counties of Merionethshire and Caernarvonshire, nor from the large estates in central east Wales, all areas with high densities of polecats (K.C. Walton pers. comm.). How this bias in returns from the National Game Bag Census data will affect the population estimate is unclear.

Two other estimates were obtained, the first by using the home range sizes presented in Blandford (1987) and the distribution given in Arnold (1984); this suggested a population of 19,200 polecats. The second assumed that polecats in Wales were more or less confined to rivers, and at densities of 1 per km of river. This calculation suggested a total population of around 12,000. How realistic it is to assume that polecats are confined to river valleys is unclear; K.C. Walton (pers. comm.) questions the validity of assuming linear territories, and there are few data to support such an assumption. Whilst most road deaths in Wales are from river valleys, this may simply be because in Wales roads tend to follow valleys, although it may reflect prey distribution (Blandford & Walton 1991).

Whilst a variety of approaches were used to calculate population size, they all produce broadly similar estimates, and thus a minimum population estimate of 15,000 seems reasonable.

Population estimates: A total pre-breeding population of about 15,000; 2500 in England, it is not known whether the introductions to Scotland survived, and 12,500 in Wales. **Reliability of population estimate:** 3.

Historical changes: The decline and subsequent spread of polecats early this century has been documented by Langley & Yalden (1977). In the 19th century polecats were still common over most of Britain, although they were already scarce in the south-east. However, by the end of that century there had been a marked decline, with the situation being reviewed in detail by Millais (1904-1906). Their decline in Scotland was hastened by the high value of their pelts (Ritchie 1920), and it was this rather than just their impact on gamekeeping interests that led to their extirpation (A.C. Kitchener pers. comm.).

It is frequently stated that at their minimum, at the onset of the First World War, polecats were probably only common within an area of approximately 70 km radius around Aberystwyth, Dyfed. However, this area excludes the north of Caernarvonshire and Denbighshire, always polecat strongholds, and includes large areas of Dyfed that did not have polecats until the 1960s. Thus an area of approximately 70 km radius around Aberdovey would be a more realistic description of the minimum range (K.C. Walton pers. comm.). At this time polecats were either extinct or virtually so over most of England and Scotland. However, polecats never became extinct in Herefordshire and Shropshire (Langley & Yalden 1977), a view supported by gamekeepers in these counties (J.D.S. Birks pers. comm.).

Since the 1920s, however, polecats have been expanding their range and numbers. The main increase occurred in the 1950s, possibly aided by the cessation of gin-trapping for rabbits. This period of rapid increase also coincided with the rapid decline in otter numbers, so polecats may have benefited from the decline of a potential competitor. Whilst otters were suffering from the effects of organochlorine insecticides, polecats, having a predominantly mammalian diet, only accumulated very low levels of organochlorine pesticides, and so were able to rapidly increase in numbers during this critical period (Jefferies 1992). Thus, by the 1960s polecats had recolonised virtually all of Wales (Walton 1964, 1968), and in subsequent decades spread into many of the English border counties.

Population trends: The spread into England seems to be continuing (J.D.S. Birks pers. comm.), and it is assumed that this spread is associated with a continuing population increase. The situation is currently very dynamic, and there have been reports of animals as far east as Leicestershire and Northamptonshire which, in appearance, appear to be typical polecats (J.D.S. Birks pers. comm.). It has been suggested that this spread of the polecat has probably been aided by the increase in young forestry plantations (Blandford 1987) and the rise in rabbit numbers (Tapper 1992). However, K.C. Walton (pers. comm.) believes that rabbit numbers *per se* were not the major contributory factor. In the 1940s 3,000,000 rabbits per annum were sent from Cardiganshire, Carmarthenshire and Pembrokeshire to London (Thompson & Worden 1956), yet polecats were virtually unknown over much of the area. Gin-trapping rabbits was prohibited after 1958, and it was the cessation of commercial rabbit trapping rather than the increase in rabbit numbers that led to the increase in polecat numbers and distribution. However, after increasing steadily since the 1960s, the National Game Bag Census data show that the numbers of polecats (and mink) killed each year per km[2] have levelled out or decreased since 1983 (Tapper 1992). The rapid increase in polecat (and mink) numbers following the decline in otter numbers, and a subsequent reversal of this trend as otter numbers built up in Wales

and the English border counties, suggest that there may be a negative interaction here, and that if the increase in otter numbers continues, polecat numbers may expand much more slowly (Jefferies 1992).

Population threats: The future of polecats in Britain seems to be assured, and the current distribution in Britain is half as large again as 20 years ago, but it would be unrealistic to expect a full recovery (unaided) to its former range (Blandford & Walton 1991). The high incidence of road casualties is surprising, considering the relatively low density of traffic in Wales during the autumn, the main period of mortality, and the lack of foraging activity near roads (Blandford 1987). Why polecats are susceptible to road deaths is unclear; it may be because roads provide a reliable source of carcasses to scavenge (K.C. Walton pers. comm.). This susceptibility to road mortality may reduce the rate of spread into areas of England, where road traffic is heavier. However, polecats have colonised the outer suburbs of one large urban area (Llanelli) despite some road casualties (K.C. Walton pers. comm.). Extensive drainage and agricultural improvements may pose a threat in some areas (Blandford & Walton 1991). Polecats have also been reported as victims of secondary poisoning in areas where anticoagulant rodenticides were in use (Walton 1970), and in England, where polecats hunt rodents around farm buildings, some animals have accumulated high levels of second generation rodenticides (J.D.S. Birks pers. comm.). What effect this may have on numbers or the rate of spread in England is currently unclear. Finally, as the range of the polecat expands, the risk of hybridisation with feral ferrets increases; how much of a risk this will be is unknown.

Feral ferret *Mustela furo*

Status: Introduced. Established on a few islands and some mainland areas, occasionally with records elsewhere.

Distribution: Established on Harris, Islay, Mull, Shetland and the Uists. Ferrets appear to survive best on off-shore islands with lots of rabbits and few other carnivores (J.D.S. Birks pers. comm.). Whilst records of individual animals also exist for many counties in England, Scotland and Wales, these probably represent relatively recent escapes. Colonies have been reported in several places on the mainland, but their size and persistence is currently unclear. For instance, from at least 1977 to 1987 feral ferrets were present throughout Strathearn, Tayside, and it was not unusual to see more than ten on a gamekeeper's gibbet (J. & R. Green pers. comm.). On Mull, they have been present since at least the late 1920s (Pocock 1932).

Population data: None available. There is no known preferred habitat type for feral ferrets, nor has there been any attempt to estimate population density. It is also unclear whether records on the mainland represent free-living populations or a 'standing crop' of escapees.

Population estimates: The total pre-breeding population is unlikely to exceed 2500, but it is impossible to be more precise; in England 200, in Scotland 2250 and in Wales 50. **Reliability of population estimate: 5.**

Historical changes: Unknown.

Population trends: Unknown. An eradication campaign was attempted on Islay in the late 1980s. This lasted two years and had temporary success, but feral ferrets are now common again (J. & R. Green pers. comm.). There have also been attempts to reduce the numbers on Shetland, but their success, if any, is unknown.

Population threats: None known.

American mink *Mustela vison*

Status: Introduced. Although escapes from fur farms occurred from 1929, the number of animals was low in these early years and they did not establish free-living populations. The first records of wild-bred young were from Devon in 1956 (Thompson 1964). Now common and widespread.

Distribution: Widespread, with records from most areas except north-west Scotland and north-west Wales (Arnold 1993). Numbers appear to be low in East Anglia and east Yorkshire (Tapper 1992). The greatest density of records is from south-west England, Sussex, the English/Scottish border counties, and south and east Scotland (Arnold 1993). The low productivity of upland rivers may limit their spread in the Highlands (Chanin 1981). In the Outer Hebrides mink have colonised all of Lewis and Harris following their escape from fur farms in the 1960s, but have yet to extend significantly further southwards. In the Inner Hebrides they have been recorded on Mull since 1990 (Green & Green 1993). They are now also on Islay (A.C. Kitchener pers. comm.), and there are unconfirmed reports from Jura. They have been present on the Isle of Arran since their escape from fur farms in the 1960s.

Population data: Mink are found in a wide range of aquatic habitats, particularly favouring eutrophic streams, rivers and lakes with abundant waterside vegetation; they are less abundant on oligotrophic waters or where waterside cover is sparse or absent (Dunstone 1993). Relatively dense populations may also occur in undisturbed rocky coastal habitats with a broad littoral zone (Birks & Dunstone 1991). On mainland Britain, mink occupy coastal habitats around Slapton in south Devon, north-east England, the whole of the Solway Firth and the west coast of Scotland, but coastal mink are probably not as widespread as coastal otters because of their need for a wider range of prey items (mammals and birds) and their requirement for a suitable foraging habitat, i.e. relatively shallow, sloping, boulder strewn, beaches or abundant rock pools (Dunstone & Birks 1983; N. Dunstone pers. comm.).

On mainland Britain, density varies with habitat. On the River Teign, an oligotrophic river in Devon, densities were 0·46 mink per km of river when rabbits were common, but only 0·23 mink per km of river when rabbits were scarce (Birks 1989). Seasonal variations in density are influenced by vacation of territories by rutting males in the spring and re-settlement after the mating season, and by the settlement of the juveniles following dispersal in August. From studies of mink inhabiting rivers and lakes in Devon (Chanin 1976; Birks & Linn 1982), it was calculated that the mean territory length for the two sexes was 2·28 per km, i.e. 0·44 mink per km of riparian habitat. Assuming a complete overlap of the territories of the two sexes, since Birks & Dunstone (1991) say that there is 'much overlap', this gives a density of 0·88 mink per km of river/lake shore. Obviously, assuming total overlap of territories between the sexes is likely to inflate the population estimates a little, but this is probably not by a substantial amount. In each water authority region in England the percentage of sites found to be occupied by mink during the national water vole survey were: Anglian - 20·5%; North West - 39·7%; Northumbria - 55·5%; Severn Trent - 33·6% South West - 66·0%; Southern - 33·0%; Thames - 25·0%; Wessex - 52·7%; Yorkshire - 48·0%; and 27·3% in Scotland and 39·3% in Wales (Strachan & Jefferies 1993). Using these figures for percent occupation, the lengths of riparian habitats in Table 4, and a density of 0·88 mink per km, D.J. Jefferies (pers. comm.) calculated that there are 4500 mink in the Anglian area, 4500 in the North West, 5750 in the Northumbrian, 7500 in the Severn Trent, 7000 in the South West, 3500 in the Southern, 2750 in the Thames, 4250 in Wessex and 6750 in Yorkshire, a total of 46,500 in England; plus 31,250 in mainland Scotland and 9750 in Wales. These estimates exclude coastal habitats.

The number of coastal mink was calculated as follows. The main known populations in England were in Slapton, Devon, the north-east coast of England, and the south coast of Solway, occupying lengths of coastline of approximately 10, 100 and 60 km respectively (N. Dunstone pers. comm.). A study on the Solway coast found a mean territory length of

1·30 km, or 0·77 mink per km (Dunstone & Birks 1985). Again, assuming a complete overlap of the territories of males and females gives a density of 1·54 mink per km of coast i.e. about 250 coastal mink in England. On the west coast of Scotland, coastal mink are only found north to about Skye i.e. approximately 4000 km of coast (N. Dunstone pers. comm.). Assuming the same density as in Solway would give a population of about 6000 coastal mink in Scotland. Off the west coast of Scotland, the only islands with mink are the Isle of Arran and Harris and Lewis (Birks & Dunstone 1991). Nothing is known about the numbers on the Isle of Arran. For Harris and Lewis, the densities (adult females per km) were higher in coastal habitats (0·85) than rivers (0·75) or lochans (0·63); productivity was also higher in the coastal habitats (Hudson & Cox 1989). Using these figures, Hudson & Cox (1989) estimated there were about 7500 breeding female mink on Harris and Lewis. Assuming an equal number of males and non-breeding females gives a total population of about 15,000 mink.

The otter survey in England in the early 1990s suggested that coastal-living mink are much more common than the figures used in this calculation, and of 204 coastal sites examined, 63·2% had mink (R. Strachan pers. comm.). This survey also suggested that the rocky coasts and estuaries of south-west England may provide mink with better foraging and denning opportunities compared with the flatter saltmarsh and reedbed-dominated estuaries of the east coast. Thus it seems probable that relatively high densities of coastal-living mink occur in south-west England and west Wales (R. Strachan pers. comm.), and more data on these will increase the population estimate presented here.

Population estimates: A total pre-breeding population of at least 110,000; 46,750 in England, 52,250 in Scotland (plus an unknown number on the Isle of Arran) and 9750 in Wales. More data on coastal and island populations of mink are needed to enable this estimate to be improved. In addition, in 1994 there were 15 mink farms in the UK; the number of mink being kept on mink farms in the UK was 100,000 in 1987 and 47,000 in 1992 (Ministry of Agriculture, Fisheries and Food pers. comm.). **Reliability of population estimate: 3.**

Historical changes: Mink were first imported into Britain in the late 1920s, and from then until 1945 the industry was small. The business then expanded and by 1962 the number of mink keepers had risen to a peak of around 700. With the introduction of the Mink (Keeping) Regulations, 1962, the number of farms dwindled to about 240 in 1971, but annual pelt production rose steadily from 6000 in 1953 to 160,000 in 1962 and 300,000 in 1971 (Johnston 1974).

Breeding mink were discovered in Devon in the mid-1950s. Their range and numbers increased considerably in the late 1950s and early 1960s, and within three years had expanded from a few kilometres of the River Teign to an area of 2600 km² (Linn & Stevenson 1980). A similar pattern was probably occurring elsewhere, as evidenced by the number of animals being killed. Thus by 1960 wild mink had been caught in five counties in England and Wales and two in Scotland. With the introduction of the Mink (Keeping) Regulations, 1962, the efforts to control feral mink were stepped up. In 1963 wild mink had been caught in 31 counties in Britain, and by 1967 this had risen to 63 (Thompson 1968). The number of wild mink caught each year rose throughout the 1960s, and by mid-1970 4875 mink had been caught in England and Wales, mostly in Devon (1317), Lancashire (594), Sussex (411) and Wiltshire (403). In Scotland the total caught was 1946, with most from Aberdeenshire and Kirkcudbrightshire. By 1971, mink had been caught in 41 counties in England and Wales, and 29 counties in Scotland (Johnston 1974). Much of this apparently rapid spread was the result of small scale escapes in which the mink were subsequently recaught, but elsewhere new feral populations were established and counties colonised from neighbouring areas (Chanin 1981). In Scotland, the early history of mink has been reviewed by Cuthbert

(1973). By the end of the 1970s, mink were widely distributed throughout mainland Scotland south of the Great Glen. Since then expansion appears to have slowed, but mink are gradually extending northwards up the east and west coasts (Green & Green 1993). Recently there has been a clear increase in the number killed in eastern England (Tapper 1992), suggesting that numbers are also now building up in this area.

Evidence of the rate of increase in recent years comes from the otter surveys of England. In 1977-1979, mink were recorded in 196 (15·1%) of the 1300 10 x 10 km squares surveyed (Lenton, Chanin & Jefferies 1980), compared with 334 (22·3%) of the 1500 10 x 10 km squares surveyed in 1984-1986, an increase of roughly 50% in seven years. The water vole survey in 1989-1990, though stratified differently and hence not directly comparable with the otter surveys, found mink in 543 (62·8%) of 864 10 x 10 km squares surveyed in mainland Britain, and 34·4% of all 600 m stretches of waterway searched showed signs of mink (Strachan & Jefferies 1993).

Population trends: Mink are continuing to increase both in range and numbers, but probably at a reduced rate. The possibility that low otter numbers helped the spread of mink has been mooted several times, e.g. Chanin & Jefferies (1978), and there is some recent evidence to support this assertion. Firstly, in three separate areas of Britain where otters have made a significant recovery in the last ten years, the mink population has independently been described as being lower than in earlier years (Birks 1990). Also, the National Game Bag Census data show that the numbers of mink (and polecats) killed each year per km² increased steadily in several years from the 1960s, but has levelled out or decreased since 1983 in Wales and the English border (Tapper 1992). These trends coincide with the decline and subsequent increase of otters in the same area, suggesting some form of negative interaction (Jefferies 1992).

Population threats: Following the 1988 epizootic in common seals, phocine distemper virus caused distemper outbreaks in Danish mink farms in 1989 (Heide-Jørgensen *et al.* 1992). Whether the virus transferred to free-living mink in Britain is unknown, but with coastal populations of mink the risk of transmission was probably high.

Badger *Meles meles*

Status: Native and generally common, particularly in southern England (Cresswell *et al. 1989*).

Distribution: Found throughout mainland Britain, plus Anglesey, the Isle of Arran, Canvey Island, Isle of Grain, Isle of Sheppey (Kent) and Isle of Wight. Badgers are most common in areas below 100 m, and are rare in upland areas.

Population data: Early attempts to estimate population size were based on the results of the Mammal Society's sett survey. Hardy (1975) suggested that there were about 35,000 badgers in Britain, and Clements, Neal & Yalden (1988) estimated a population of 36,000 social groups or about 216,000 adult badgers. These estimates were hampered by the lack of data from many areas, and by a failure to differentiate between different types of sett. Based on a stratified survey of 2455 1 x 1 km squares from November 1985 to February 1988, in which setts were classified into one of four types, the number of social groups was estimated to be 41,894 $\pm$ 4404 (95% confidence limits) (Reason, Harris & Cresswell 1993). Mean densities for different land classes range from 0 to 0·646 $\pm$ 0·135 (s.e.) social groups per km² of land. Locally, densities may reach six social groups per km² (Kruuk 1978). Mean group size from a number of studies averaged six adults (Cresswell, Harris & Jefferies 1990), although individual group sizes of as few as two in Speyside (Kruuk & Parish 1987) and more than 20 adults in Gloucestershire have been recorded (C.L. Cheeseman pers. comm.). In areas of low population density mean group size may be smaller (Skinner, Skinner & Harris 1991). Assuming a mean group size of

six adults, the total British badger population is approximately 250,000 adult badgers, and 172,000 cubs are born each spring (Harris *et al.* 1992). Of the total British badger population, 24·9% is in south-west England and 21·9% in south-east England, with overall 76.1% in England, 9.9% in Scotland and 14.0% in Wales (Cresswell *et al.* 1989).

Population estimates: A total pre-breeding population of about 250,000; 190,000 in England, 25,000 in Scotland and 35,000 in Wales. In addition there are about 172,000 cubs born each year. **Reliability of population estimate: 2.**

Historical changes: The distribution and numbers of badgers in Britain are clearly dependent on the pattern of agriculture (Reason, Harris & Cresswell 1993). The effects of changing patterns of agriculture on badger numbers since the Domesday Book of 1086 have been discussed by Cresswell *et al.* (1989). Even in the last 150 years, badgers have undergone major changes in status and possibly also distribution; these changes are summarised by Cresswell, Harris & Jefferies (1990). At the turn of the century, badgers were probably rarer than they had been 100 years earlier or would be half a century later, almost certainly the result of persecution by gamekeepers. Millais (1904-1906) described them as 'somewhat scarce'. During this century badger numbers have increased overall, although in East Anglia in the early 1960s badger deaths were recorded as a result of dieldrin poisoning (Cramp, Conder & Ash 1962; Jefferies 1969), and whilst the full effects of these insecticides on the badger population in East Anglia are unknown, a number of well-known setts became inactive for extended periods, and some still remain so (Cresswell, Harris & Jefferies 1990).

Population trends: At present these are unclear. Griffiths & Thomas (1993) have suggested that the British badger population may be stable, although a definitive estimate of population changes will not be available until the national badger survey is repeated. However, in some areas the rates of sett loss are substantial, and in the absence of a comparable rate of establishment of new setts, the badger population is likely to be declining, at least locally. In Essex, for instance, in the 20 year period up to the mid-1980s, 36% of known setts disappeared, and of those remaining, the number occupied by badgers fell to 14%. Also, the modal sett size declined from six holes to three. In south and west Yorkshire, 81% of 278 setts were occupied in the mid-1970s, but only 38% in 1978 (Paget & Patchett 1978). Conversely, in parts of the south-west anecdotal reports suggest that the badger population may be expanding, at least locally, in some areas.

Population threats: Annual adult mortality is believed to total approximately 61,000 animals, while annual cub mortality is 64,500 pre-emergence and 41,500 post-emergence (Harris *et al.* 1992). The pre-emergence cub mortality is thought to be largely due to infanticide (Cresswell *et al.* 1992). Road deaths are probably the next major cause of death, with approximately 50,000 badgers killed per annum. Whilst this figure may seem high, a comparable figure (60,000) is obtained by extrapolating the results of the Surrey road deaths survey (R. Ramage pers. comm.); see the hedgehog account for details of the survey. In addition, an estimated 10,000 badgers are killed illegally by diggers and a further 1000 killed each year in an attempt to control bovine tuberculosis in cattle in the south-west (Harris *et al.* 1992). Despite these various mortality factors, cub survival to the end of the first year approximately equals adult mortality, and so mortality at the individual level (i.e. ignoring sett losses and their associated mortality - see below) is probably not affecting population size (Harris *et al.* 1992). Persecution by badger diggers and other forms of illegal killing probably have had only a minor impact on population size in recent years, although there was a more substantial impact earlier this century (Cresswell, Harris & Jefferies 1990). In the absence of past persecution, it has been estimated that there could be 43,437 $\pm$ 4731 badger social groups in Britain, an increase of 3·7% on the present population. Most of this

loss occurred in Norfolk and Suffolk as a consequence of persecution by gamekeepers last century (Harris 1993; Reason, Harris & Cresswell 1993).

However, sett losses, rather than mortality of individual badgers, probably pose the most significant population threat. Sett destruction often involves the death of the resident badgers, and where this is the main sett, can lead to the loss of an entire social group. Landscape changes, particularly those associated with agricultural activities, were the major cause of sett losses in Essex in the 20 years up to the mid-1980s (Skinner, Skinner & Harris 1991), and Reason, Harris & Cresswell (1993) estimated that small increases in landscape diversity (in the absence of past persecution) could produce an increase in the badger population to 58,284 $\pm$ 5640 social groups, an increase of 40%. Obviously, this is a theoretical calculation. It assumes that any population increase will occur in a linear fashion in response to increasing habitat availability, an assumption that may not hold true. However, it does serve to show that with small habitat improvements, there could be substantial increases in badger populations. Fragmentation of populations by loss of setts or new road schemes, particularly in low density areas, may pose a substantial threat (Skinner, Skinner & Harris 1991).

Otter *Lutra lutra*

Status: Native. Localised, but generally increasing.

Distribution: In England otters are absent from the central area, rare in the east, north-west and south, but reasonably common in the south-west, north-east and the English counties bordering central Wales. They are found throughout most of Scotland, but with reduced numbers in areas of intensive agriculture and the industrial central lowland belt. In Wales, they are absent from parts of the south and Anglesey.

Population data: These were calculated for England, Scotland and Wales from the length of river in each water authority region and the percent of occupation of sites in the latest published otter surveys, using 1984-1986 data for England (Strachan *et al.* 1990), 1984-1985 data for Scotland (Green & Green 1987) and 1984-1985 data for Wales (Andrews & Crawford 1986). From these surveys, the site occupation rate for each water authority region was as follows: Anglian - 1.1%; North West - 9.3%; Northumbria - 9.8%; Severn Trent - 3.6%; South West - 43.8%; Southern - 3.0%; Thames - 0%; Wessex - 0.6%; Yorkshire - 2.2%; and 65.0% in mainland Scotland and 38.0% in Wales. The density of otters in different habitat types is unclear. D.J. Jefferies (pers. comm.) used the following data to calculate the otter population size. A study of rehabilitated otters in East Anglia found that three adults (one male, two females) occupied a minimum polygon range of 74.7 km² (Jefferies *et al.* 1986), and in Perthshire four adult otters (one male, three breeding females, plus some juveniles) occupied a minimum convex polygon range of 57.4 km² (Green, Green & Jefferies 1984). This gave an estimated 24.9 km² per adult otter in low density areas such as England and Wales, and 14.4 km² per adult otter in high density areas such as Scotland. From the figures for the length of all waterways in Table 4, and the area covered by each water authority, there were 1.10 km of waterway per km² in England and Wales, and 1.66 km of waterway per km² in Scotland, i.e. 27.32 km of waterway per adult otter in England and Wales (minimum convex polygon range multiplied by the length of waterways per km²) and 23.77 km of waterway per adult otter in Scotland. Using these figures, the lengths of all waterway (Table 4) and the percentage occupation to give the occupied length of waterway in each region, produced an estimated total adult otter population of about 350 in England (Anglian - 10, North West - 42, Northumbria - 43, Severn Trent - 34, South West - 196, Southern - 13, Thames - 0, Wessex - 2 and Yorkshire - 13), 3567 in mainland Scotland and 391 in Wales. These figures do not include of the number of immature animals living on their natal range.

To estimate the otter population in Shetland, Kruuk *et al.* (1989) conducted a stratified survey of holts, covering 35% of the coast. In smaller, intensively-studied areas, they found there were 0.331 resident female otters per holt, and that resident females comprised 54.5% of the otter population. Allowing for sampling errors and statistical errors, they concluded that there were 700-900 adult otters in Shetland in 1988. There are no reliable data on which to calculate the number of adult otters in other coastal regions of Scotland, but D.J. Jefferies (pers. comm.) has provisionally estimated these as 1000 on the west coast of Scotland from the Mull of Kintyre north to Cape Wrath and 1200 on Orkney and the Western Isles by assuming densities comparable to those found in Shetland.

In a recent study in north-east Scotland, Kruuk *et al.* (1993) argued that area of waterway, rather than length of waterway, should be used when calculating the amount of waterway per otter, since there was an exponential decline in otter utilisation with mean stream width. This finding is very similar to a possible relationship they noted between fish biomass and river width (smaller streams showed much larger fish productivity). Thus, if it was possible to calculate the area of waterways, it should produce a more accurate otter population estimate. In an area where otters were common Kruuk *et al.* (1993) calculated a median value of one otter per 15.1 km of stream. If this figure is used, it suggests a population of 5600 otters in mainland Scotland. However, since their data are based on the proportion of spraints deposited by otters marked with radionuclides, their estimate is likely to include spraints from unmarked otters of a variety of ages, not just adults, as was used in the calculation above. Furthermore, the calculation presented here is based on occupancy levels in the mid-1980s, since when the population has increased (see below). Thus the results from the study in north-east

Scotland suggest that the estimate presented here for the adult population is probably reasonably accurate.

Population estimates: A total pre-breeding population in the mid-1980s of about 7350; 350 in England, 6600 in Scotland (3600 on the mainland and 3000 on the islands) and 400 in Wales. When the results of the current otter resurveys are all available, they will produce significantly higher population estimates, since there has been an increase in the levels of occupancy since the mid-1980s, e.g. Northumbria 9·8% to 25·8%, Thames 0% to 2·2%, Wessex 0·6% to 12·3% and Yorkshire 2·2% to 9·3% (J. & R. Green pers. comm.). **Reliability of population estimate: 3.**

Historical changes: These are described by Chanin & Jefferies (1978) and Jefferies (1989). Otter populations were relatively high until at least the mid-18th century. Otter hunting with hounds had started by 1796 (Bell 1874), and in the 18th and 19th centuries otters were increasingly persecuted for fishery protection and sport. Local declines in otter populations in the 18th century accelerated, and by the end of the 19th century these had become so severe that in some areas there was a shortage of otters to hunt (Jefferies 1989). There are few data on the effects of persecution on otter populations, but severe local effects did occur. For example, between March 1831 and March 1834 the Duchess of Sutherland's estate paid five shillings each for 263 otters (Ritchie 1920), and otters were entirely exterminated from the Inner Hebridean islands of Colonsay and Oronsay by keepers; otters did not return to these islands until the 1950s (J. & R. Green pers. comm.). In fact, persecution for pelts was widespread and led, for instance, to the development of 'otter-houses' on Shetland in which the animals were periodically trapped.

However, during the First World War the cessation of hunting and reduced pressure from gamekeepers led to a small population increase. Intensive hunting with packs of hounds during the 1920s and 1930s altered the age structure of the population, and

probably had a significant population impact; in the 1930s the annual kill was around 400 animals. This declined to an annual mean of 199 in the 1950s (Chanin 1991). A catastrophic decline occurred simultaneously over England, southern Scotland and Wales, but most severely in the south-east, starting in 1957-1958. This was due to a combination of hunting pressure and the pollution of rivers by organochlorine insecticides. The trough in this decline seems to have occurred around 1977-1979. In the mid-1970s the population in Norfolk was down to 17 pairs (Macdonald & Mason 1976), and on the Somerset Levels in 1983/84 there were only about 12 otters (Scott 1985). There was markedly less decline in Scotland. Green & Green (1980) showed that in 1979 the otter population in southern Scotland was fragmented, but that the Northern and Western Isles, the Inner Hebrides, the west coast and south-west Scotland supported good otter populations.

Population trends: A recovery seems to have commenced in the early 1980s, although the population in East Anglia continued to decline (Chanin 1992). This general increase seems to be continuing, and a survey of England in progress in 1993 reported many new areas with signs of otters (R. Strachan pers. comm.). In Scotland a survey underway in 1994 showed substantial increases in distribution, particularly in the central and eastern lowlands, and that there is now a significant urban otter population, most markedly within Greater Glasgow (J. & R. Green pers. comm.). Improvements in water quality and good baseline populations seem to be major factors leading to this rapid recolonisation of Scotland. However, whilst otters seem to have a good future in those areas with established populations, current pollutant levels in lowland areas of England may prevent consolidated range expansion (Mason & Macdonald 1992). A study in Wales and the west midlands suggested that the colonisation of lowland areas of England is inhibited by the organochlorine pesticide residues in the otter's food chain, but that if contamination levels can be reduced, otters will spread rapidly (Mason & Macdonald

1993a). Furthermore, levels of PCBs in some lowland areas may be sufficiently high to adversely affect the reproduction or physiological competence of otters so that such populations may not be self-sustaining (Mason & Macdonald 1993b).

Because the otter population in East Anglia did not follow the general pattern of increase, a restocking programme commenced in 1983 (Jefferies *et al.* 1986), and up to the end of 1989 18 animals had been released at six localities in East Anglia (Wayre 1989). By that time it was considered that suitable habitat for any further releases was limited (Anon. 1989), and the current East Anglian otter population is derived largely, if not entirely, from these releases (Mason & Macdonald 1993c). Subsequently, a further six animals were released at two sites in the Lee catchment north of London (Mason 1992). In addition a few otters have been released in south-west England not far from the zone of expansion of the wild population. In East Anglia it has been claimed that there have been 21 litters, 19 from released animals and two from second generation females (Wayre 1989). However, the value of these releases and the reported successes have been seriously questioned by Mason (1992).

Population threats: Otters are relatively short-lived animals with, on average, a short breeding life-span in which to produce sufficient cubs to sustain the population. Hence any factor which reduces either otter survival or breeding success, even by only a small amount, could be detrimental to the survival of otter populations (Conroy 1992). Thus road mortalities may be important to isolated relict populations. Natural, as opposed to violent, mortality appears to be highest during times of food shortage. This applies to both Shetland (Kruuk & Conroy 1991) and north-east Scotland (Kruuk *et al.* 1993), and it is at these times that most alternative prey items (mammals and birds) occur in spraints (Kruuk *et al.* 1993). However, samples from a range of habitats do not reflect this seasonal pattern of violent mortality (Mason & Madsen 1990).

One study in riparian habitats in Scotland showed that food is limited (Kruuk *et al.* 1993), with the otters taking 60-118% of the mean standing crop or 53-67% of the annual production of salmonids. This finding has important implications for the conservation of otters, since if otters are food limited, improving otter habitats (e.g. by providing bankside vegetation, reducing human disturbance, etc.) may not be of value unless fish biomass is also raised (Kruuk *et al.* 1993). Similarly, events that lower fish stocks, such as short-term pollution or commercial fishing, are more likely to affect otter populations if they happen at those times of the year when the food supply is critical.

Pollution of rivers and seas may still be a significant threat to otters, particularly in lowland areas. Mason (1989) has reviewed all the various pollution threats to British (and other) otters. Mason & Macdonald (1992) argue that in many lowland areas both rivers and fish are still too contaminated to support otters, and PCB levels alone appear sufficient to cause reproductive problems. In mink, reproductive failure occurs when PCB concentrations exceed 50 mg per kg fat (Jensen *et al.* 1977), and such concentrations have been exceeded in otters from eastern England and elsewhere in Europe where numbers have declined sharply. In contrast, thriving otter populations, such as that in northern Scotland, have generally contained low levels of PCBs (Foster-Turley, Macdonald & Mason 1990). Some high PCB levels have been recorded in very young animals. For instance, a cub born in eastern England to a mother released as part of a restocking programme was killed by a car when only 11 weeks old and not yet weaned. It had already accumulated 62 mg of PCBs per kg fat in its liver (Jefferies & Hanson 1987). Two animals from eastern England, containing high concentrations of PCBs, exhibited pathological symptoms such as ulcers and skin abnormalities (Keymer *et al.* 1988). These symptoms were similar to those recorded in Baltic seals where PCB-induced adrenocortical hyperplasia is thought to have resulted in a failure of the immune system

(Bergman & Olsson 1986). Mason & Macdonald (1993c) concluded that contamination, particularly by PCBs, may mean that the otter populations in East Anglia may not be viable without repeated releases of captive-bred animals.

In south-west Scotland and northern England, there was an increase in dieldrin, DDE and PCBs in otter scats from west to east, suggesting that organochlorines may still be having an impact on otters (Mason 1993). A similar negative correlation between mean PCB concentrations and otter population performance was found in Wales and the adjacent English counties (Mason & Macdonald 1993d). However, interpreting the significance of PCB residues is not easy, and residues in otters from East Anglia are as high as those from parts of Wales, where otter numbers are increasing (D.J. Jefferies pers. comm.). Whether the absence of otters in much of lowland England is due to an absence of otters to colonise the area, a lack of suitable habitat or a high level of pollutants is as yet unclear.

In both Scotland and Wales, acidification of upland rivers reduces invertebrate populations, and hence reduces the fish population on which the otters feed, possibly leading to local population declines (Mason & Macdonald 1989; Green & Green 1993) rather than a contraction in distribution (Mason 1991). It has been suggested that in lowland areas, increased public pressure on waterside amenities means that disturbance and destruction of bankside vegetation renders many areas unsuitable for otters. However, Jefferies (1987) showed that the effects of disturbance may be overrated. He found that the behaviour of males was little affected, but females were more affected, using more underground holts than hovers, and that the effects of disturbance were most pronounced on females with cubs. The loss of wet woodlands, carrs and riverside trees, habitats favoured as resting sites by otters, may be particularly significant (Macdonald & Mason 1983; Jefferies et al. 1986).

With current legal protection and with improvements in water quality, population increases should continue, although the changes in waterside habitats probably mean that otters will never regain their former numbers. Where numbers have reached very low levels, restocking may aid population growth (Jefferies et al. 1986; Jessop 1992). For those areas where numbers are low, heavy losses in commercial fish and crustacean traps (Jefferies, Green & Green 1984) may be significant, although, generally, violent deaths have not posed a serious threat to otter populations. The potential impact of oil spills, such as the *Esso Bernicia* spill in Sullom Voe in 1978 and the *Braer* incident in Shetland in 1993, could be considerable on coastal otter populations. One major incident in this area could destroy a significant proportion of the British otter population.

Wildcat *Felis silvestris*

Status: Native. Uncommon but wildcats increased in numbers and range throughout much of this century following a reduction in persecution (Langley & Yalden 1977).

Distribution: Wildcats are only found in Scotland north of a line between Edinburgh and Glasgow (Easterbee, Hepburn & Jefferies 1991), and are normally confined to low altitudes. Since 1987 there have been a number of reports from Galloway; whether these represent true wildcats, and if so whether a natural colonisation or an undocumented release, remain to be determined (J. & R. Green pers. comm.).

Population data: Only two density estimates are available. In east Scotland, Corbett (1979) estimated a density of 30·3 wildcats per 100 km² in Glen Tanar, Deeside. In west Scotland, R. Scott (pers. comm.) estimated about 8·0 per 100 km² in Ardnamurchan. These two estimates were obtained about 15 years apart. Whether wildcats are still present in Deeside at the densities prevalent when Corbett was working there is unclear, and it is possible that there has been an overall decline in density to the approximate levels currently seen in Ardnamurchan (R. Scott pers. comm.). Analysing the data collected by N. Easterbee during 1983-1987, D.J. Jefferies (pers. comm.) found that wildcats were rare or absent in the central area, with density increases to the north, south, east and west. The density in the east (based on the number of sightings per five year period) was still higher than in Ardnamurchan. Thus within their current range, density appears to decline from east to west and possibly from south to north (R. Scott pers. comm.). If wildcats occur throughout their current range at the lower density (8·0 per 100 km²), the total population would be 2800, and if at the higher density (30·3 per 100 km²), the total population would be 10,700.

An independent estimate was supplied by D.J. Jefferies (pers. comm.), who used the distribution of wildcats on a 10 x 10 km square basis as shown in Easterbee, Hepburn & Jefferies (1991). Each occupied 10 x 10 km square was allocated to one of four status categories based on the frequency of sightings (which was known for 82% of the occupied squares), and the status in particular squares was related to the known density in the two field study sites described above. This produced an estimated population of about 3500 wildcats. This estimate was of animals of independent-age (over five months old) and of wildcat appearance, although it undoubtedly included some hybrids (D.J. Jefferies pers. comm.).

Population estimates: A total pre-breeding population of about 3500, all in Scotland.
Reliability of population estimate: 3.

Historical changes: Wildcats were once widespread, but persecution and loss of habitat led to a population decline (Langley & Yalden 1977). In 1800 wildcats were still widespread in Scotland and Wales, and they were present in at least six, and possibly eight, English counties. By the mid-1800s, they were extinct or virtually so in England, although there is one apparently reliable record from Hutton Roof, Cumbria, in 1922; two wildcats

were seen, and one was shot and preserved (Arnold 1993). The last reliable record from Wales was probably in 1862. The wildcat's decline in Scotland continued into the early 20th century. It reached its nadir around the First World War, when wildcats were confined to a small area of north-west Scotland. Ritchie (1920) supposed that it still survived in Argyll, Inverness-shire, Sutherland and Wester Ross, but was not optimistic about its future.

The range expansion earlier this century was undoubtedly associated with an increase in numbers. After the First World War, wildcats expanded their range, and by the end of the Second World War occupied much of their current range (Taylor 1946). A questionnaire survey in the early 1960s showed that wildcats were increasing in abundance (Jenkins 1962), but since the 1960s there has been little range expansion.

Population trends: These are unclear. The recent survey by Easterbee, Hepburn & Jefferies (1991) found that wildcats were reported to have declined in 34% of the occupied 10 x 10 km squares in the years before the survey, whereas they had increased in only 8%. Interpreting subjective data is difficult, but Easterbee, Hepburn & Jefferies (1991) concluded that most populations of wildcats in Scotland were showing little change. Relatively few population increases were recorded and these were mostly in the areas where wildcats were classified as established, whereas the areas where wildcats were occasional and rare showed few increases, but frequently showed a decrease, of 32% and 44% respectively.

It appears that most of the suitable habitat in Scotland north of the central industrial belt has now been recolonized by wildcats, and that further opportunities for spread or population expansion are limited. It seems unlikely that wildcats will cross the central industrial belt naturally, although there is a substantial area of suitable habitat which could support wildcats in south Scotland (Easterbee, Hepburn & Jefferies 1991).

Population threats: During the 1983-1987 survey, persecution was found to be widespread, and 19% of reported cases affected established populations, whereas 81% affected lower density populations. The Game Conservancy's National Game Bag Census return for 1984/85 recorded the killing of 274 wildcats on 40 shooting estates in central, eastern and north-eastern Scotland. This figure, which excludes many estates and persecution from other sources, still amounts to an annual mortality of nearly 10% of the population estimated by D.J. Jefferies (see above). This level of persecution was recorded prior to wildcats receiving legal protection in 1988. Current levels of persecution are unquantified but are still thought to be high in some areas (McOrist & Kitchener 1994). The continued persecution of low density populations could lead to localised population declines and even extinctions, since many of the populations are small and isolated (Easterbee, Hepburn & Jefferies 1991). Furthermore, some of these decreases have been in the relict population in the north-west highlands, which was thought to have least hybridisation with domestic cats.

Overall, hybridisation with domestic cats is believed to pose the major conservation problem, and is probably a continuing event which commenced several centuries ago (French, Corbett & Easterbee 1988). Recent genetic studies (Hubbard *et al. 1992*) have suggested that much interbreeding is occurring with consequent DNA hybridisation; of 42 putative wildcats from remote areas of northern and western Scotland, only eight showed clear genetic differences from domestic cats. However, discriminant analysis of skull measurements of Scottish wildcats suggests that in the last 30 years there has been a reduction in hybridisation with natural selection for the original wildcat skull morphology (French, Corbett & Easterbee 1988; Kitchener 1992). Hybridisation was most frequent from 1940-1965, when wildcats were rapidly expanding their range but numbers were low and hence there was a shortage of potential mates. Since 1965 the skulls of wildcats have partially reverted in size and shape to those of wildcats collected before 1940 (French, Corbett & Easterbee 1988). It is unknown whether wildcats will fully revert to their original wild-type morphology, or whether they have evolved a new skull morphology after a period of hybridisation with domestic cats.

Other threats include accidental killing by dogs, snares, poison baits set for other species, and road traffic accidents. Corbett (1979) found that on the Glen Tanar estate 58% of wildcat deaths were due to snaring, 8% were shot, 8% were killed by cars, 8% trapped, and only 17% were due to natural causes. Most viral diseases in domestic cats seem to readily infect wildcats. Active feline leukaemia virus infections have been found in several wildcats from Scotland (McOrist *et al.* 1991).

Since wildcats are mostly found in the less developed and more remote areas, development programmes and road building to boost local economies could be detrimental to wildcat populations (McOrist & Kitchener 1994). Although increasing afforestation helped the spread of wildcats, as forest plantations mature they become less suitable for the small mammals on which wildcats prey (Easterbee, Hepburn & Jefferies 1991). Forestry management should therefore aim to diversify the age of plantations. Finally, two wildcats collected in Aberdeenshire had significant levels of dieldrin in their livers, and one other contained traces of DDE (McOrist & Kitchener 1994). If dieldrin is still present in the food chain of wildcats, it may constitute an additional threat to populations already under pressure.

Feral cat *Felis catus*

Status: Introduced. The term 'feral cat' is widely applied, and difficult to define precisely. Cats living independently of humans vary from totally free-living populations on islands, through urban colonies that are at least in part provisioned, to straying individuals in urban areas and cats loosely associated with farms.

Distribution: Feral cat colonies are most common in six areas of Britain. These are Cleveland, Durham, Northumberland and Tyne and Wear; Greater London and south-east England; Greater Manchester, Humberside, Lancashire, Merseyside and Yorkshire; the midlands; the central lowlands of Scotland; and South Wales (Rees 1981). The majority of colonies (69%) were found on hospital, industrial and private residential sites (Rees 1981). They are found on most (if not all) inhabited islands, including those such as Lundy with very small human populations (Rees 1981). They have been deliberately introduced to many islands, e.g. Holm of Melly, Noss and South Havra in the Shetlands in the 1890s to control rats, and St Kilda in 1930, although they are now extinct on St Kilda. There are truly feral populations on some uninhabited islands, e.g. the Monach Isles, Outer Hebrides, where they were introduced to control rabbits (Corbett 1979; Macdonald 1991).

Population data: Of 287 colonies, nearly 50% consisted of ten or fewer cats, and only 7% consisted of more than 50 cats (Rees 1981). Occasionally very large colonies occur. In Portsmouth dockyard, colony size varied from 252-351 over three years, and adult population size from 164-203, an average density of over 2 per ha (Dards 1981). Rural densities are much lower. On Devon farmland and the Monach Isles densities of 6 per km² were recorded (Macdonald & Apps 1978; L.K. Corbett unpubl.). A survey found that about two-thirds of English farms had cats that were, to varying extents, independent or semi-feral, and that the mean colony size was four (Macdonald *et al.* 1987).

In the 1980s it was estimated that there were over 6,000,000 cats in Britain, and a widely quoted figure was that about 20% of these, i.e. 1,200,000, were feral (e.g. Tabor 1981). However, this figure was derived from a questionnaire survey that located 704 colonies, and it was suggested that the total

number of animals thought to occur in these colonies (12,302) represented 1% of the total feral cat population, which might therefore number 1,200,000 (Rees 1981). There was no quantitative evidence for this assessment. Therefore, to calculate the size of the feral cat population in Britain, it was assumed that their density was 6 per km² in rural habitats in the arable and pastoral land class groups but that feral cats were absent from marginal upland and upland land class groups. This gave a rural population of 600,000 feral cats in England, 125,000 in Scotland and 55,000 in Wales. To calculate the size of the urban feral cat population, four detailed surveys in Bristol, Oldham, Swindon and the Wirral and Ellesmere Port were used. In these surveys, feral cat colonies were located and the number of cats present in each was estimated, suggesting a mean density of around 1·4 feral cats per km² (R.J.C. Page pers. comm.). This density was applied to all the built up areas in England, Scotland and Wales.

Population estimates: A total pre-breeding population of about 813,000; 625,000 in England (600,000 in rural areas, 25,000 in urban areas), 130,000 in Scotland (125,000 in rural areas, 5,000 in urban areas) and 58,000 in Wales (55,000 in rural areas, 3,000 in urban areas). These must be minimum figures, since there are no data on the numbers of free-living cats in urban areas that are loosely or temporarily associated with households, and which do not live in colonies. **Reliability of population estimate: 4.**

Historical changes: Feral cats have probably been present in Britain in considerable numbers for a long time, having possibly arrived in Britain with the Normans in the 11th century (Zeuner 1963). Hudson (1898) estimated that there were at least 500,000 cats in London, of which 80,000-100,000 were feral, and Matheson (1944) estimated that there were 30,000 cats in Cardiff, of which 6,600 were feral. Both these estimates suggest that in the period up to the Second World War about 20% of the total urban cat population was feral. Current estimates suggest that this proportion has declined dramatically, and with improved welfare, particularly the neutering of entire colonies (Neville 1989), this proportion should decline further.

Population trends: Possibly declining in urban areas due to neutering of animals in colonies. However, recently the Cats Protection League (1993) estimated that 25% of United Kingdom families (i.e. 5,400,000 households) owned at least one domestic cat, and that the total domestic cat population was approximately 7,600,000 animals. It was estimated that this will approach 8,000,000 by the year 2000. Whether this will also lead to a growth in the feral cat population, particularly in the number of free-living urban cats that do not live in colonies but are loosely associated with particular households, is unknown. There is no evidence to indicate any change in the size of the rural population of feral cats.

Population threats: None known. Neutering of colonies (Neville 1989) will locally reduce problems and limit the growth of individual colonies, but is unlikely to have a significant impact on the total number of feral cats in Britain, especially since the technique is usually applied to urban colonies, and most feral cats are found in rural habitats.

Order: Pinnipedia

Common seal *Phoca vitulina*

Status: Native; locally common.

Distribution: The coasts of east England, east Scotland, north and west Scotland, the Hebrides, Orkney and Shetland. There are very few records from Wales (Arnold 1993), and breeding colonies are only found in England and Scotland.

Population data: Until 1984 population estimates were based on haul-out counts made from boats at the end of the pupping season. However, common seal pups are capable of swimming within hours of birth, so at any one time a proportion of pups will not be observed

(Reinjders & Lankester 1990). Also, the pupping season is lengthy, so early born pups will disperse before late ones are born. Therefore, common seals are now counted between late July and mid-August during the annual moult (Thompson *et al.* 1989), when the largest number of seals are usually recorded. An aerial survey in Orkney in 1985 during the moult produced a mean population estimate approximately three times that obtained in previous surveys; much of this increase was due to the change of survey period rather than any change in common seal numbers (Thompson & Harwood 1990). The relationship between the number of seals counted and total population size has yet to be established owing to the uncertainty over the proportion that is at sea at any given time, although this is only a small proportion of the total population (Thompson 1989; Thompson & Harwood 1990). However, so long as standardised survey techniques are used for different areas, improved methods can be used to re-evaluate old survey data (Thompson & Harwood 1990).

Because the breeding grounds and moulting sites of common seals are more dispersed than those of grey seals, common seal surveys are made less frequently and several areas have yet to be covered using the more effective moult surveys (Thompson 1992). In July/August 1991 an aerial survey was carried out in Shetland, the north coast of Scotland and reference locations on the west coast of Scotland using a helicopter and a thermal imager. A thermal imager was used because it is difficult to discriminate seals on rocky shores. Separate counts are needed to estimate pup production, and thermal imaging is also used here, since it helps differentiate between dead and live pups; failure to recognise dead pups can lead to over-estimates of pup production (Thompson & Harwood 1990). Sites where common seals haul-out on to sandbanks, such as the Wash, Firth of Tay and Moray Firth, are surveyed using a fixed-wing aircraft (Hiby, Duck & Thompson 1993).

By these means, the minimum number counted was 24,640. Studies of common seals in Orkney fitted with radio-transmitters have shown that almost all males and 42-75% of females are likely to be counted in aerial surveys in August. If the behaviour elsewhere in Britain is the same as that observed in Orkney, total population sizes could be 23-59% higher than these values (Sea Mammal Research Unit unpubl.). Thus the population could be between 30,310 and 39,180. Individual counts were: 1551 in the Wash in 1991; 1663 on the east coast of Scotland in 1991; 8205 on the north and west coast of Scotland and Inner Hebrides in 1988-1991; 1300 in the Outer Hebrides in 1974; 7137 in Orkney in 1989; 4784 in Shetland in 1991 (Hiby, Duck & Thompson 1993).

Population estimates: A total pre-breeding population of about 35,000; 2200 in England, 32,800 in Scotland and none in Wales (based on colony counts, although there are occasional sightings of animals off the Welsh coast). **Reliability of population estimate: 2.**

Historical changes: Common seals were once more widely distributed around the coasts of Britain, with colonies on the Isle of Wight in the 19th century and in the Bristol Channel until quite recently (Bonner 1972; Bonner & Thompson 1991). Their disappearance from these two areas is probably due to increased human pressure (Anderson 1990). Similarly in the early years of the 19th century, common seals bred in great numbers in the mouth of the River Tees, and from around 1820 or 1830 about 1000 frequented the mouth of the Tees, but by 1862 the number had been reduced to three (Millais 1904-1906). Thorburn (1920) described common seals as constantly persecuted, and only abundant in the Hebrides, Orkney and Shetland. They were thought to be thinly distributed on the western coasts of England, and on the east coast there were some on the Farne Islands, Northumberland but they were rare south of the Wash.

Lockley (1966) suggested a minimum population of common seals in Britain of 8000, excluding pups. This rose to 11,000-12,000 by the early 1970s (Bonner 1972). However, following the introduction of grey seal hunting in the 1960s, hunting was soon extended to common seals on the west coast of Scotland and in the Wash, and the long-established hunt in the Shetlands intensified, since common seal pups produced a much more valuable pelt (Bonner 1989a). In the Wash, the annual kill of pups averaged 607 from 1962 to 1970, and never rose above 870 (Vaughan 1978). This represented only 38% of the calculated production (Bonner 1976), and was not thought to seriously endanger common seals in the Wash (Bonner 1989a). The same applied to kills of 400-600 in the west of Scotland. However, in Shetland before 1960 the cull probably accounted for about 300-400 pups, but after 1962 the number killed increased substantially until, in 1968, about 900 young seals were taken, a very high proportion of the annual production of pups (Bonner, Vaughan & Johnston 1973). A survey of Shetland in 1971 (Bonner, Vaughan & Johnston 1973) found that the common seal population had declined, possibly at a rate of around 7·5% per annum over the previous 15 years. Public antipathy to these hunts led to the introduction of the Conservation of Seals Act 1970, which for the first time provided a close season for common seals. Comparisons of surveys conducted in Shetland in 1971 and 1984 showed that the population still had not fully recovered from the effects of hunting by the mid 1980s.

Population trends: These are unclear. Counts made on the Wash between late July and early August showed an average increase of 3·5% per annum between 1969 and 1988 (Hiby, Duck & Thompson 1993). Conversely, in Shetland a helicopter count in 1991 showed almost exactly the same population size as estimated in 1984 from boats (4784 compared to 4700 in 1984), yet helicopter surveys generally have yielded substantially higher counts than those obtained from boats. Thus the 1991 result may suggest that common seals in Shetland have declined since 1984 (C. Duck pers. comm.).

In 1988, the phocine distemper epizootic killed more than 18,000 common seals in the North Sea, the Kattegat-Skagerrak and the southern Baltic (Heide-Jørgensen *et al*. 1992). Populations in Denmark and Sweden were reduced by up to 60% in 1988, but are expected to reach pre-epizootic levels by 1995 (Heide-Jørgensen *et al*. 1992). In the Wash the common seal population was reduced by about 50% following the epidemic, and counts since that time have not shown any recovery in numbers. Populations on the east coast of Scotland were thought to have experienced 10-20% mortality. Common seals in Orkney, Shetland and the west coast of Scotland, however, were not significantly affected by the epizootic (Harwood *et al*. 1991; Thompson & Miller 1992; Hiby, Duck & Thompson 1993). Prior to the phocine distemper virus outbreak, the British common seal population may have been 46,000-47,000 (P.M. Thompson pers. comm.). Overall, however, the effect of the epizootic on the total British population was much less than elsewhere in Europe (Sea Mammal Research Unit unpubl.).

Population threats: The effects of the observed levels of organochlorine contamination are not fully understood (Thompson 1992). Reijnders (1986) demonstrated reproductive suppression in common seals from the Netherlands as a result of PCB contamination, but these pollutant levels were some 200 times (PCBs) and four times (total DDTs) greater than those found in British seals. However, during illness or starvation, the mobilisation of fat reserves and the consequent increase in circulating PCBs may be sufficient to compromise an animal's physiology (Law, Allchin & Harwood 1989). Evidence to support this assumption was provided by Hall *et al*. (1992), who found significantly greater concentrations of organochlorines in the blubber of common seals which died as a result of contracting phocine distemper virus, than in live seals which had been exposed to the virus. However, it is possible that the dead animals were already ill and mobilising their fat reserves at the time they contracted the virus, and so the higher concentrations of organochlorines could have been the consequence of fat metabolism entirely unrelated to the events that caused their deaths. The high mortality rates seen during the phocine distemper virus epizootic were probably the consequence of introducing a highly pathogenic virus into a naive population with no specific immunity to the infectious agent. Thus no contributory external factors are necessary to explain the severity of the outbreak, but synergistic effects due to organochlorine pollution or crowding of seals at haul-out sites may have exacerbated the impact of the disease in some areas (Heide-Jørgensen *et al*. 1992). Whilst the epizootic led to a marked reduction in common seal populations in several parts of the North Sea, they appear to have recovered remarkably well (Thompson & Hall 1993).

Harwood & Hall (1990) have discussed the rôle of periodic mass mortalities in managing marine mammal populations. They argued that these events are the most important factor determining the long-term average population size in the absence of human exploitation. Density-dependent mechanisms such as small changes in infant survival or in the fecundity of the youngest age classes will serve to set an upper limit on population size, but the pattern of phocid social behaviour, such as periodic aggregations to breed or feed, exacerbates the risk of disease spread irrespective of total population density. However, long-term fidelity to particular breeding sites limits the exchange of individuals between neighbouring breeding groups, and hence limits the spread of disease.

The Scottish populations are susceptible to oil spills. Whilst seals have short hair which may become coated in oil, they do not preen and ingest that oil (Thompson 1992). However, should these animals be in the vicinity of a recent spill, the inhalation of toxic fumes could result in neural damage (Geraci 1990). Also, domestic sewage may contain toxic chemicals as well as human pathogens which may survive in sea-water and are known to cause infections in captive seals (Thompson 1992).

Common seals are particularly susceptible to disturbance at breeding sites, since mothers and pups can become separated, and the time available to nurse pups, already limited by their preference for inter-tidal haul-out sites, may be reduced (Thompson 1992). This may account for their disappearance from the Isle of Wight and Bristol Channel. Plans to reclaim areas of the Wash pose a threat to one population, both due to the loss of inter-tidal haul-out sites and increased levels of disturbance; this occurred in the Tees estuary during the 1960s (Thompson 1992). It is possible that the poor rate of increase in the number of common seals in Shetland over the past 20 years is in part due to the intensive fishing activities, particularly industrial fisheries, in the area (F.G.L. Hartley pers. comm.).

The seal epizootic in 1988 was not a new phenomenon to British common seals; similar events were recorded in Orkney in 1813, 1836 and 1869/70, and Shetland in the 1930s (Harwood & Hall 1990). The British common seal population is still under threat from a recurrence of the phocine distemper epizootic, since a large proportion of the population has not come into contact with the infection and has yet to develop an immune response (Harwood et al. 1989; Harwood & Grenfell 1990; Carter et al. 1992). However, whilst common seal mortality from the phocine distemper virus was only 10-20% in the Moray Firth, the high prevalence of antibodies in the survivors suggests that the low mortality in this area was not due to the seals lacking contact with the virus. It is possible that the seals in that area are either more resistant to the phocine distemper virus, or else the virus had mutated to a less virulent form (Thompson & Miller 1992; Thompson et al. 1992).

Grey seal *Halichoerus grypus*

Status: Native; locally common.

Distribution: There are important colonies in the Farne Islands, Northumberland, south-west Wales, Firth of Forth, Hebrides, Orkney and Shetland, with smaller populations in south-west England, Donna Nook/the Wash and the Humber Estuary.

Population data: The main grey seal breeding colonies on the Isle of May in the Firth of Forth, the Hebrides and Orkney are surveyed annually during the breeding season using conventional aerial photography. Each colony is covered three to five times during the pupping season, with pups counted from the photographs. In addition, the colony on the Farne Islands, Northumberland is counted from the ground. Since the breeding season exceeds the period that any one pup remains ashore, the counts only provide figures for the maximum number of pups at the site at any one time, and mathematical models incorporating life history parameters have been applied to the data since 1988 (Harwood et al. 1991). A maximum likelihood model is used to derive pup production figures from these counts (Ward, Thompson & Hiby 1987). Total pup production from these main colonies accounts for some 85% of all pups born in Britain each year. The total female population and total production figures are derived from models based on the overall pup production in each breeding area (Sea Mammal Research Unit unpubl.). It is believed that the 95% confidence intervals for the pup production estimates are within 10% of the point estimate. Those for the estimate of the number of adult females are within 35% below and 73% above the point estimates. It is not possible to give 95% confidence limits for the number of males, but these are almost certainly at least as large as for the female part of the population (Sea Mammal Research Unit unpubl.). In addition, less frequent counts are carried out of the numbers of pups born in the Humber Estuary, south-west Britain, mainland Scotland and Shetland but confidence limits cannot be provided for these population estimates (Hiby, Duck & Thompson 1993).

Overall, these counts suggest a total population of 93,500 grey seals at the start of the 1991 pupping season, when approximately 27,000 pups were born. Of the total population, 7100 were around England and Wales (Farne Islands, Northumberland - 3200; Humber Estuary - 800; south-west Britain - 3100) and 86,400 around Scotland (mainland Scotland - 3500; Inner Hebrides - 8700; Outer Hebrides - 37,500; Isle of May - 4200; Orkney - 29,000; Shetland - 3500) (Hiby, Duck & Thompson 1993).

Population estimates: A total pre-breeding population of about 93,500; 5500 in England, 86,400 in Scotland and 1600 in Wales.
Reliability of population estimate: 1.

Historical changes: In the early part of this century, grey seals were rather rare in England and Wales. A fair-sized colony inhabited the Isles of Scilly, a few still persisted on the Farne Islands, Northumberland and some were found on the Pembrokeshire coast. In Scotland they were much more plentiful, especially on the north-western coasts and the Hebrides, Orkney and Shetland (Thorburn 1920). However, at the time of the enactment of the Grey Seal Protection Act 1914, the British grey seal population was put at only 500 animals, although this was undoubtedly a significant under-estimate. In 1928 the population was estimated to have reached 4000-5000 (Rae 1960), and by 1932, when a new Act extended the close season for grey seals, the population was put at 8,000, again with no information as to how this estimate was derived (Bonner 1982).

In the 50 years up to 1980, several populations of grey seals showed dramatic increases (Bonner 1981). It is unclear to what extent this increase in grey seal numbers was due to a reduction in hunting pressures, the change in economic circumstances which reduced the human population in the areas frequented by the seals (the abandonment of islands such as the Monachs in the Outer Hebrides and Holm of Faray in Orkney provided new secure breeding places for the seals), or the almost total disappearance of the crofter-fisher lifestyle which regarded seals as a valuable asset, thereby allowing the seals to exploit their new breeding places in comparative safety (Bonner 1982). Whatever

the relative importance of the various factors, grey seal populations improved. For example, pup production on the Farne Islands, Northumberland increased from less than 100 in the early 1930s to 751 in 1956 and 2010 in 1971 (Coulson & Hickling 1964; Bonner 1975) and on the Monach Isles from about 50 in 1961 to 1400 in 1974 (Bonner 1976). Overall, the British grey seal population doubled from 34,200 in the mid-1960s (Smith 1966) to 69,000 in the mid-1970s (Summers 1978).

The growth in seal numbers led to concern over their impact on fish stocks. The grey seal and fisheries controversy has been described in detail by Bonner (1982; 1989b). In 1959 the Nature Conservancy set up a Consultative Committee on Grey Seals and Fisheries, which in 1963 recommended (Nature Conservancy 1963) that grey seal numbers should be reduced by 25% in the Orkneys and the Farne Islands to preserve fish stocks. At that time, the population of grey seals in Scotland was estimated to be 29,500. The Farne Island population was culled from 1963 to 1965 under the auspices of the Ministry of Agriculture, Fisheries and Food, but thereafter the cull was halted because the National Trust argued that the fisheries case, as it related to the Farne Islands, Northumberland, was insufficiently proven. The cull in Orkney continued, whilst that on the Farne Islands was reintroduced in 1972 because increasing seal numbers were damaging the fragile environment and leading to increased pup mortality. The benefits and failures of these control programmes are discussed by Bonner (1982). Reviewing the pattern of population growth, Harwood & Greenwood (1985) concluded that in the years up to the early 1980s, some undisturbed grey seal populations had grown at rates of 6-7% per annum, whereas others had not. Thus for the Inner Hebrides, from 1976-1981, the increase was 7% per annum (Natural Environment Research Council 1982), for the Outer Hebrides 6·5% per annum from 1969-1975 (Summers 1978), and for Orkney until 1969 6% per annum, when the effects of pup culling became apparent, and thereafter 3% per annum (Summers 1978). For the Farne Islands, the growth rate was 8% per annum from the 1930s until 1951 (Coulson 1981), and then 7% per annum from 1951 to 1971, with a decline thereafter as a result of control measures.

Renewed controversy over the impact of seals on fisheries led, in 1977, to an annual culling programme being introduced in Orkney and the Outer Hebrides, with the aim of reducing grey seal numbers in these populations from 50,000 to 35,000 by 1982. Originally planned as an annual cull of 4000 moulted pups and 900 breeding cows and other pups (Summers 1979; Bonner 1982), it was revised after the first year to a pup-only hunt because of widespread public concern. Also, the effects of culling adults at breeding colonies was not as predicted; around 15% of cows were deterred from coming ashore, and of those that did come back, some deserted their pups if the colony was disturbed again and some of the cows failed to return to breed in subsequent years. At the colonies where cows were culled in 1977, pup production in 1978 was up to 40% lower than in 1971 (Harwood & Greenwood 1985).

Population trends: The grey seal population is continuing to increase and the 1991 count was 9·9% higher than equivalent figures for 1990 (Hiby, Duck & Thompson 1993). The number of pups born each year in Orkney has increased more than 60% since 1984, although not all the Orkney colonies have increased at the same rate. Whilst some have shown a steady increase, others have declined and some have shown little change; reasons for this disparity are unknown (Sea Mammal Research Unit unpubl.). The 1988 phocine distemper virus had less impact on grey than common seals. Although only a few grey seal carcasses were found, it was estimated that there was a substantial but undetected mortality of 12%. This led to pup production in 1988 being 24%, 20% and 13% lower than expected for Orkney, the Isle of May and the Farne Islands respectively (Harwood et al. 1991; Hall, Pomeroy & Harwood 1992; Hiby, Duck & Thompson 1993). Since 1989, pup

production has risen steadily at all sites except the Farne Islands, although it is still lower than expected. The reasons for the continued reduction in pup production at the Farne Islands are unknown.

Harwood & Prime (1978) showed that both juvenile and adult survival are probably affected by the density of animals within a breeding assembly, and thus as long as suitable breeding sites are available, there is a mechanism to ensure that the density at any one site does not rise to a level which would significantly affect the rate of increase of the population. However, since many potential grey seal breeding sites have yet to be occupied, it is likely that the British grey seal population will continue to increase.

Population threats: Bonner (1981) reviewed the literature on pollutant levels in grey seals, and concluded that generally they have not suffered any toxic effects from the levels of pollutants found, even though levels in blubber can be quite high (Blomkvist et al. 1992). However, recent studies of seals in the Baltic suggest that very high pollutant burdens may cause pathological changes which could ultimately affect reproductive performance (Olsson, Karlson & Ahnland 1992). Other work has shown that trace metal and organochlorine levels in grey seals on the eastern coast of Britain were considerably lower than those from grey seals that had suffered reproductive disorders elsewhere in the North Sea (Reijnders 1986; Law, Allchin & Harwood 1989; Law et al. 1991). Also organochlorine contaminants in grey seals from the Farne Islands in 1988 were lower than in 1972, suggesting a gradual decline with time (Law, Allchin & Harwood 1989). As for common seals, the risks posed by the discharge of untreated sewage are unknown (Thompson 1992).

Grey seals are potentially at risk from oil spills. Although in general seals seem able to avoid oil patches at sea, they often become stained by crawling over oil-covered rocks (Bonner 1972). Thus when the *Torrey Canyon* discharged 119,000 tonnes of crude oil off south-west England in 1967, there were an estimated 200-250 grey seals in the area affected by the spillage, but few seal deaths were reported (Bonner 1972). Whilst the *Exxon Valdez* incident in North America demonstrated that substantial seal mortality can be caused by massive releases of crude oil in enclosed waters, this type of pollution is unlikely to affect British seals, as shown by the *Braer* incident in Shetland (W.N. Bonner pers. comm.).

Grey seals are very sensitive to disturbance of their breeding sites; hence the dramatic increase in use of islands off north-west Scotland following depopulation of the area (Summers & Harwood 1979). Unlike common seals, nearly all grey seals now show immunity to the phocine distemper virus (Carter *et al.* 1992; Hiby, Duck & Thompson 1993), and so it would appear unlikely that a recurrence of this disease will have a significant impact on grey seals in the near future.

Order: Artiodactyla

Red deer *Cervus elaphus*

Status: Native, with a number of feral populations in England and Scotland. Deer from native stocks are only confirmed in parts of Scotland and north-west England (Lowe & Gardiner 1974); all other populations are introduced. Common and increasing.

Distribution: Cumbria, East Anglia, Hampshire, south-west England, south-west Scotland, Scotland north of the central industrial belt, and with scattered records from elsewhere in England and Wales. Red deer are also found on numerous Scottish islands (Staines 1991).

Population data: They are found on open moorland, and in coniferous and deciduous forest. Densities vary with the quality and structure of the habitat. Densities of 5-40 (exceptionally) per km² occur in forestry plantations, and 12-15 per km² are typical for hill land, although densities from less than 10 to over 30 per km² occur (Ratcliffe 1984; Stewart 1985; A.J. de Nahlik pers. comm.; B. Staines pers. comm.). In Hampshire, the size of the herd in the New Forest and Avon Valley was estimated from counts to be around 300, with two-thirds of these in the New Forest area (M. Clarke and R.J. Putman pers. comms). In north-west Essex the population was estimated subjectively by N.G. Chapman (pers. comm.) to be around 50. In Breckland in 1992, 100 were counted on Forestry Commission land and surrounding estates within an 8 km radius (R. Whitta pers. comm.), and in the Dunwich area of Suffolk there were 200 in 1994 (E. Calcott pers. comm.). In northern England, the population in Cumbria numbered about 1000 (J. Cubby and V.P.W. Lowe pers. comms), with the 600 in the southern part of the Lake District so extensively hybridised with sika deer *Cervus nippon* that it was unlikely that any pure red deer remained in the area (Lowe & Gardiner 1975). The Peak District population was estimated subjectively and by sign (rutting-stand) surveys to be around 200 (D.W. Yalden unpubl.). In addition, there are scattered records and small populations in England from north Staffordshire northwards, but these populations are generally small, and the total number is probably less than 300. In south-west England the population size on Exmoor was estimated in 1991/92 by a combination of faecal counts, vantage point counts and a simultaneous vantage point count over the whole area (Langbein & Putman 1992) and on the Quantocks in 1989/90 by assessing faecal density (F. Winder & P.R.F. Chanin unpubl.). These gave a spring population of 4750 in the Exmoor National Park, a further 1000 within 10 km of the park boundary, 800-900 on the Quantocks (Langbein & Putman 1992), plus an unknown number elsewhere from mid-Devon to Cornwall, suggesting a population in south-west England of at least 10,000 (R.J. Putman pers. comm.). In addition, red deer roam large distances from these main centres of distribution, and records are widely scattered (Arnold 1993). Thus, allowing for some animals away from the main areas, the total

English population lies at around 12,500. Red deer have also been recorded occasionally in Wales (Arnold 1993).

In Scotland, the population size in the Highlands was estimated for 1986 by Clutton-Brock & Albon (1989) using the Red Deer Commission's census figures and standardised counts of different blocks within a common time frame, using a multiple regression model that included both year and block identity as independent variables. This approach suggested an early spring population of $297,000 \pm 40,000$, compared with the Red Deer Commission's estimate of 265,000 for the highlands. Of these, 30% were in three contiguous areas in the eastern and central Highlands. Populations in Scottish woodlands were estimated by Staines & Ratcliffe (1987) to be 27,000-50,000, using vantage point counts and indices of faecal abundance. Since deer are notoriously difficult to count in woodlands, it is likely that the population lies at the upper end of this range.

Hingston (1988) estimated that there were approximately 5000-6000 red deer in parks, whilst J. Langbein (pers. comm.) put this figure at 7500. In addition there were 18,500 red deer on farms in Scotland in 1989 (Callander & MacKenzie 1991) and 33,625 farmed red deer in England and Wales in 1993 (Ministry of Agriculture, Fisheries and Food pers. comm.).

Population estimates: A total pre-breeding population of about 360,000; 12,500 in England, 347,000 in Scotland and fewer than 50 in Wales. In addition, there are a further 7500 in parks and 52,125 on farms.
Reliability of population estimate: 2.

Historical changes: The red deer herd in north Devon and west Somerset was estimated to number 250 in 1871, and over 500 in the early 1900s. In Cumbria it was thought that there were about 300 at the turn of the century, although they had been much rarer fifteen years earlier (Millais 1904-1906). The number of red deer in English parks at the turn of the century was around 6000

(Whitaker 1892). In Scotland, deforestation of native woodlands and persecution led to the probable extinction of all native stocks in the lowlands by the 17th century (Ritchie 1920). Red deer only survived on remote hill lands of the Scottish Highlands and islands. Red deer numbers were probably lowest at the end of the 18th century, but increased in the 19th century with a rising interest in deer stalking (Staines & Ratcliffe 1987) and introductions. From a peak around 1914, numbers are thought to have declined during the First World War. The situation in the 1920s and 1930s is unclear, but the population may still have been 200,000 at the start of the Second World War, following which the population declined by up to 50% to approximately 100,000 by 1950 (Callander & MacKenzie 1991). Red Deer Commission census figures for Scotland since 1960 have shown a steady increase in numbers, suggesting that the population has doubled in the last 30 years, with a possible temporary reduction in the late 1970s due to increased natural mortality during two severe winters (Callander & MacKenzie 1991). In 1975, Gibbs *et al.* (1975) estimated the total red deer population in Britain to be 190,000, but gave no details as to how this estimate was obtained.

Population trends: Until recently, the red deer population in Scotland was continuing to increase due to a number of factors. These included lower than average levels of natural mortality, reduced competition with hill sheep and the underculling of hinds (Clutton-Brock & Albon 1989; Callander & MacKenzie 1991). However, with an annual cull now in excess of 50,000 and perhaps the effects of winter weather, the red deer population in Scotland may now be relatively stable (C.B. Shedden pers. comm.). Red deer are also increasing in both range and numbers in south-west England. Lloyd (1975) estimated that there were 500-800 red deer in the Exmoor National Park during the 1970s, and Allen (1990) estimated 1500 during the 1980s. Using faecal pellet counts over limited areas and extrapolating these to the rest of the Park, Malcolm *et al.* (1984) suggested a figure of around 1900 red deer in the early 1980s. All these figures were undoubtedly gross under-estimates. Based on a retrospective analysis of current rates of population growth, Langbein & Putman (1992) suggest that the population was around 1400 in 1975, rising to just under 3000 by 1985, with a further 50% increase over the last seven years. Continued growth at the same rate would produce a population in excess of 9000 in the Exmoor National Park by the turn of the century. Elsewhere, numbers are low, and populations seem to be stable or declining slightly. Reasons for this remain unclear, but poaching is thought to maintain the Peak District population at around 200 (D.W. Yalden unpubl.).

Population threats: In some areas there is hybridisation with the increasing populations of sika deer (see below). However, red deer populations in Galloway, south-west Scotland and most English populations (except Cumbria) are non-native. Almost all of the English populations are of park origin, and most of the park herds were of continental rather than Scottish origin. In addition, many were probably red deer-wapiti crosses (R.J. Putman pers. comm.). Since these populations are not pure native stock, further hybridisation in these areas may not be a major conservation issue. More recent information suggests that hybridisation is occurring between native red and sika deer, and introgression of genes from sika to red deer seems likely to increase. Also, sika-like hybrids seem to be better competitors in dense woodland, and so it is possible that sika-like deer may completely replace red deer in such habitats (Balharry *et al.* 1994).

Sika deer *Cervus nippon*

Status: Introduced; locally common.

Distribution: Large populations occur in Argyll, Inverness-shire, Peeblesshire, Ross and Cromarty and Sutherland. Small populations occur in Cumbria, Dorset (including Brownsea Island in Poole Harbour), Hampshire, Lancashire and Northamptonshire, with a few deer in Bedfordshire. The Dorset population now extends into east Devon,

particularly around Axminster (J. Langbein pers. comm.). A small population is maintained on the island of Lundy.

Population data: Sika deer are found in dense woodland and scrub, and the thicket stages of coniferous forests. In England, populations are still small enough to be estimated by counts. Transect counts, adjusted for areas of different habitats, and population reconstruction from cull data, suggested there were about 200 in the New Forest in the 1980s (Mann 1983; Putman 1986), although this population has recently been subjected to a heavy cull and may now only number about 100 (R.J. Putman pers. comm.). The Dorset population is expanding into parts of Devon; based on counts of the main sub-populations, the total number, including those on Brownsea Island, was less than 2000 (R.J. Putman pers. comm.) in the early 1990s. There were a further 200 in the Forest of Bowland in Lancashire (J. Cubby pers. comm.) and around 40 on Lundy. Thus the total population of sika deer in England is under 2500.

In Scotland approximately 140,000 ha are colonised by sika (P.R. Ratcliffe pers. comm.). Assuming that at any one time *circa* 25% of this area is suitable for sika deer, this gives 35,000 ha of suitable habitat with densities of 20-25 deer per km^2 (A. Chadwick pers. comm.). This suggests 7000-8750 sika occur in Scotland. The Red Deer Commission put the number of sika in Scotland at 10,000 (Scottish Development Department 1990), although there are no details as to how this figure was calculated.

In addition, Hingston (1988) suggested there were about 500 Japanese sika in parks, plus approximately another 400 of the Formosan and Manchurian subspecies. J. Langbein (pers. comm.) estimates a total of 1500 for all subspecies since Hingston (1988) did not include all the parks with sika deer.

Population estimates: A total pre-breeding population of about 11,500; fewer than 2500 in England, 9000 in Scotland and none in

Wales. In addition, there are a further 1500 in deer parks. **Reliability of population estimate:** 2.

Historical changes: The first Japanese sika to reach Great Britain were a pair presented to the Zoological Society of London in 1860. In the same year, a stag and three hinds were imported to Enniskerry, Co. Wicklow, and they formed the source for a number of parks in England and Scotland (Lever 1977). However, at the turn of the century they were still held in fewer than ten English (and some Scottish) deer parks, and numbered only a few hundred (Whitaker 1892). Details of the early introductions to deer parks in Britain are given in Whitehead (1964), who also documented the early range extensions. In the mid-1970s, Gibbs *et al.* (1975) estimated a total population in Britain of 1000, but no details are given as to how this estimate was obtained. Data on their range expansion has been updated by Ratcliffe (1987). The origins and genetic identity of the sika deer in Britain are discussed by Ratcliffe (1987), Ratcliffe *et al.* (1991) and Putman & Hunt (1993).

Population trends: The increases in some populations but not others reflect the availability of suitable habitat (young coniferous plantations) for colonisation. Whilst the populations in the New Forest, Ross and Cromarty and Argyll are spreading only slowly, most populations in northern Scotland are expanding their range rapidly in areas where there is suitable habitat. Juvenile males will apparently travel long distances, and colonisation by stags can precede the appearance of hinds by up to 10 years. The rate of range expansion in Argyll was 3-5 km per year (Ratcliffe 1987).

Population threats: It would appear that where substantial populations of both red and sika deer occur, hybridisation is rare (Harrington 1982). However, once a first cross has been established, further introgression is rapid, and other than F1 hybrids, it is very difficult to distinguish hybrid stock from pure red or pure sika deer (Putman & Hunt 1993). Thus selective culling of

apparent hybrids is not an effective management practice. Multivariate analysis of skull measurements shows that the only population that can be considered to be pure is that in Peeblesshire, because the original introductions (to Dawyck in 1908) came directly from Japan and native red deer do not occur in the area. Similarly, the sika deer in the New Forest appear to have retained their identity, perhaps also reflecting an introduction of purer stock and their relative isolation from the red deer in the area (Putman & Hunt 1993). The high degree of variability in the Lake District population reflects the high numbers of hybrid deer observed there during the last 10-20 years, and the population in the Lake District may now be comprised entirely of hybrids between sika and red deer. It seems that the remaining sika deer populations were derived from mainland Asiatic deer which had previously hybridised with red deer (*Cervus elaphus xanthopygus*), and all the Scottish populations other than that in Peeblesshire have been exposed to some hybridisation with red deer since their introduction (Ratcliffe 1987; Ratcliffe *et al.* 1991; Putman & Hunt 1993).

Since only the populations in the New Forest and Peeblesshire appear to be relatively pure bred, there could be a case for managing these to ensure their continuing genetic integrity.

Fallow deer *Dama dama*

Status: Introduced; widespread and locally common.

Distribution: Found throughout much of England and in parts of Wales. Local in Scotland, where its distribution includes three west coast islands. Fallow deer prefer deciduous/mixed mature woodland and conifer plantations with open areas.

Population data: There are very few reliable population estimates from any habitats, except Forestry Commission counts from large areas of continuous woodland. Densities normally range from 18-43 fallow deer per km^2 (N.G.

Chapman pers. comm.). However, these populations are often heavily managed, and so the density is maintained at a particular level that is not related to the carrying capacity of that habitat type but often at a level that is subjectively believed to limit their grazing impact (R.J. Putman pers. comm.). Since these populations are maintained at an arbitrary level (e.g. 2400 in the New Forest), any density estimates or extrapolations based on these counts are largely meaningless. Even where accurate counts are available, it is rarely possible to relate these counts to the areas covered by the deer. In agricultural landscapes, densities are particularly hard to estimate, since they can vary tremendously with no apparent environmental cause, although levels of human disturbance and intensity of culling may be more important here than environmental quality *per se* (R.J. Putman pers. comm.). Thus in one agricultural area in Lincolnshire there was a minimum of 40 per km² based on minimum counts (R.J. Putman pers. comm.). However, more typical densities for agricultural land in Hampshire, based on transect counts adjusted for the area of each habitat sampled, were 8·0 per km² in an arable landscape with small fields and scattered small copses, 6·8 per km² on rolling downs with scattered coverts and copses and 4·6 per km² in an area of mixed arable and pasture with more extensive woodlands (Thirgood 1990). Pellet counts in a mixed agricultural woodland and moorland area of Devon suggested *circa* 17·5 fallow deer per km² (J. Langbein pers. comm.).

It is difficult to relate fallow deer numbers to land classes, or to particular habitat types, although density does change with habitat (Putman 1986; Chapman & Putman 1991). Many populations are still centred on ancient deer forests, or around the parks from which they originally escaped (J. Langbein & R.J. Putman pers. comm.); see, for example, Chapman (1977) for a description of the situation in Essex. Thus, despite being a long-standing introduction, their distribution is patchy and their numbers and distribution are dominated by human influence, and so it was not possible to use habitat characteristics to estimate population size. Therefore the recorded distribution and estimated density were used to calculate population size. B. Mayle (pers. comm.) calculated a population size of 32,400 in 1986, based on the distribution given by Arnold (1984) and the results of the Forestry Commission's survey of its own woodlands. She based her calculation on a figure of 50 deer in each of the 648 10 x 10 km squares believed to contain fallow deer. This figure is a minimum estimate, since the current distribution map almost certainly under-estimates the number of 10 x 10 km squares containing fallow deer, and because fallow deer populations also are very clumped and locally can reach very high densities. For most of the recorded range, densities will be much higher than 0·5 per km². Gibbs *et al.* (1975) estimated that the total fallow deer population in Britain was 50,000, although they gave no details as to how this figure was obtained. A third figure was produced by Gliksten (1993), who estimated 60,000-70,000 fallow deer, based on a subjective estimate of density and the known distribution. The Red Deer Commission put the number of fallow deer in Scotland at 1000-2000 (Scottish Development Department 1990), although there is no information as to how this figure was calculated.

Whilst this approach was subjective, it is hard to be more precise. R.J. Putman (pers. comm.) tried to produce a quantitative estimate based on the areas of known distribution, the areas of suitable habitat, and densities estimated in a variety of habitats. However, the estimate produced by this means was unrealistically high because the available data on densities are heavily biased due to the clumped distribution of the species. In view of all the problems in trying to calculate a population size, and since most attempts to count fallow deer numbers under-estimate them, it is probable that the total population is about 100,000, but it is impossible to be more precise.

In addition, Hingston (1988) estimated that there were 11,580 fallow deer in 81 parks, but some parks were not included at the request of the owners. J. Langbein (pers. comm.) estimates that there are 17,000 in parks. In 1993 there were 6,710 farmed fallow deer in England and Wales (Ministry of Agriculture, Fisheries and Food pers. comm.). Gliksten (1993) estimated that 15% of all farmed deer are fallow. Based on the number of farmed red deer in Scotland in 1989 (Callander & MacKenzie 1991), this would suggest about 3250 farmed fallow deer in Scotland.

Population estimates: The best estimate possible is that the total pre-breeding population is about 100,000; in England 95,000, in Scotland fewer than 4000 and in Wales fewer than 1000. In addition, there are a further 17,000 in parks and about 10,000 on farms. **Reliability of population estimate: 4.**

Historical changes: Their early history in Britain is described by Whitehead (1964). By the middle of the 17th century, there were over 700 parks in England that held fallow deer. During the Civil War, many were broken up and the deer escaped and, although the majority were killed, a few survived in the more inaccessible areas to establish feral populations. In the 18th century there was renewed interest in establishing deer parks, and by the end of last century there were about 390 parks in England with 71,000 fallow deer (Whitaker 1892). The number of parks with fallow deer subsequently declined, and in 1988 only about 120 remained (J. Langbein pers. comm.).

At the turn of the century the number of feral fallow deer herds was small. Millais (1904-1906) described a number of herds, and although his list is not exhaustive, it does suggest that feral fallow deer were comparatively few. In Essex, for instance, Laver (1898) only refers to the herd in Epping Forest, yet eighty years later Chapman (1977) showed that there were many feral herds, all centred around deer parks. It is probable that fallow deer numbers throughout Britain have increased this century as a result of repeated escapes from parks.

Population trends: Numbers are possibly slowly increasing, but the magnitude of the increase is unknown and is believed to vary between different areas. Gill (1992) considered that fallow deer were possibly the only species of deer in Britain not increasing either in range or numbers.

Population threats: Fallow deer have been established for around nine centuries, possibly from a relatively small founder stock. Certainly, electrophoretic studies of blood proteins have so far failed to reveal any evidence of genetic polymorphism in British fallow deer (Pemberton & Smith 1985). A second sub-species of fallow deer (*Dama dama mesopotamica*) is larger and has a different antler morphology, and has been hybridised with *Dama dama dama* on deer farms in New Zealand, the United States of America and elsewhere, either by natural or artificial methods. A cross-bred herd exists in Kent, and stock has been advertised for sale in Britain. Free-ranging fallow deer populations are often in close proximity to deer parks and farms, and escapes do occur. Thus there is a potential risk of hybrid or pure Persian fallow deer cross-breeding with the long-established stock, and at present there are no measures to reduce this risk (N.G. Chapman pers. comm.).

In some areas, such as Cannock Chase in Staffordshire (P. James pers. comm.) and Epping Forest, Essex (Chapman & Chapman 1969), road mortalities can be high, and these may lead to local population reductions.

Roe deer *Capreolus capreolus*

Status: Native in Scotland. Roe deer became extinct in England during the 18th century, and populations in south, east and north-west England were re-established by reintroductions in the 19th century.

Distribution: Roe are the most widely distributed species of deer in Britain. They are found throughout Scotland and northern England, southern England and parts of East Anglia, with scattered records from Wales and the English counties along the Welsh border. They occur on a few of the larger islands in the Inner Hebrides and the Clyde Islands (Arnold 1993).

Population data: Roe deer are found in open mixed coniferous and purely deciduous woodland, in agricultural landscapes, and, in some parts of Scotland, on moorland without access to cover. Woodland density estimates vary from 0.5 ± 0.5 (95% confidence interval) to 24.8 ± 0.5 per km^2, based on pellet counts at 20 sites in Scotland (J. Latham pers. comm.). Densities in sitka spruce forests in the Scottish borders and the pine forests of East Anglia range from 8-25 deer per km^2, with densities being greatest (25 per km^2) in stands 5-15 years old, declining to 8 deer per km^2 prior to the first thinning, and subsequently rising to 15 per km^2 as the forest is further thinned (Loudon 1982; Staines & Ratcliffe 1991). Locally, densities of 75 deer per km^2 have been recorded in isolated woods in southern England (Loudon 1982), but such estimates probably only include part of the animals' ranges (A.L. Johnson pers. comm.). At Porton Down, Wiltshire, in an area of open downland, there were 6.9 per km^2, as determined by helicopter and ground-based counts (Johnson 1984). At Alice Holt, Hampshire, an area of mixed broadleaved and coniferous forest, there were 12.8 deer per km^2 as estimated by pellet counts (K. Otim unpubl.). Other than these, there are few density estimates on which to base a population estimate.

B. Mayle (pers. comm.) estimated the number of roe deer in Britain to be 62,950 by assuming a density of 50 animals for each of the 1259 10 x 10 km squares thought to contain roe deer, as indicated by Arnold (1984) and from the Forestry Commission's own surveys. However, this is almost certainly a very substantial under-estimate, since it assumes a mean density of only 0.5 deer per km^2. If it is assumed that for the 1237 10 x 10 km squares in which roe deer are currently recorded (Arnold 1993), 5-10% of the habitat was suitable for roe deer at a mean density of 15 per km^2, the population would number

93,000-186,000. However, even 186,000 is likely to be a significant under-estimate. The Red Deer Commission for Scotland obtained an estimate for the Scottish population in 1980 of 125,000-175,000, and in 1990 the figure was put at 200,000 (Scottish Development Department 1990), although there is no information as to how this figure was calculated. Shedden (1993) believed this figure to be a substantial under-estimate for the following reasons. Scottish roe deer populations have relatively low levels of recruitment, and so a 15% cull should prevent population growth. Since the roe deer population in Scotland was expanding, the cull must have been under 15%. Shedden (1993) therefore calculated a roe deer population in Scotland of 305,000-400,000 based on the number of stalkers, the estimated cull size, and the assumption that this represented 10% of the total roe deer population in Scotland. Despite the number of assumptions, this probably provides the most realistic population estimation for Scotland. Assuming that the true population in Scotland is around 350,000, based on the distribution of roe deer in Britain as a whole, it is probable that the total population in Britain is around 500,000.

Population estimates: A total pre-breeding population of about 500,000; 150,000 in England, 350,000 in Scotland and around 50 in Wales. **Reliability of population estimate: 3.**

Historical changes: Once widespread, in historical times roe deer became extinct throughout much of Great Britain, and by the beginning of the 18th century were thought to survive only in remnant woodlands in parts of the central and north-west Highlands of Scotland (Ritchie 1920). The reasons for this decline are unclear; several explanations have been put forward, but none are convincing. An increase in woodlands during the 18th century led to a range expansion in Scotland, with roe deer reaching the Scottish border by 1840. Roe deer of unknown origin were re-introduced to Milton Abbas, Dorset, in 1800, and Millais (1904-1906) estimated that at the start of the century there were 300-400 in

Dorset, and that they were still spreading. At that time there were also populations in the New Forest, Surrey and Sussex, and they were re-introduced to Epping Forest, Essex, although these did not persist. The population in East Anglia originated from an introduction of German deer to the area between Brandon and Thetford in 1884 (Chapman *et al.* 1985), and the roe deer in the Lake District are thought to be of Austrian origin (Staines & Ratcliffe 1991). From these centres, roe deer have spread throughout much of eastern, northern and southern England during the course of this century. Full details of these changes are given by Whitehead (1964). By the mid-1970s, Gibbs *et al.* (1975) estimated the total roe deer population in Britain to be 200,000, although no details are given as to how this figure was obtained.

Population trends: Still increasing in range in England, and this range increase is almost certainly associated with an increase in numbers, although the rate of increase is unknown.

Population threats: None known.

Chinese muntjac *Muntiacus reevesi*

Status: Introduced. Locally common and rapidly increasing in numbers.

Distribution: Following the original introduction to Woburn Park, Bedfordshire in 1894, Chinese muntjac are now established in most of southern England as far north as Derbyshire, Lincolnshire and Nottinghamshire, including some urban areas. In addition, there are scattered records outside this range, including Cheshire, Cumbria, Northumberland, South Yorkshire and in Scotland, although a number of the Scottish records have yet to be confirmed (Chapman, Harris & Stanford 1994), and parts of north Wales and most of the counties along the south Wales coast. They have also been introduced to Steep Holm, in the Bristol Channel.

Population data: Muntjac seek areas of cover (Chapman *et al.* 1985) and are most common in deciduous woodland, mixed/coniferous woodland and areas of scrub. However, despite their wide distribution (which includes virtually every English county plus several in Wales and possibly in Scotland), their distribution is very clumped. A recent survey, in which large numbers of records were collected from members of the public, found that 50% of the reports came from just five counties - Berkshire, Buckinghamshire, Hertfordshire, Oxfordshire and Warwickshire. Elsewhere numbers were low and/or populations were scattered, either due to recent colonisation, or deliberate or accidental releases outside the main area of distribution (Chapman, Harris & Stanford 1994). This patchy distribution makes estimating population size particularly difficult. In addition, there are few detailed density estimates, but in one area of coniferous woodland in East Anglia, densities of up to 30 animals per km^2 were recorded (K. & M. Claydon pers. comm.). This high density occurred in the absence of culling. A similar high density was recorded in a small (43.5 ha) deciduous wood in Oxfordshire (Harding 1986). However, where populations are heavily managed, densities are likely to be lower.

Population size was estimated as follows. For the counties of Berkshire, Buckinghamshire, Hertfordshire, Oxfordshire and Warwickshire, adult densities were assumed to be 30 per km^2 in prime habitats (semi-natural broadleaved and mixed woodlands, young plantations and scrub) and 15 per km^2 in broadleaved, coniferous and mixed plantations. For this calculation, adults were taken to be animals that had reached adult size, i.e. they were at least seven months of age. Based on the distribution of records, the estimated number of muntjac in these five counties was taken to represent 50% of the total population in Britain.

Population estimates: A total pre-breeding population of about 40,000; in England around 40,000, in Scotland fewer than 50 and in Wales fewer than 250. Whilst muntjac are widely recorded in Wales, most of these records are of scattered individuals, and the population is unlikely to exceed 250 adult animals. It must also be remembered that muntjac breed throughout the year, with no evidence of seasonal trends in productivity or survival (Chapman, Chapman & Dansie 1984). Thus at any time of the year there will also be a number of fawns and immature animals in the population, and one study (Claydon, Claydon & Harris 1986) suggested that these would add about 30% to the total population, i.e. around 12,000 animals that have not reached adult size. **Reliability of population estimate:** 3.

Historical changes: Their spread is documented in detail by Lever (1977), Anderson & Cham (1987) and Chapman, Harris & Stanford (1994). The first feral muntjac was observed at Wrest Park, 11 km east of Woburn, Bedfordshire in 1922, and another a few years later at Ashridge Park, Hertfordshire, 19 km south of Woburn (Lever 1977). In the first 60 years the spread was relatively slow, extending to a radius of 72 km from Woburn (Whitehead 1964). By the early 1990s this had extended to 300 km to the south-west, 200 km to the north and north east, and 120 km to the south-east (Chapman 1991). However, natural spread only seems to occur at a rate of about 1 km per year, and the wide distribution is in large part due to many deliberate and accidental releases (Chapman, Harris & Stanford 1994). In the mid-1970s, Gibbs *et al.* (1975) estimated that the total population in Britain was 5000, although no details are given as to how this figure was obtained.

Population trends: Numbers are increasing rapidly, and in many parts of the current range numbers are still well below carrying capacity. The population model detailed below gives an intrinsic rate of population growth of almost 10% per year; thus at current rates the population will double in less than 8 years. However, modelling work has suggested that the potential for further natural range expansion is more limited than generally

perceived, and most spread is likely to be in Kent and Sussex, and to a lesser extent north in Lincolnshire, Nottinghamshire and South Yorkshire, and west into Cheshire and Shropshire (Chapman, Harris & Stanford 1994).

Whilst the estimate presented here may seem large considering the small size of the founder population (Chapman, Harris & Stanford 1994), and the slow early spread, a population of 40,000 is entirely feasible. A simple population growth model based on certain assumptions (that the founder population was introduced at the turn of the century; there were 24 animals with equal numbers of bucks and does; that all does bred; that culling was not introduced until 1925 and that until then all animals died at eight years of age) and demography data supplied by N.G. Chapman from several sites in southern England (sex ratio of the population is equal; 47% of fawns die before two months of age; mortality by 1 year is 56%, by 2 years 69%, by 3 years 75%, by 4 years 81%, by 5 years 88%, by 6 years 94%, by 7 years 95% and by 15 years 100%; an interbirth interval of 8 months; no does are pregnant before 6 months of age, 60% are pregnant at 10 months, 80% at 12 months, 100% at 15 months) showed that the muntjac population in 1993 could have reached 292,000 animals (S. Wray pers. comm.). Obviously not all of the assumptions in the model would have been met. For example, not all the does in the founder population would have bred, not all would have lived to 8 years, etc., but the model does serve to show the potential rapid rate of growth, and also that the estimate of 40,000 is a long way below the maximum number that could have been achieved in a hundred years.

There are several reasons why the population is well below the theoretical maximum that could have been achieved. In particular, the population growth model made no allowance for the effects of the severe winters of 1939/1940, 1946/1947 and 1962/1963 on the muntjac population, although there was a very significant level of mortality (Pickvance & Chard 1960; Chapman, Harris & Stanford

1994). Three large die-offs in a quarter of a century must have had a significant impact on the rate of population growth and hence rate of spread, especially since muntjac had not long been established outside Woburn Park (Chapman, Harris & Stanford 1994). The rapid spread since 1963 is probably in part due to the long period without winters severe enough to induce high levels of mortality. The other significant factor in limiting the rate of spread is the high level of culling that often occurs when muntjac are first colonising an area, which is often undertaken in an attempt to prevent the species becoming established.

Population threats: A field study in East Anglia estimated that 47% of fawns die before the age of two months, probably largely due to predation (K. & M. Claydon pers. comm.). For older animals, culling and road traffic accidents are probably the main causes of mortality, and heavy culling can severely limit the rate of spread into some areas. Although extreme winter conditions, and in particular long periods of snow cover such as in 1962/1963, may cause heavy mortality, there is no evidence of increased fawn mortality in most winters, and it is unlikely that adverse weather conditions will limit population growth other than temporarily.

Chinese water deer *Hydropotes inermis*

Status: Introduced; uncommon and local.

Distribution: Free-living populations occur in Bedfordshire/Hertfordshire, Berkshire, Cambridgeshire, Norfolk and Suffolk. Records elsewhere (Arnold 1993) relate to individual animals rather than established populations.

Population data: There are few density estimates. At Whipsnade Park, Bedfordshire, densities of 2 per ha have been recorded, and at Woodwalton Fen, Cambridgeshire 0·3 per ha (Farrell & Cooke 1991). The population in Bedfordshire/Hertfordshire was estimated to be 40-100 by field censuses (Nau 1992); the population at Shinfield, Berkshire, was estimated by sightings to be about 20 (S.

Wray pers. comm.); that in Cambridgeshire in the area around Woodwalton Fen, Holme Fen and Monks Wood was estimated to be 100-200 by A.S. Cooke & L. Farrell (pers. comm.) based on personal observations; the population near Newmarket, Suffolk, was estimated to be about 20 based on sightings (N.G. Chapman pers. comm.); that at Minsmere, Suffolk, was estimated by counts to be three (L. Farrell pers. comm.); and that on the Norfolk Broads was estimated at about 300 based on sightings, although this may be an under-estimate (R. Engeldow pers. comm.). Thus the free-living population is approximately 480-650. However, in addition there are a number of itinerant animals not included in these figures. Since there are reports well away from the main centres of distribution, and other small populations have arisen from escapes from collections, the true figure probably lies at the upper end of this range.

There are also 400-600 free-roaming in Whipsnade Park on the Bedfordshire Downs and 200-300 at Woburn Park.

Population estimates: The total pre-breeding population probably lies around 650, all in England. **Reliability of population estimate: 2.**

Historical changes: Chinese water deer were introduced to Woburn Park around the turn of the century, and from 1929 to 1931 a total of 32 were transferred to Whipsnade Park. From these populations animals were sent to a number of parks around England, including two in Hampshire, one in Montgomeryshire, one in Norfolk, two in Shropshire and one in Yorkshire, amongst others (Lever 1977). Some of these led to free-living populations, not all of which persisted, and the early history of these is summarised by Whitehead (1964) and Lever (1977). The populations in Hampshire had died out by 1963, and those in Northamptonshire and Shropshire also appear to have died out. The populations in Berkshire and Suffolk originated in the 1980s.

Population trends: The low numbers (especially when compared with muntjac, which were introduced at around the same time), widely scattered records of vagrant/itinerant animals, and impermanence of many feral populations, suggest that conditions are not ideal for the establishment of this species, and that numbers are likely to remain low.

Population threats: Harsh winters can cause heavy mortality, and fox predation may be a significant cause of mortality of young animals. Road casualties are probably also significant. Whether any of these mortality factors pose a threat to population survival is unknown.

Reindeer *Rangifer tarandus*

Status: The native population became extinct approximately 9500 years ago. Swedish stock was re-introduced to the Cairngorms in 1952, when there were 15 animals (4 bulls, 9 cows, 2 calves). Subsequently there have been additional introductions of Norwegian and Russian reindeer.

Distribution: Until May 1991 the whole herd was kept in the Cairngorms, where The Reindeer Company leases approximately 2400 ha. However, since May 1991 the herd has been split into two approximately equal sized groups, the second being on a 200 ha hill farm on the Glenlivet Estate near Tomintoul, Grampian.

Population data: Herd numbers are taken from actual counts and recorded in annual herd lists (E. Smith pers. comm.). Thus in February 1993 there were 77 animals in total, with an expected calving in May of about 30 animals.

Population estimates: A pre-breeding population of up to 80 animals, all in Scotland. **Reliability of population estimate:** 1.

Historical changes: The early history of the herd is summarised by Whitehead (1964). From 1952 to 1960, the herd remained below 25 animals. There was a period of slow increase in the 1960s, and since 1970 the herd has been maintained at approximately constant size (E. Smith pers. comm.).

Population trends: A constant herd size is maintained, with a maximum number in June just after calving of around 100 animals.

Population threats: None.

Park cattle *Bos taurus*

Status: A number of herds of park cattle survived to the beginning of this century, but their origins are unknown. Their status at the turn of the century was summarised by Anon. (1887). The principal strains which survive today are Cadzow, Chartley, Chillingham, Dynevor and Vaynol. All are horned cattle. Only the Chillingham herd has been kept pure; they are remarkably homozygous and show no affinity with any other breed (Hall & Hall 1988). All the other strains have been, or are being, crossed with other breeds, including longhorn and highland cattle, to produce the white park breed, which must be distinguished from the Chillingham cattle (Hall 1991). Whilst the Vaynol cattle were at one time considered to be part of the white park breed, they are now considered to be separate (Anon. 1993). The conformation of the white park is that of a typical early 20th century British beef breed, but skeletally the Chillingham cattle resemble mediaeval British cattle. Whilst Chillingham and white park cattle are horned, British white cattle are genetically hornless and arose from another park herd. In addition, since 1978 a herd of Aberdeen Angus cross shorthorn cattle has been allowed to run feral on the island of Swona (Orkney). The Chillingham cattle and the Swona herd are among the very few cattle in the world that are completely feral, i.e. with a natural sex ratio and age distribution (Hall & Moore 1986).

Distribution: Chillingham cattle were found only in Chillingham Park, Northumberland, until a reserve herd was established in Morayshire in 1972. White park cattle are mostly found in farm parks, whereas the British white is becoming a commercial proposition (Hall 1991). The Swona herd is confined to Swona, Orkney.

Population data: Data are available from herd counts. In addition, the white park, Vaynol and British white cattle are fully pedigreed (S.J.G. Hall pers. comm.). Thus in March 1993 the Chillingham Park herd of Chillingham cattle consisted of 19 males and 26 females, and the reserve herd in Morayshire contained four males and six females. In February 1993 there were six male and 17 female cattle of the Vaynol strain. In January 1993 there were 24 male and 250 female white park cattle, and in September 1992 there were 83 male and 730 female British white cattle. Precise numbers of the Swona herd are unknown, but there are 20 at most (S.J.G. Hall pers. comm.).

Population estimates: In March 1993 the number of Chillingham cattle was 55: 45 in England, 10 in Scotland and none in Wales. **Reliability of population estimate:** 1.

Historical changes: Chillingham cattle declined to only 13 animals in 1947. The number then increased steadily to about 40 around 1970, since when numbers have fluctuated between 40 and 65. The sex ratio is biased because of better survival of adult females (Hall 1991).

Population trends: The numbers of white park cattle are increasing, but only slowly. British white cattle are increasing more rapidly. The size of the Swona herd fluctuates and numbers have reached the low 30s in the past (Hall & Moore 1986).

Population threats: None known. The reserve herd of Chillingham cattle is self-sustaining, and no animals are moved from this herd to Chillingham or anywhere else, although occasionally calves are sent from

Chillingham to join the herd. The reserve herd is maintained as a nucleus to repopulate Chillingham Park in the event of the latter herd being wiped out by disease. In March 1993 semen was being stored from three Vaynol cattle and six white park cattle.

Feral goat *Capra hircus*

Status: Introduced; well established.

Distribution: Generally hilly and mountainous areas of England, Scotland and Wales plus a number of islands (Bute, Cara, Colonsay, Holy Island (Isle of Arran), Islay, Jura, Lundy, Mull, Rathlin and Rum (Bullock 1991).

Population data: Populations are generally small and discrete. Unless otherwise stated, population estimates were based on visual counts that include kids of the year. In southern England there are the following populations: Brean Down, Somerset - maintained at 15-20 animals by culling (M. Oates pers. comm.); Lundy, Devon - in 1991 the population of six was augmented by the introduction of six from the Valley of the Rocks to give a total of 12; Valley of the Rocks, Devon - since 1988 the maximum number of goats has never risen above 40, and in 1991 six were removed to Lundy and in 1992 nine were removed to the Isle of Wight; Ventnor, Isle of Wight - in 1992 nine goats were introduced to Bonchurch Down for scrub control. In northern England/southern Scotland feral goats occur at: College Valley, Northumberland - 34; Nether Hindhope, Roxburgh - 43; Kielderhead Moors, Borders Region and Northumberland - in 1992 about 100 but a cull was planned to reduce the population to about 75; Langholm-Newcastleton Hills, Dumfries & Galloway and Borders - estimated 130, with a maximum of 145; Moffat Hills, Dumfries & Galloway - 184. Feral goats are found in south-west Scotland as follows: Cairnsmore of Fleet, Dumfries & Galloway - on the whole massif, *circa* 400; 'Wild Goat Park', Dumfries & Galloway - an enclosure established by the

Forestry Commission with 35 goats in 1992 and the number maintained at between 30 and 50 (J. Livingstone pers. comm.); Glentrool, Central Galloway - 200; Corserine and the Rhinns of the Kells, Central Galloway - 150; Loch Dee and Loch Doon, Central Galloway - 150-200 (all J. Livingstone pers. comm.). Western Scotland supports several populations. In the Clyde area there were estimated to be 355 in the mid-1980s, and subsequent counts of parts of the area suggested there had been little change or a small increase. For the period 1960-1978 the population on Rum showed six-yearly cycles, with population estimates ranging from 98-185 (Boyd 1981). In 1981 the population was estimated to be 200 (R.I.M. Dunbar pers. comm.), and although there are no recent data, the population on Rum is unlikely to have decreased and may be as high as 300. From Islay, Jura, Mull and the west coast of mainland Scotland there is an estimate of over 400 in the mid-1980s. In the central and north Scottish Highlands, information from the 1980s suggests a population of over 300. Since 1980 several new populations of feral goats have been established in Scotland in the interests of trophy hunting and/or the cashmere industry but no data are available on these herds (D.J. Bullock pers. comm.). In Wales a survey in Snowdonia in 1991 estimated 282 goats, and there is thought to be a similar number in the Rhinogau/Maentwrog area (Hellawell 1992).

Population estimates: A total pre-breeding population of over 3565. About 315 in England, over 2650 in Scotland and 600 in Wales. **Reliability of population estimate:** 2.

Historical changes: Goats were probably one of the earliest domesticated animals to be introduced to Britain. The early history and distribution of feral goats in Britain is documented by Whitehead (1972).

Population trends: Probably there is little overall change. No populations have declined since 1980 (D.J. Bullock pers. comm.) and the Scottish population has remained constant since the late 1960s (Greig 1969). The severe

winter of 1978/1979 caused significant losses, but a series of milder winters up to 1992/1993 has led to an increase in many populations that are not controlled by culling. Between 1980 and 1990 a number of populations were culled in the interests of afforestation, and these culls were augmented by large scale removals (more than 20 goats at a time) for the cashmere industry, although demand for the latter declined after 1990 (D.J. Bullock pers. comm.).

Population threats: None known.

Feral sheep *Ovis aries*

Status: Introduced; long-standing feral populations.

Distribution: Soay sheep are found on Soay and Hirta, St Kilda, and there have been introductions to Ailsa Craig (Strathclyde), Cardigan Island (Dyfed) and a number of other Welsh Islands, Holy Island (Isle of Arran), Lundy (Devon) and Sanda Island (Strathclyde). Boreray blackface sheep are confined to Boreray, St Kilda.

Population data: Soay sheep numbers are based on population counts in May/June and include the surviving lambs of the year. The population of Soay sheep on Hirta fluctuates in a cyclical manner between about 600 and nearly 1600 (Clutton-Brock *et al.* 1991). The population on the neighbouring island of Soay may cycle in synchrony with the one on Hirta. In 1966 the minimum size of the population on the island of Soay was 115, and 140-160 in 1967 (Jewell, Milner & Boyd 1974). Recent counts have been made from the neighbouring island of Hirta, from which most of the grazings can be seen. In summer 1991 the count was 250-300, in August 1992 it was 110-120 (A. MacColl & I. Stevenson pers. comm.); the true numbers would be no more than 30 more. The population on Cardigan Island was reduced to about half in October 1990 and now numbers less than 100. There are no recent counts for the population on Holy Island, and the Lundy population is managed at around 150 by annual culls. There are three or four on Sanda Island (B. Zonfrillo pers. comm.). The size of the sheep population on the island of Boreray was estimated by land- and sea-based counts in 1992 to be 302 (A. MacColl & I.R. Stevenson pers. comm.).

Population estimates: The average size of the pre-breeding Soay sheep population is around 1800; 150 in England, 1550 in Scotland and 100 in Wales. The total pre-breeding feral population probably never exceeds 2500 animals. There are also many in parks, in farm parks, and on some farms. The pre-breeding population of Boreray sheep is around 300, all in Scotland. **Reliability of population estimate:** 1.

Historical changes: The Soay sheep resemble the original wild species and the domesticated Neolithic sheep brought to Britain about 5000 BC. Those on Soay may be the direct descendants of these sheep, although there is a faint possibility that they were originally introduced by the Vikings in the 9th and 10th centuries AD (Campbell 1974). When St Kilda was evacuated in 1930, the Soay sheep were left on the island of Soay, as were the flock of primitive blackface sheep on Boreray. In 1932, 107 Soay sheep were transferred from Soay to the larger island of Hirta by the St Kildans, who returned annually to tend the sheep on Boreray and Hirta until the outbreak of the Second World War, when the Soay sheep on Hirta were said to number about 500. In 1947 the flock was said to number 400-450 and in 1948 650-700 (Lever 1977). Annual counts from 1955 to 1973 showed that the Soay population on Hirta fluctuated between 610 and 1783 (Boyd 1974). Nine counts of the Boreray blackface sheep between 1951 and 1971 showed that the minimum flock size varied between 330 and 466 (Lever 1977). In 1934 six Soay sheep were introduced to Skokholm, in 1944 eight were introduced to Cardigan Island, two to Middleholm Island in 1945, four to St Margaret's Island near Tenby in 1952, and in 1958 a few were introduced to Skomer. In 1975 the only Welsh island still to have Soays

was Cardigan, where there were 80. Soay sheep were introduced to Lundy around 1927, and by 1959 numbered over 80. The Soays on Ailsa Craig were introduced direct from St Kilda in the 1930s; in 1956 they numbered 14 (Lever 1977), but do not persist today.

Population trends: The Soay sheep on Hirta, and possibly those on Soay, show cyclical changes in numbers and these are probably density-dependent. Thus on Hirta, high winter mortality occurs every three to four years following summers when population density exceeds 2·2 sheep per ha. During these die-offs, more than 50% of adults, 70% of yearlings and 90% of lambs die and population density falls by around 65% (Clutton-Brock *et al.* 1992). Despite these perturbations, there are no long-term population changes. On Hirta, changes in population size occur as a result of high over-winter mortality from starvation and this is particularly pronounced among lambs and rams (Clutton-Brock *et al.* 1991), thereby giving an adult population with a varying bias towards females. Recent calculations, taking into account this unusual demography, suggest that the effective population size of the Hirta Soay sheep is in the range 200-250 (D.R. Bancroft pers. comm.).

Population threats: None known. Despite their isolation and population dynamics, the Soay sheep on Hirta have substantial genetic variation at the phenotypic and molecular level (Jewell, Milner & Boyd 1974; J.M. Pemberton & D.R. Bancroft pers. comm.), a conundrum that is the subject of current research. There is the potential threat from diseases or parasites introduced from the mainland. An example is the presence of the nematode *Nematodirus battus* on the island. It was first identified in England in 1951, and it is unclear whether the parasite was a recent introduction or had previously been over-looked. Yet this parasitic worm was found in most of the 120 Soay sheep carcasses examined on Hirta in 1989/1990, despite these sheep being separated from mainland stocks since the 1930s (Gulland 1991; I.R. Stevenson pers. comm.). Also, Gulland (1991) reported that

50% of the Soay sheep examined had cysts of the tapeworm *Taenia hydatigena*, yet there are no carnivores on the island and the last resident dog left with the islanders in the 1930s.

Discussion

Current status: It should be clear from the extent of extrapolation required to achieve most of our population estimates that we do not intend the figures to be accepted uncritically. However, we feel that they indicate the likely order of magnitude of the numbers of each species, and therefore they have allowed the species to be ranked in order of abundance much more objectively than has been done previously (Table 14). One problem with this ranking, however, is that species should not be compared on a simple numerical scale, especially where a relatively non-mobile species is isolated into a number of sub-populations. Large species obviously have a greater biomass and economic impact, and so whilst roe deer and common dormice may be of comparable numerical status, they are very different in both biomass and economic importance. Equally, they differ in mobility, and so in their vulnerability to habitat fragmentation. This problem was considered by Bright (1993), who used five life-history traits to identify the species of mammal most at risk from habitat fragmentation. These were primarily low density, slow breeding, often poorly mobile species associated with semi-natural habitats, and included all riparian mammals.

For our assessment of the pre-breeding population of each species, a reliability grading has been included, and the implications of these gradings need to be considered in relation to the ranking in Table 14. For example, the field vole is listed as the commonest British mammal, but on the basis of one of the least reliable population estimates because population size had to be calculated relative to other species of small mammal. In general, the rarer species are often those with the most reliable population estimates, and confidence can be placed in the order of magnitude of these estimates. The greatest problems arose with the commonest and most widespread species. Invariably, population sizes were calculated from only a few density estimates, and in all but a few cases these did not include more than a few

habitats and rarely included any from Scotland or Wales. Other species for which the estimates have a low reliability rating are those which are relatively thinly spread over a wide variety of habitats, such as the hedgehog. Other problems occurred for species which locally can be very abundant, yet for which typical densities were virtually unknown, such as the harvest mouse.

Thus one aspect of this exercise has been to highlight the lack of basic data on population densities for many, if not most, species of mammal in Britain. More field data, particularly from unusual habitats and/or from Scotland and Wales, will allow the estimates for all species to be improved, and increase the confidence that can be placed both on individual estimates and the ranking of all the species.

Changing status: In judging conservation priorities, absolute population size is one important criterion, but its use is tempered by what is known of recent changes in status. No species has a stable population size, and we have tried to document the likely pattern of recent trends. Many species were reduced by persecution (e.g. polecat) or overhunting (e.g. roe deer) in previous centuries, and are slowly recovering their range and status. Others have been more recently reduced by pollution (e.g. otter) or disease (e.g. rabbit). What time span is important in assessing change? We have taken the last 30 years, that being the period over which the Biological Records Centre has been accumulating data (Arnold 1993). This at least provides some possibility of measuring trends, and this period is also well-covered by the Game Conservancy Trust's National Game Bag Census (Tapper 1992). This choice of time frame produces some surprises. The rarer carnivores, including the otter, have probably been increasing their ranges during this period, albeit from low levels; the greater horseshoe bat has probably been stable; and the species of most conservation concern in respect of recent declines are the red squirrel and the water vole.

Relative status: With the mammals arranged in relative order of abundance, it is possible to make comparisons with other vertebrates, particularly those of conservation interest. For birds, Schedule 1 of the Wildlife and Countryside Act 1981 lists those of special concern, and they are discussed further by Batten *et al.* (1990). Mostly, they have fewer than 1000 breeding pairs. For example there are 52 pairs of red kite *Milvus milvus*, 75 'pairs' of marsh harrier *Circus aeruginosus*, and 424 pairs of golden eagle *Aquila chrysaetos*. Few British mammals are so rare, but also few, if any, are so well documented, and none are so mobile. Generally, the rarest mammals are an order of magnitude more numerous. At the other end of the range, the most abundant breeding birds are the wren *Troglodytes troglodytes* with 7,100,000 pairs, the chaffinch *Fringilla coelebs* with 5,400,000 pairs, the blackbird *Turdus merula* with 4,400,000 pairs and the robin *Erithacus rubecula* with 4,200,000 pairs (Gibbons, Reid & Chapman 1993). Similarly, the commonest mammals, (rabbits and five of the small mammals) are roughly an order of magnitude more common. Of comparable abundance, however, are some of the domestic mammals. There are 41,050,000 sheep *Ovis aries*, 10,330,000 cattle *Bos taurus* (Government Statistical Service 1992), 7,300,000 domestic dogs *Canis familiaris* (Pet Food Manufacturers' Association pers. comm.) and 7,600,000 domestic cats *Felis catus* (Cats Protection League 1993). The abundance of these species must reduce their wild counterparts by competitive exclusion, e.g. dogs and urban foxes (Harris 1981) or sheep and red deer (Clutton-Brock & Albon 1989). The relative ecological impacts of wild and domestic mammals may also be judged from these population sizes. Of the 41,050,000 sheep in Britain, approximately 60% are in upland areas. These clearly have more impact on upland ecosystems than around 360,000 red deer.

Three species of reptile and amphibian are rare enough to be of conservation concern. It has been estimated that there are 20,000 natterjack toads *Bufo calamita*, 7000-8000 sand lizards *Lacerta agilis* and 2000 smooth snakes *Coronella austriaca* in Britain (Nature Conservancy Council 1983). These compare numerically with the rarer mammals, but suffer even more the problems imposed by small size and limited mobility.

European status: The conservation status of each species under British and European legislation is shown in Table 15. Whilst this summarises the protection thought to be required for each species, for most the information on their status across Europe is even worse than for Britain, which precludes most direct comparisons of population size. However, we can put British species into a European perspective by assessing the proportion of their range which Great Britain represents, since detailed distributions were given by Niethammer & Krapp (1978-1990) for the Insectivora, Rodentia and Artiodactyla, and all species were mapped by Corbet (1978). For this, we have considered 'western Europe' to include that area west of the former USSR, a total area of 4,909,989 km² (Novotny & Pankova 1981). Iceland and Ireland have been excluded since, being islands, their mammal fauna is limited. Some northern species extend south to the Alps and Pyrenees, but are largely absent from 'Mediterranean' countries (Albania, Bulgaria, Greece, Italy, Portugal, Spain and what was Yugoslavia), an area of 1,425,082 km². Similarly, some southern species are largely absent from 'Scandinavia' (Finland, Norway and Sweden), an area of 1,110,916 km². What we will term 'north-west Europe' ('western Europe' minus the 'Mediterranean' and 'Scandinavian' countries) covers an area of 2,373,991 km². The area covered in this review thus forms approximately 9·7% of 'north-west Europe', 6·6% of 'northern Europe' ('north-west Europe' and 'Scandinavia'), 6·1% of 'southern Europe' ('north-west' and 'Mediterranean' Europe) and 4·7% of 'western Europe'. These percentages form the basis of the entries in Table 14. A species with more than 4·7% of its European range in Britain is more important from a European perspective than would be expected from the area available. Inherent inaccuracies in these figures (for example, whether the species' range includes islands such as Corsica, Ireland, Sardinia and Sicily) are relatively trivial, given the approximations being attempted.

The insectivores are probably about as common in the rest of Europe as in Britain, though the hedgehog is replaced in the east by the eastern hedgehog *Erinaceus concolor*, and the common shrew is similarly replaced in France, Italy and Spain by three species: Millet's shrew *Sorex coronatus,* the Appenine shrew *Sorex samniticus* and the Spanish shrew *Sorex granarius* respectively. In Europe generally, as in Britain, the water shrew is much rarer than either the common or pygmy shrews. The lesser white-toothed shrew is obviously represented here in a minuscule segment of its overall range, but its density (in the absence of any competitors) is probably much higher in the Isles of Scilly than elsewhere.

Most of the rare Chiroptera are at the edge of their ranges in Britain, and are relatively much more common in southern Europe. This applies particularly to the greater and lesser horseshoe and grey long-eared bats. In a European context, therefore, their British populations are even less significant than suggested by the small proportions of their European ranges which Britain contributes. Bechstein's bat is an exception to this, being rare everywhere. Saint Girons (1973), for instance, listed only 29 records for France, three for Belgium and one for the Netherlands; Benzal, Paz & Gisbert (1991) gave only 17 records for Iberia; and Pucek (1981) gave only 12 records for Poland. The barbastelle bat is as rare in France and Iberia, with only 27 recent records (Benzal, Paz & Gisbert 1991), as in Britain. Pucek (1981) considered it rare also in Poland, but mentioned a wintering group of about 50, and large numbers wintering elsewhere, suggesting that it is either more numerous or more obvious further east than in Britain.

Of the lagomorphs, the brown hare population appears to be more important in a European context because it is largely absent from Scandinavia, and also from Iberia, where it is replaced by the African hare *Lepus capensis*. Moreover, populations of the brown hare have also declined over much, if not all, of its European range. Conversely, the mountain hare is probably more numerous in Scandinavia, where it is certainly widespread, and the British population is not especially significant. The rabbit, paradoxically in view of its Mediterranean origin, seems very strongly represented in Britain, though it is not so markedly 'over represented' here as various more recent introductions such as the grey squirrel, American mink, sika deer, Chinese muntjac and Chinese water deer.

Among the Rodentia, most of the common species have about 6-7% of their European ranges in Britain. The red squirrel, yellow-necked mouse, harvest mouse and common dormouse are less well distributed in Britain, and their populations are probably also much smaller than elsewhere in Europe. In Britain the red squirrel has lost much of its British range to competition from the introduced grey squirrel, and this decline is likely to continue. Whilst the European red squirrel population is currently not under threat, the grey squirrel has been introduced to two areas in Italy, and in 30-40 years has spread over some 200 km². There is also a risk that they may be deliberately or accidentally translocated over the Alps elsewhere into Europe, or into other parts of Italy. Thus there is a real risk that the pattern of species replacement recorded in Britain may be repeated in Europe (Gurnell & Pepper 1993). The yellow-necked mouse is much more abundant in eastern Europe, where it may replace the wood mouse completely in forested localities. Conversely, in Britain the field vole is numerically much more important than the 6·2% of its European range would imply, because it is frequently displaced on the mainland by its competitors, the common vole *Microtus arvalis* and the burrowing vole *Terricola subterraneus*, particularly in agricultural areas.

The rarer British carnivores owe their current status to past levels of persecution which have not been equalled elsewhere in Europe. The British pine marten and polecat populations are not especially significant on a European scale. For the otter, however, the factors which have adversely affected its English distribution have also reduced its range across much of central Europe (Mason & Macdonald 1986). As a consequence, 'fringe' populations in Iberia, Ireland, and Scandinavia are strongest, and the British - principally Scottish - population is a significant element in this European population. Although both foxes and badgers are distributed widely across western Europe, their European populations have been reduced by rabies and the associated control measures, as well as by hunting. When reviewing the status of the badger in western Europe, Griffiths & Thomas (1993) estimated that in 6% of the area badger numbers were probably or possibly declining, in 15% they were thought to be stable, they were increasing in 59% of western Europe, and no information was available for 21% of the area. They concluded that many European badger populations were recovering from population decreases during the rabies outbreak. When looking at population densities, badgers were particularly abundant in Ireland, Sweden and Great Britain, and Griffiths (1991) estimated that Great Britain had 17% of the total European badger population. The only country believed to contain more badgers was Ireland (Smal 1993). The impact of hunting on badger populations in Europe is reviewed by Griffiths & Kryštufek (1993). Badger hunting is most frequent in Norway, Sweden and Switzerland, although nowhere is the level high enough to affect the badger population.

The two seals are, in a European context, two of the most important of our mammals, a status emphasised even more by the fact that some populations elsewhere (e.g. the common seal in the Waddensee, the grey seal in the Baltic) are known to be declining due to pollution, the phocine distemper virus outbreak and other causes. Thus the common seal population in Britain in 1991 was about 5% of the total world stock, and 40% of the European sub species (Hiby, Duck &

Thompson 1993), while the grey seals in United Kingdom waters constitute over 55% of the world population (Bonner 1981).

Populations of Artiodactyla have been severely altered by overhunting, protection and introductions. Estimating the size of deer populations is notoriously difficult and in Europe a variety of techniques have been used, most of which significantly under-estimate population size (Gill 1990). Thus it is difficult to put our deer populations into a European perspective. Niethammer & Krapp (1986) suggest a partial total for the European population of red deer of 811,000 in the 1970s, excluding France, Greece, Italy and Portugal. More recently, Gill (1990) has estimated that the total European red deer population in 1984 was at least 1,250,000. Of this, the British population contributed just under 30%. Of the other European deer, range considerations would suggest that 6·6% of the roe deer and 5·8% of the fallow deer should be in Britain. For roe deer, Gill (1990) estimated a European population in the early 1980s (excluding Great Britain, Greece, Portugal and Spain) of around 5,500,000. However, one study suggested that the estimate for Switzerland was 50-80% less than the actual population (Gill 1990). If the same level of under-estimation applied to the rest of Europe, the actual roe deer population would probably have been nearer 7,750,000-10,000,000, and the proportion in Britain is roughly what the range estimates would predict. For fallow deer, however, it is ironic that, having been introduced from Europe, numbers in Europe are now comparatively low and Ueckermann (1984) suggested that Britain has more free-living fallow deer than any other country in Europe. Gill (1990) estimated that the total European population of free-living fallow deer was only around 125,000 in the early 1980s, excluding Great Britain, Ireland and Spain. Thus Britain has about 40% of the entire European fallow deer population. Conversely, the introduced reindeer are insignificant in a European context: in 1984 there were estimated to be 51,000 wild reindeer in Norway and 600 in Finland (Gill 1990). In Europe, most of the introduced Asian deer are confined to Britain. Muntjac are not found elsewhere in Europe, and there were fewer than 6000 sika in the rest of Europe in 1984 (Gill 1990).

For the feral caprines, there are two centres of distribution in Europe: the Mediterranean and Great Britain and Ireland. The 'wild' sheep on Corsica and Sardinia (*Ovis aries musimon*) and Cyprus (*Ovis aries ophion*) are the result of ancient introductions of domesticated stock, and so are technically feral. The Corsican population is, at the most, in the low thousands, in Sardinia in 1983 there were between 1150 and 1590 mouflon (Cassola 1985), and in the mid-1980s the total number on Cyprus was estimated to be 800 (Maisels 1988). Apart from the many introductions of Corsican/Sardinian mouflon to mainland sites, there are no other feral sheep populations in Europe (D. Bullock pers. comm.). As with the 'wild' Mediterranean sheep, the 'wild' Mediterranean goat populations are all believed to have their origins in anciently introduced domesticated stock and so are also technically feral. It also seems likely that all the goat populations have been genetically mixed with recently feral goats, although some populations, such as on Theodorou Island, off Crete, seem to be phenotypically close to the true wild goat *Capra aegagrus* (D. Bullock pers. comm.). The total Cretan population, including the off-shore islands, is probably at the most in the low thousands, with a similar population in all the other Aegean islands, and less than 1000 in the Parnitha Reserve on the

Peloponnese, Greece (D. Bullock pers. comm.). In 1971 there were 300-350 feral goats on Montecristo Island, Italy (Spagnesi *et al.* 1986). There are undoubtedly other feral goat populations in the Mediterranean of more recent origin. However, excluding these and the recent mouflon introductions to Europe, the Mediterranean feral caprine populations that are of ancient origin comprise fairly small, discrete units and for neither species is the total likely to exceed 5000 (D. Bullock pers. comm.). Thus roughly similar sized populations of feral caprines of ancient origin occur in the Mediterranean and in the British Isles. However, populations of feral sheep, such as the Soay and Boreray, and feral goats close to the 'old English goat', are unique to Britain.

In summary, most of the mammals we regard as rare in Britain are not rare in Europe. Two bats, Bechstein's and barbastelle, are certainly of conservation concern across the whole of western Europe. On a European scale, the wild mammals for which the British populations are most important are undoubtedly the badger, otter, common seal, grey seal, red deer and fallow deer; we are responsible for around 17%, a substantial but unknown proportion, 40%, 78%, 30% and 40%, respectively, of their western European populations. The populations of feral caprines that are of ancient origin are of particular interest, as the populations in Britain are unique, and constitute approximately half the ancient feral caprines in Europe.

Table 1. The number of 1 x 1 km squares, area of each land class (i.e. excluding the area of sea) in the survey area (i.e. Great Britain excluding the Channel Islands and the Isle of Man), the number of squares in each land class surveyed for habitat data and the proportion of each land class that was urban and rural.

Land class	Number of 1 x 1 km squares	Area of land (km²)	% of total land area	Number of squares surveyed for habitat data	% of total number of squares surveyed for habitat data	% of land area rural	% of land area urban
1	14,159	14,147	6·14	215	1·52	84·13	15·87
2	14,463	14,461	6·28	139	0·96	86·45	13·55
3	15,452	15,448	6·71	127	0·82	86·26	13·74
4	9012	8696	3·77	122	1·35	78·18	21·82
5	3870	3839	1·67	118	3·05	84·18	15·82
6	10,021	9961	4·32	104	1·04	89·69	10·31
7	2468	1325	0·58	78	3·16	90·43	9·57
8	4310	2749	1·19	77	1·79	79·81	20·19
9	11,781	11,666	5·06	128	1·09	81·83	18·17
10	13,905	13,826	6·00	107	0·77	84·59	15·41
11	8895	8895	3·86	44	0·49	87·47	12·57
12	3543	3540	1·54	43	1·21	85·05	14·95
13	7257	7094	3·08	92	1·27	83·59	16·41
14	933	721	0·31	43	4·61	76·12	23·88
15	4188	4175	1·81	57	1·36	87·07	12·93
16	3089	3072	1·33	46	1·49	87·66	12·34
17	12,998	12,998	5·64	147	1·13	95·11	4·89
18	6580	6580	2·86	66	1·00	97·44	2·56
19	5421	5421	2·35	51	0·94	98·06	1·94
20	2508	2508	1·09	54	2·15	96·74	3·26
21	9717	9716	4·22	50	0·51	98·78	1·22
22	12,549	12,549	5·45	107	0·85	99·02	0·98
23	6951	6951	3·02	46	0·66	99·50	0·50
24	7207	7206	3·13	43	0·60	98·67	1·33
25	10,552	10,512	4·56	93	0·88	95·06	4·94
26	6876	6748	2·93	87	1·27	85·14	14·86
27	6881	6839	2·97	82	1·19	89·83	10·17
28	7464	7353	3·19	57	0·76	96·67	3·33
29	5465	2461	1·07	87	1·59	95·67	4·33
30	4254	3475	1·51	42	0·99	96·35	3·65
31	3016	1750	0·76	31	1·03	95·10	4·90
32	3779	3685	1·60	37	0·98	98·73	1·27
Totals	239,564	230,367	100·00	2620	1·09	90·04	9·96

Table 2. The distribution of land classes, number of 1 x 1 km squares and the area of land (km²) in each land class in England, Scotland and Wales. Total number of squares 239,564, total land area 230,367 km².

Land class	England		Scotland		Wales	
	Frequency of occurrence	Area of land	Frequency of occurrence	Area of land	Frequency of occurrence	Area of land
1	13,105	13,094	-	-	1054	1053
2	14,459	14,457	-	-	4	4
3	15,360	15,356	-	-	92	92
4	8954	8640	-	-	58	56
5	2471	2451	12	12	1387	1376
6	7276	7232	10	10	2735	2719
7	1375	738	262	141	831	446
8	3214	2050	258	165	838	534
9	11,027	10,919	53	53	701	694
10	13,641	13,564	129	128	135	134
11	8895	8895	-	-	-	-
12	3542	3539	1	1	-	-
13	4792	4684	1804	1764	661	646
14	603	466	301	233	29	22
15	1390	1386	336	335	2462	2454
16	2451	2438	315	313	323	321
17	3934	3934	63	63	9001	9001
18	2069	2069	3571	3571	940	940
19	3193	3193	2186	2186	42	42
20	1235	1235	1028	1028	245	245
21	9	9	9708	9707	-	-
22	3296	3296	9250	9250	3	3
23	844	844	6066	6066	41	41
24	197	197	7010	7009	-	-
25	2012	2004	8540	8508	-	-
26	1192	1170	5683	5577	1	1
27	1499	1490	5382	5349	-	-
28	962	948	6502	6405	-	-
29	-	-	5465	2461	-	-
30	-	-	4254	3475	-	-
31	-	-	3016	1750	-	-
32	-	-	3779	3685	-	-
Totals	132,997	130,298	84,984	79,245	21,583	20,824

Table 3. The area of the principal habitat types in England, Scotland, Wales and for the whole of Great Britain (excluding the Channel Islands and the Isle of Man). The habitat types are described by Cresswell, Harris & Jefferies (1990). Figures for hedgerows, treelines and linear waterways are in km, the rest are in km².

	England	Scotland	Wales	Great Britain
Hedgerows	429,504	36,008	62,104	527,616
Treelines	76,886	13,711	12,434	103,031
Ditches and drains	62,593	11,722	3907	78,222
Semi-natural broadleaved woodland	5135	1390	783	7308
Broadleaved plantations	1119	54	87	1260
Semi-natural coniferous woodland	249	365	6	620
Coniferous plantations	3825	7125	895	11,845
Semi-natural mixed woodland	1082	426	69	1577
Mixed plantations	640	177	86	903
Young plantations	550	1682	119	2351
Recently felled woodland	182	148	29	359
Parkland	675	162	53	890
Tall scrub	385	86	62	533
Low scrub	785	261	176	1222
Bracken	723	976	461	2160
Coastal sand dunes	221	270	58	549
Coastal sand or mud flats	608	506	129	1243
Coastal shingle or boulder beaches	429	653	71	1153
Lowland heaths	482	16	45	543
Heather moorlands	2812	11,845	1314	15,971
Blanket bog	1557	10,198	413	12,168
Raised bog	40	143	9	192
Marginal inundation	290	132	76	498
Coastal marsh	122	30	21	173
Wet ground	506	490	241	1237
Standing natural water	221	1059	46	1326
Standing man-made water	547	314	55	916
Running natural water	575	460	104	1139
Running canalised water	90	13	7	110
Upland unimproved grassland	4686	12,824	2459	19,969
Lowland unimproved grassland	2107	458	319	2884
Semi-improved grassland	13,109	6461	3311	22,881
Improved grassland	18,104	5683	3771	27,558
Arable land	48,158	9573	3280	61,011
Amenity grassland	1571	175	126	1872
Unquarried inland cliffs	250	1187	82	1519
Vertical coastal cliffs	45	217	17	279
Sloping coastal cliffs	87	77	30	194
Quarries and open-cast mines	470	137	67	674
Bare ground	275	93	13	381
Built land	17,586	3379	1934	22,899
Totals, excluding linear features	130,298	79,245	20,824	230,367

Table 4. Lengths of riparian habitats (km) in the water authority regions in England, and in Scotland and Wales.

	Length of river systems[1]	Length of streams[2]	Length of canals[3]	Length of lake shores[4]	Total length of riparian habitats
England					
Anglian	3771	20,424	125	373	24,693
North West	1091	10,907	4	457	12,459
Northumbria	983	10,771	-	109	11,863
Severn Trent	1115	23,048	990	375	25,528
South West	2002	10,138	29	68	12,237
Southern	1442	9875	41	186	11,544
Thames	174	11,799	210	340	12,523
Wessex	1020	8161	82	85	9,348
Yorkshire	874	14,751	268	257	16,150
Total for England	12,472	119,874	1749	2250	136,345
Scotland					
Mainland	17,021	109,271	-	4165	130,457
Jura	800	1980	-	178	2958
Orkney	110	130	-	110	350
Outer Hebrides	1320	2870	-	1642	5832
Shetland	1510	2980	-	278	4768
Total for Scotland	20,761	117,231	-	6373	144,365
Wales	3873	23,708	152	403	28,136

[1,2] Figures calculated from the length of waterway for each water authority region in England plus Wales obtained by adding all the lengths for each hydrometric area (from digitised 1:50,000 map data supplied by the Institute of Hydrology); this includes rivers from their primary sources to drainage channels, and from the numbers of rivers and streams given by Smith & Lyle (1979).

[3] From National Rivers Authority (1991).

[4] Calculated using the median point for each size group of lakes given by Smith & Lyle (1979) and using this figure to calculate a total circumference for each lake.

Table 5. Relative proportion of different species of small mammals in bird of prey pellet samples from different regions of Britain. Figures marked * are calculated back from percentages.

	Common shrew	Pygmy shrew	Water shrew	Bank vole	Field vole	Wood/yellow-necked mouse	Harvest mouse	House mouse	Common shrew: pygmy shrew	Common shrew: water shrew	Pygmy shrew: water shrew	Field vole: bank vole	Wood/yellow-necked mouse: bank vole	Field vole: wood/yellow-necked mouse	Wood/yellow-necked mouse: harvest mouse	Wood/yellow-necked mouse: house mouse	Common shrew: wood/yellow-necked mouse	Common shrew: field vole
Barn owl																		
South-east England (n = 6725)[1]	1526	320	62	235	3650	784	78	70	4·8	24·6	5·2	15·5	3·3	4·7	10·1	11·2	2·0	0·4
South-west England (n = 9463)[1]	2305	576	202	459	4762	1046	36	77	4·0	11·4	2·9	10·4	2·3	4·6	29·1	13·6	2·2	0·5
East England (n = 7307)[1]	1792	273	86	308	3728	783	92	245	6·6	20·8	3·2	12·1	2·5	4·8	8·5	3·2	2·3	0·5
Midlands (n = 4536)[1]	1384	186	57	279	2103	461	38	28	7·4	24·3	3·3	7·5	1·7	4·6	12·1	16·5	3·0	0·7
North England (n = 4256)[1]	1382	246	46	146	2121	298	0	17	5·6	30·0	5·3	14·5	2·0	7·1	-	17·5	4·6	0·7
Scotland (n = 7427)[1]	2494	484	81	256	3355	720	0	37	5·2	30·8	6·0	13·1	2·8	4·7	-	19·5	3·5	0·7
Wales (n = 4424)[1]	1346	247	40	193	2187	379	4	28	5·5	33·7	6·2	11·3	2·0	5·8	94·8	13·5	3·6	0·6
Total for Great Britain (n = 44,138)[1]	12,229	2332	574	1876	21,906	4471	248	502	5·2	21·3	4·1	11·7	2·4	4·9	18·0	8·9	2·7	0·6
Surrey (n = 151)[2]	12	9	2	9	82	24	1	12	1·3	6	4·5	9·1	2·7	3·4	24·0	2·0	0·5	0·2
Devon (n = 553)[3]	98	27	8	56	194	149	15	6	3·6	12·2	3·4	3·5	2·7	1·3	9·9	24·8	0·7	0·5
East Norfolk (n = 15,324)[4]	3882	762	214	532	8290	1014	519	111	5·1	18·1	3·6	15·6	1·9	8·2	2·0	9·1	3·8	0·5
Sheffield and Peak District (n = 1818)[5]*	473	91	36	91	909	182	18	18	5·2	13·1	2·5	10·0	2·0	5·0	10·1	10·1	2·6	0·5
Peak District (n = 2400)[6]	582	87	6	496	1044	174	0	11	6·7	97·0	14·5	2·1	0·4	6·0	-	15·8	3·3	0·6
South Westmorland (n = 2023)[7]	889	74	13	25	898	123	0	1	12·0	68·4	5·7	35·9	4·9	7·3	-	-	7·2	1·0
Pembroke (n = 5574)[8]	796	150	154	518	2767	965	0	224	5·3	5·2	1·0	5·3	1·9	2·9	-	4·3	0·8	0·3
Mid-Wales (n = 3997)[9]	807	404	10	32	2573	168	0	3	2·0	80·7	40·4	80·4	5·3	15·3	-	56·0	4·8	0·3

119

Table 5 continued

	Common shrew	Pygmy shrew	Water shrew	Bank vole	Field vole	Wood/yellow-necked mouse	Harvest mouse	House mouse	Common shrew: pygmy shrew	Common shrew: water shrew	Pygmy shrew: water shrew	Field vole: bank vole	Wood/yellow-necked mouse: bank vole	Field vole: wood/yellow-necked mouse	Wood/yellow-necked mouse: harvest mouse	Wood/yellow-necked mouse: house mouse	Common shrew: wood/yellow-necked mouse	Common shrew: field vole
Long-eared owl																		
Britain and Ireland (n = 249)[10]	201	99	6	854	3679	1397	1	12	2·0	33·5	16·5	4·3	1·6	2·6	-	1164·4	0·1	0·1
Sheffield and Peak District (n = 748)[5]*	45	75	1	30	500	96	0	1	0·6	45·0	75·0	16·7	3·2	5·2	-	96·0	0·5	0·1
Peak District (n = 920)[6]	61	157	2	6	573	118	0	3	0·4	30·5	78·5	95·5	19·7	4·9	-	39·3	0·5	0·1
South Lancashire (dunes) (n = 608)[11]	0	6	0	65	154	382	0	1	-	-	-	2·4	5·9	0·4	-	-	-	-
South Scotland (upland) (n = 504)[12]	46	51	0	0	407	0	0	0	0·9	-	-	-	-	-	-	-	-	0·1
Short-eared owl																		
Britain and Ireland (n = 3302)[13]	101	77	1	57	2657	393	6	10	1·3	101·0	77·0	46·6	6·9	6·8	65·5	39·3	0·3	<0·1
Sheffield and Peak District (n = 76)[5]*	3	4	0	1	55	13	0	0	0·8	-	-	55·0	13·0	4·2	-	-	0·2	0·3
Peak District (n = 117)[6]	12	14	0	1	87	3	0	0	0·9	-	-	87·0	3·0	29·0	-	-	4·0	0·1
Clwyd (n = 630)[14]	145	298	0	47	64	76	0	0	0·5	-	-	1·4	1·6	0·8	-	-	1·9	2·3
Tawny owl																		
New Forest (n = 69)[15]	6	0	0	8	8	47	0	0	-	-	-	1	5·9	0·2	-	-	0·1	0·8
London/Surrey (n = 936)[16]	31	2	2	110	454	301	1	35	15·5	15·5	1·0	4·1	2·7	1·5	-	8·6	0·1	0·7
Wytham Woods (n = 8330)[17]	1146	174	38	2920	1269	2783	0	0	6·6	30·2	4·6	0·4	1·0	0·5	-	-	0·4	0·9
Sheffield and Peak District (n = 450)[5]*	64	9	1	46	220	105	0	5	7·1	64·0	9·0	4·8	2·3	2·1	-	21·0	0·6	0·3
Peak District (n = 325)[6]	49	26	2	20	150	75	0	3	1·9	24·5	13·0	7·5	3·8	2·0	-	25·0	0·7	0·3
Aberdeen (n = 180)[18]	23	2	1	16	90	48	0	0	11·5	23·0	2·0	5·6	3·0	1·9	-	-	0·5	0·3

Table 5 continued

	Common shrew	Pygmy shrew	Water shrew	Bank vole	Field vole	Wood/yellow-necked mouse	Harvest mouse	House mouse	Common shrew: pygmy shrew	Common shrew: water shrew	Pygmy shrew: water shrew	Field vole: bank vole	Wood/yellow-necked mouse: bank vole	Field vole: wood/yellow-necked mouse	Wood/yellow-necked mouse: harvest mouse	Wood/yellow-necked mouse: house mouse	Common shrew: wood/yellow-necked mouse	Common shrew: field vole
Kestrel																		
Sheffield and Peak District (n = 164)[5]*	20	11	0	16	112	5	0	0	1·8	-	-	7·0	0·3	22·4	-	-	4·0	0·2
Yorkshire (n = 119)[19]	9	0	2	0	101	7	0	0	-	4·5	-	-	-	14·4	-	-	1·3	0·1
Yorkshire (upland) (n = 644)[20]	53	138	0	30	352	65	0	6	0·4	-	-	11·7	2·2	5·4	-	10·8	0·8	0·2
South Cumbria (n = 200)[21]	50	11	0	24	105	10	0	0	4·5	-	-	4·4	0·4	10·5	-	-	5·0	0·5
Pembroke (n = 111)[22]		8	0	23	78	2	0	0	-	-	-	3·4	0·1	39·0	-	-	4·0	0·1

[1] Glue (1974); [2] Teagle (1963); [3] Linn & Scott (1980); [4] Buckley & Goldsmith (1975); [5] Clinging & Whiteley (1980); [6] Yalden (1985); [7] Webster (1973); [8] Bowman (1980a); [9] Bowman (1980b); [10] Glue & Hammond (1974); [11] South (1966); [12] Village (1981); [13] Glue (1977); [14] Roberts & Bowman (1986); [15] Hirons (1984); [16] Beven (1965, 1967, 1982); [17] Southern (1954); [18] N.D. Redgate (pers. comm.); [19] Ellis (1946); [20] Simms (1961); [21] Yalden & Warburton (1979); [22] Davis (1975).

N.B. Some of the data collected in the regional samples are also included in the samples from Britain as a whole, so there is a very small amount of replication in the data presented.

Table 6. Relative proportions of different species of small mammal in bottle samples from different regions of Britain.

	Common shrew	Pygmy shrew	Water shrew	Bank vole	Field vole	Wood/yellow-necked mouse	Harvest mouse	House mouse	Common shrew: pygmy shrew	Common shrew: water shrew	Pygmy shrew: water shrew	Field vole: bank vole	Wood/yellow-necked mouse: bank vole	Field vole: wood/yellow-necked mouse	Wood/yellow-necked mouse: harvest mouse	Wood/yellow-necked mouse: house mouse	Common shrew: wood/yellow-necked mouse	Common shrew: field vole
Britain (n = 2054)[1]	886	52	57	542	82	419	2	14	17·0	15·5	0·9	0·2	0·8	0·2	209·5	29·9	2·1	10·8
Surrey (n = 805)[2]	313	13	11	218	43	205	0	2	24·1	28·5	1·2	0·2	0·9	0·2	-	102·5	1·5	7·3
Essex (n = 1031)[3]	526	38	32	254	22	154	1	4	13·8	16·4	1·2	0·1	0·6	0·1	154·0	38·5	3·4	23·9
Peak District (n = 1029)[2]	615	66	17	110	78	143	0	0	9·3	36·2	3·9	0·7	1·3	0·6	-	-	4·3	7·9
Sheffield (n = 2151)[4]	1215	141	39	279	167	308	0	2	8·6	31·2	3·6	0·6	1·1	0·5	-	154·0	3·9	7·3
Lake District (n = 153)[2]	84	7	3	44	1	14	0	0	12·0	28·0	2·3	<0·1	0·3	0·1	-	-	6·0	84·0
North and central Wales (n = 323)[2]	128	5	7	93	21	69	0	0	25·6	18·3	0·7	0·2	0·7	0·3	-	-	1·9	6·1

[1]P.A. Morris (unpubl.); [2]Whiteley & Yalden (1976); [3]Corke & Harris (1972); [4]Clinging & Whiteley (1980).

N.B. Some of the data collected in the regional samples are also included in the sample from Britain as a whole, so there is a very small amount of replication in the data presented.

Table 7. Relative proportion of different species of small mammals in trapping samples from different regions of Britain. All figures are the actual number of captures.

	Common shrew	Pygmy shrew	Water shrew	Bank vole	Field vole	Wood mouse	Yellow-necked mouse	Harvest mouse	House mouse	Common shrew: pygmy shrew	Common shrew: water shrew	Pygmy shrew: water shrew	Field vole: bank vole	Wood/yellow-necked mouse: bank vole	Field vole: wood/yellow-necked mouse: house mouse	Wood/yellow-necked mouse: harvest mouse	Wood/yellow-necked mouse: house mouse	Common shrew: wood/yellow-necked mouse	Common shrew: field vole
England and Wales (n = 8693)[1]	2104	191	35	2156	174	3912	52	43	26	11·0	60·1	5·5	<0·1	1·8	<0·1	92·2	152·5	0·5	12·1
Hampshire (n = 2198)[2]	44	7	0	396	0	1253	484	7	7	6·3	-	-	-	4·4	-	248·1	248·1	<0·1	-
Hampshire and Oxfordshire (n = 630)[3]	192	9	8	91	5	311	0	9	5	21·3	24·0	1·1	<0·1	3·4	<0·1	34·6	62·2	0·6	38·4
Arundel, Sussex[4] (n = 117)	10	0	0	25	0	82	0	0	0	-	-	-	-	3·3	-	-	-	0·1	-
Rogate, Sussex (n = 1613)[5]	202	181	0	314	126	653	0	137	0	1·1	-	-	0·4	2·1	0·2	4·8	-	0·3	1·6
Bookham Common, Surrey (n = 443)[6]	80	9	3	118	88	141	0	4	0	8·9	26·7	3·0	0·8	1·2	0·6	35·3	-	0·6	0·9
Windsor Park, Berkshire (n = 199)[5]	11	9	0	21	39	114	0	5	0	1·2	-	-	1·9	5·4	0·3	22·8	-	0·1	0·3
Silwood Park, Berkshire (n = 1254)[7]	82	33	0	15	965	157	0	2	0	2·5	-	-	64·3	10·5	6·1	78·5	-	0·5	0·1
Essex (general survey) (n = 852)[8]	174	16	3	125	48	421	13	15	37	10·9	58·0	5·3	0·4	3·4	0·1	28·1	11·4	0·4	3·6
Essex (Coptfold Estate) (n = 1965)[8]	65	5	2	531	1	1041	318	0	2	13·0	32·5	2·5	<0·1	2·0	<0·1	-	520·5	0·1	65·0
Matching Green, Essex (n = 1852)[9]	32	8	0	557	0	1215	40	0	0	4·0	-	-	-	2·3	-	-	-	<0·1	-
East Bergholt, Suffolk (n = 1174)[10]	40	6	8	788	1	288	42	1	0	6·7	5·0	0·8	-	0·4	-	-	-	0·1	-

123

Table 7 continued

	Common shrew	Pygmy shrew	Water shrew	Bank vole	Field vole	Wood mouse	Yellow-necked mouse	Harvest mouse	House mouse	Common shrew: pygmy shrew	Common shrew: water shrew	Pygmy shrew: water shrew	Field vole: bank vole	Wood/yellow-necked mouse: bank vole	Field vole: wood/yellow-necked mouse	Wood/yellow-necked mouse: harvest mouse	Wood/yellow-necked mouse: house mouse	Common shrew: wood/yellow-necked mouse	Common shrew: field vole
Sheffield (overnight) (n = 726)[11]	44	16	0	232	16	418	0	0	0	6·3	-	-	0·1	1·8	<0·1	-	-	0·1	2·8
Sheffield (day time) (n = 207)[12]	20	10	0	122	10	44	0	0	1	2·0	-	-	0·1	0·4	0·2	-	-	0·5	2·0
Sheffield and Peak District (n = 726)[13]	45	8	8	330	94	240	0	0	1	5·6	5·6	1·0	0·3	0·7	0·4	-	240·0	0·2	0·5
Peak District (n = 559)[14]	25	4	7	289	85	148	0	0	1	6·3	3·6	0·6	0·3	0·5	0·6	-	148·0	0·2	0·3
Peak District (n = 717)[15]	45	7	1	397	51	216	0	0	0	6·4	45·0	7·0	0·1	0·5	0·2	-	-	0·2	0·9
York, North Yorkshire (n = 1048)[16]	7	24	0	126	0	891	0	0	0	0·3	-	-	-	7·1	-	-	-	<0·1	-
North Yorkshire Moors (n = 108)[11]	22	10	0	25	6	45	0	0	0	2·2	-	-	0·2	1·8	0·1	-	-	0·5	3·7
Filey, North Yorkshire (n = 217)[17]	86	24	27	3	60	17	0	0	0	3·6	3·2	0·9	20·0	5·7	3·5	-	-	5·1	1·4
Knaresborough, North Yorkshire (n = 301)[18]	41	3	0	133	13	110	0	0	1	13·7	-	-	0·1	0·8	0·1	-	-	0·4	3·2
Loch Tay, Perthshire (low altitude) (n = 422)[19]	43	0	1	108	229	41	0	0	0	-	43·0	-	2·1	0·4	5·6	-	-	1·0	0·2
Loch Tay, Perthshire (high altitude) (n = 131)[19]	7	0	0	0	124	0	0	0	0	-	-	-	-	-	-	-	-	-	0·1
Clova, Angus (low altitude) (n = 155)[19]	9	0	0	1	142	3	0	0	0	-	-	-	-	3·0	47·3	-	-	-	-

Table 7 continued

	Common shrew	Pygmy shrew	Water shrew	Bank vole	Field vole	Wood mouse	Yellow-necked mouse	Harvest mouse	House mouse	Common shrew: pygmy shrew	Common shrew: water shrew	Pygmy shrew: water shrew	Field vole: bank vole	Wood/ yellow-necked mouse: bank vole	Field vole: wood/ yellow-necked mouse	Wood/ yellow-necked mouse: harvest mouse	Wood/ yellow-necked mouse: house mouse	Common shrew: wood/ yellow-necked mouse	Common shrew: field vole
Clova, Angus (high altitude) (n = 100)[19]	14	1	0	11	74	0	0	0	0	14·0	-	-	6·7	-	-	-	-	-	0·2
Sunart, Argyll (n = 317)[19]	29	0	0	59	155	74	0	0	0	-	-	-	2·6	1·3	2·1	-	-	0·4	0·2
North-west Scotland (n = 383)[20]	60	5	3	92	13	210	0	0	0	12·0	20·0	1·7	0·1	2·3	0·1	-	-	0·3	4·6

[1]ADAS unpubl., from Cambridgeshire, Essex, Gloucestershire (two sites), North Yorkshire, Northumberland, Oxfordshire (two sites), Powys (two sites), Warwickshire (two sites); [2]Tarrant *et al.* (1990); [3]Tew (1989); [4]Toms (1990); [5]S.E. Randolph (pers. comm.); [6]Lord (1961); [7]Brown (1954); [8]Corke & Harris (1972); [9]A. Gudgion (pers. comm.); [10]S. Bullion (pers. comm.); [11]Brown (1980); [12]Lazenby, Johnson & Whiteley (1986); [13]Clinging & Whiteley (1980); [14]Whiteley & Yalden (1976); [15]Shore (1988); [16]Zhang & Usher (1991); [17]G.L. Woodroffe (pers. comm.); [18]Fraser (1988); [19]Corbet (1960); [20]Delany (1961).

Table 8. Summary of the data in Tables 5-7 showing the ratios of various species of small mammal in pellet, bottle and trapped samples.

	Common shrew	Pygmy shrew	Water shrew	Bank vole	Field vole	Wood/yellow-necked mouse	Harvest mouse	House mouse	Common shrew: pygmy shrew	Common shrew: water shrew	Pygmy shrew: water shrew	Field vole: bank vole	Wood/yellow-necked mouse: bank vole	Field vole: wood/yellow-necked mouse	Wood/yellow-necked mouse: harvest mouse	Wood/yellow-necked mouse: house mouse	Common shrew: wood/yellow-necked mouse	Common shrew: field vole
Barn owl pellets																		
Totals (n = 75,978)	19,768	3936	1017	3635	38,663	7270	801	888	5·0	19·4	3·9	10·6	2·0	5·3	9·1	8·2	2·7	0·5
Long-eared owl pellets																		
Totals (n = 9029)	353	388	9	955	5313	1993	1	17	0·9	39·2	43·1	5·6	2·1	2·7	-	117·2	0·2	0·1
Short-eared owl pellets																		
Totals (n = 4125)	261	393	1	106	2863	485	6	10	0·7	261·0	393·0	27·0	4·6	10·5	80·8	48·5	0·5	0·1
Tawny owl pellets																		
Totals (n = 10,290)	1319	213	44	3120	2191	3359	1	43	6·2	30·0	4·8	0·7	1·1	0·7	-	77·0	0·4	0·6
Kestrel pellets																		
Totals (n = 1230)	132	160	2	93	748	89	0	6	0·8	66·0	80·0	8·0	1·0	9·4	-	14·8	1·5	0·2
Bottle samples																		
Totals (n = 7546)	3767	322	166	1540	414	1312	3	22	11·7	22·7	1·9	0·3	1·1	0·3	37·3	59·6	2·9	9·1
Trapping samples																		
Totals (n = 27,107)	3533	586	106	7065	2519	12,994	223	81	6·0	33·3	5·5	0·4	1·8	0·2	58·3	160·4	0·3	1·4
Overall totals																		
(n = 135,305)	29,133	5998	1345	16,514	52,711	27,502	1035	1067	4·9	21·7	4·5	3·2	1·7	1·9	26·6	25·8	1·1	0·6

Table 9. Percentages of different species of bat from various British samples (excluding vagrants). Samples from local studies are excluded.

	Enquiries from public to NCC May 1982-December 1983 (n = 628)[1]	Relative frequency of each species recorded in houses (n = 1807)[2]	Enquiries from public to NCC 1983-1992 (n = 11,152)[3]	Recorded in bat boxes in six forests 1976-1990 (n = 3054)[4]	Number of post-1960 10 x 10 km square records (n = 4271)[5]	Number of post-1960 records received by BRC (n = 11,482)[6]	Bat carcasses submitted for testing for rabies (n = 1194)[7]
Greater horseshoe bat	0·3	0·4	1·0	0	2·7	3·6	0·3
Lesser horseshoe bat	1·8	2·1	4·4	0	5·6	7·6	0·3
Whiskered bat				0·4			
Brandt's bat				0·2			
Whiskered bat/ Brandt's bat*	3·2	3·4	2·9		7·7	6·5	3·5
Natterer's bat	1·4	1·2	2·8	7·6	7·8	6·3	3·0
Bechstein's bat	0	<0·1	<0·1	0	0·4	0·8	0·1
Daubenton's bat	0·2	1·0	1·7	0	6·9	5·8	1·6
Serotine	3·6	4·1	4·9	0	3·0	2·2	2·3
Noctule	0·3	1·2	1·2	6·3	4·7	3·4	2·0
Leisler's bat	0·2	0·1	0·3	1·1	1·0	0·8	0·2
Pipistrelle	58·4	54·9	49·2	22·5	33·7	37·9	66·2
Nathusius' pipistrelle	-	-	-	-	-	-	1·0
Barbastelle	0·2	<0·1	<0·1	0	1·0	1·2	0
Brown long-eared bat				62·0			19·3
Grey long-eared bat				0			0·3
Brown long-eared bat/ Grey long-eared bat*	30·4	30·3	31·3		25·6	24·3	

[1] Mitchell-Jones *et al.* (1986); [2] Mitchell-Jones *et al.* (1989); [3] A.J. Mitchell-Jones (pers. comm.); [4] Stebbings & Walsh (1991); [5,6] Arnold (1993) and H.R. Arnold (pers. comm.); [7] A.M. Hutson (pers. comm.).

* Figures are averages between two species that are difficult to differentiate.

Table 10. The reliance of British species of bat on buildings, trees and caves (and other underground sites) as roost sites, excluding vagrant and migrant species. From Hutson (1993).

Species	Reliance on buildings	Reliance on trees	Reliance on caves	Status	Distribution
Greater horseshoe bat	5	1	5	4	5
Lesser horseshoe bat	5	1	5	4	4
Whiskered bat	?3	?	3	3	2
Brandt's bat	?3	?	3	3	2
Natterer's bat	?4	?	4	3	2
Bechstein's bat	?2	?	3	5	5
Greater mouse-eared bat	?3	?	5	5	5
Daubenton's bat	3	4	4	2	1
Serotine	5	1	1	2	4
Noctule	1	5	1	2	2
Leisler's bat	3	?5	1	4	3
Pipistrelle	4	2	1	1	1
Barbastelle	1	?	2	5	3
Brown long-eared bat	4	3	2	2	1
Grey long-eared bat	4	?	2	5	5

The reliance of British species of bat on basic roost types and their relative status and distribution. Each category is scored out of 5: a score of 5 is high reliance, rare status or restricted distribution; a score of 1 indicates low reliance, common status or widespread distribution.

Table 11. Comparison of the relative number of records and population size for British bats (excluding vagrants).

	Relative proportion (%) of records (mean of columns 3,4,6,7 in Table 9)	Population size	Relative proportion (%) of total British bat population	Bat carcasses submitted for testing for rabies (%) (n = 1194)[1]
Greater horseshoe bat	1·2	4000	0·2	0·3
Lesser horseshoe bat	3·1	14,000	0·5	0·3
Whiskered bat		40,000		
Brandt's bat		30,000		
Whiskered bat/ Brandt's bat*	3.3		2.7	3.5
Natterer's bat	5·0	100,000	3·8	3·0
Bechstein's bat	0·2	1500	0·1	0·1
Daubenton's bat	2·2	150,000	5·7	1·6
Serotine	2·4	15,000	0·6	2·3
Noctule	3·2	50,000	1·9	2·0
Leisler's bat	0·6	10,000	0·4	0·2
Pipistrelle	44·5	2,000,000	76·3	66·2
Nathusius' pipistrelle	(0·8)[2]	?	?	1·0
Barbastelle	0·3	5000	0·2	0
Brown long-eared bat		200,000	7·6	19·3
Grey long-eared bat		1000	<0·1	0·3
Brown long-eared bat/ Grey long-eared bat*	33·9			

[1]A.M. Hutson (pers. comm.); [2]figures only available from one source and so this percentage is not averaged over the four samples.
* Figures that lie between lines are averages between two species that are difficult to differentiate.

Table 12. Population trends since 1978 in counts of bats from colonies in houses. These data are summer counts of nursery roosts and are predominantly, but not exclusively, pipistrelle colonies. Population trends are shown by assuming a colony size of 100 in 1978. Data from R.E. Stebbings (pers. comm.).

Area (and mean colony size ± s.e. in 1978)	1978	1979	1980	1981	1982	1983	1984	1985	1986	1987	1988	1989	1990	1991	1992
South-east England (105 ± 17, n = 34)	100	60·4	51·2	55·2	44·4	49·6	44·7	39·3	36·2	39·3	38·0	37·2	34·4	27·6	23·5
South-west England (105 ± 13, n = 10)	100	77·1	78·1	84·3	64·6	63·9	72·8	57·9	68·5	59·0	51·0	47·3	52·2	45·0	41·9
Midlands (123 ± 23, n = 25)	100	48·2	33·7	26·2	21·6	25·8	24·0	27·1	28·1	22·9	25·6	26·0	27·0	27·4	22·3
North England (116 ± 54, n = 5)	100	86·4	130·6	146·9	130·3	75·2	75·8	82·9	82·0	70·1	80·8	84·1	68·5	56·9	46·3
Scotland (94 ± 26, n = 3)	100	114·9	51·0	86·7	71·8	108·6	124·9	163·1	175·7	176·0	168·2	169·0	165·5	177·9	185·9
Wales (296 ± 116, n = 4)	100	60·0	40·9	42·8	38·9	46·4	34·6	19·0	20·1	20·1	20·0	19·9	19·3	15·0	16·1
Britain (119, n = 81)	100	61·4	47·3	48·5	40·3	44·3	42·0	36·2	37·4	35·3	35·5	35·4	32·6	29·4	26·8

Table 13. Population trends since 1980 in counts of bats from colonies in houses. These data are summer counts of nursery roosts and are predominantly, but not exclusively, pipistrelle colonies. Population trends are shown by assuming a colony size of 100 in 1980. Data from R.E. Stebbings (pers. comm.).

Area (and mean colony size ± s.e. in 1980)	1980	1981	1982	1983	1984	1985	1986	1987	1988	1989	1990	1991	1992
South-east England (52 ± 7, n = 57)	100	108·0	86·9	97·1	86·2	75·9	70·0	76·1	73·5	72·0	66·5	53·3	45·5
South-west England (55 ± 7, n = 48)	100	107·9	82·7	81·8	93·3	74·3	87·9	75·8	65·5	60·7	67·0	57·8	53·8
Midlands (41 ± 6, n = 71)	100	77·6	63·9	76·5	71·3	80·4	83·3	68·0	76·0	77·2	80·3	81·3	66·3
North England (45 ± 9, n = 16)	100	112·5	99·8	57·6	58·1	63·6	62·8	53·7	61·9	64·4	52·4	43·5	35·4
Scotland (59 ± 18, n = 8)	100	170·0	140·8	213·0	245·0	320·0	344·6	345·3	330·1	331·8	324·8	349·2	364·9
Wales (97 ± 26, n = 14)	100	104·7	95·1	113·5	84·6	46·4	49·1	49·5	49·0	48·7	47·3	36·8	39·4
Britain (52 ± 4, n = 214)	100	102·5	85·1	93·5	88·5	76·4	78·9	74·4	74·8	74·6	68·8	62·0	56·5

Table 14. Estimated pre-breeding population size and conservation status of the 64 species and one sub-species of mammal included in this review. Due to the different methods used to obtain the population estimates, direct comparisons between species should be made with caution. The numbers after the total population estimates denote the reliability of the estimate, where [5] is thought to be least, and [1] most, reliable; see the text for further details. The numbers after the population estimate for each of the three countries denote the rank order of abundance for that country, with [1] being the rarest.

	Population size				Changing status (see footnote)	British range (see footnote)	European status (see footnote)	Population threats (see footnote)
	Total	England	Scotland	Wales				
Greater mouse-eared bat	E[1]	0	0	0	− −	5	?	—
Coypu	E[1]	0	0	0	− −	172	?	—
Nathusius' pipistrelle	?	?	?	?	±?	?	?	—
Red-necked wallaby	29[1]	3[1]	26[2]	0	− −	14	100	R
Park cattle	45[1]	45[2]	10[1]	0		—	?	—
Reindeer	80[1]	0	80[4]	0	+	—	?	—
Chinese water deer	650[2]	650[9]	0	0	+| +	33	95*	Cl,Pr?,R?
Grey long-eared bat	1000[3]	1000[11]	0	0	+|	19 +	0.4	Cl,H,P
Ship rat	1300[2]	<750[10]	<550[8]	0	− −	23 1	6.1	K,P
Bechstein's bat	1500[4]	1500[12]	0	?0	+|	19	0.7	H,P
Feral sheep	2100[1]	150[4]	1850[10]	100[5]	+| +	—	?	D?
Feral ferret	2500[5]	200[5]	2250[11]	50[2=]	+| +	166	?	—
Wildcat	3500[3]	0	3500[13=]	0	+| +	347	4.6	I,K,P?
Feral goat	>3565[2]	315[6]	>2650[12]	600[11]	+| +	113	?	—
Pine marten	3650[2]	<100[3]	3500[13=]	50[2=]	+	262	1.8	C?,K
Greater horseshoe bat	>4000[2]	3500[16]	0	500[9=]	− −	114	0.4	H,P
Barbastelle	5000[5]	4500[17]	0	500[9=]	−?	41	4.8	H,P
Skomer vole	7000[1]	0	0	7000[15=]	+| +	1	100	C?
Otter	>7350[3]	350[7]	6600[16]	400[8]	+| +	1308 1	7.8	H,P,R
Leisler's bat	10,000[4]	9750[20]	250[5=]	?0	+| +	41	4.9	H?,P?
Fat dormouse	10,000[3]	10,000[21]	0	0	+	9	0.003	—
Sika deer	11,500[2]	<2500[14]	9000[17]	0	++	153	32.3	I,K
Lesser white-toothed shrew	14,000[4]	14,000[23]	0	0	+|	3	0.0007	—
Lesser horseshoe bat	14,000[2]	7000[19]	0	7000[15=]	±?	238	1.3	Cl?,H
Serotine	15,000[4]	14,750[24]	0	250[7]	±?	128	2.0	H?,P?

Table 14 continued

	Population size				Changing status (see footnote)	British range (see footnote)	European status (see footnote)	Population threats (see footnote)
	Total	England	Scotland	Wales				
Polecat	15,000 [3]	2500 [15]	?0 [7]	12,500 [22=]	+	235	0·5	C?,H,I?,K?,R?
Brandt's bat	30,000 [5]	22,500 [25]	500 [7]	7000 [15=]	–?	43 [+]	6·3	H,P
Common seal	35,000 [2]	2200 [13]	32,800 [22]	0	+	387	40*	D,P
Whiskered bat	40,000 [4]	30,500 [27]	1500 [9]	8000 [18]	–?	112 [+]	4·2	H,P
Chinese muntjac	40,000 [3]	40,000 [28]	<50 [3]	<250 [6]	++	417	100*	Cl,K?
Noctule	50,000 [3]	45,000 [29]	250 [5=]	4750 [14]	––	199	4·6	H?,P?
Grey seal	93,500 [1]	5500 [18]	86,400 [25]	1600 [13]	++	553	78*	K,P?
Natterer's bat	100,000 [4]	70,000 [31]	17,500 [18]	12,500 [22=]	±?	331	7·6	H,P
Fallow deer	100,000 [4]	95,000 [32=]	<4000 [15]	<1000 [12]	±?	546	40*	I?,K?,R
American mink	>110,000 [3]	46,750 [30]	52,250 [24]	9750 [19]	++	1051	21·6	C?
Daubenton's bat	150,000 [4]	95,000 [32=]	40,000 [23]	15,000 [24]	±?	293	7·6	H?,P?
Red squirrel	160,000 [3]	30,000 [26]	121,000 [27]	10,000 [20=]	––	386 [1]	1·7	C,F,H
Brown long-eared bat	200,000 [4]	155,000 [35]	27,500 [21]	17,500 [25]	––?	436 [+]	6·3	H,P
Red fox	240,000 [4]	195,000 [36=]	23,000 [19]	22,000 [26]	+	1744	4·7	K
Badger	250,000 [2]	195,000 [36=]	25,000 [20]	35,000 [27=]	±?	1800	17*	F?,H,K,R
Mountain hare	350,000 [3]	500 [8]	350,000 [34=]	0	++	363	5·0	Cl?,F,H?,K
Red deer	360,000 [2]	12,500 [22]	347,000 [33]	<50 [1]	++	783	30*	I,K
Weasel	450,000 [4]	308,000 [39]	106,000 [26]	36,000 [29]	–	1490	4·7	C?,K?
Stoat	462,000 [4]	245,000 [38]	180,000 [29]	37,000 [30]	–	1514	6·6	K
Common dormouse	500,000 [3]	465,000 [40]	0	35,000 [27=]	––?	352	1·1	Cl?,F,H
Roe deer	500,000 [3]	150,000 [34]	350,000 [34=]	50 [2=]	++	1237	6·6	–
Yellow-necked mouse	750,000 [4]	662,500 [43]	0	87,500 [34]	–	219	0·5	F,H
Feral cat	813,000 [4]	625,000 [42]	130,000 [28]	58,000 [32=]	±?	–	?	–
Brown hare	817,500 [2]	572,250 [41]	187,250 [30]	58,000 [32=]	––	1594	7·0	D?,H,K,Pr?
Orkney vole	1,000,000 [1]	0	1,000,000 [41]	0	––	16	0·04	H
Water vole	1,169,000 [3]	752,000 [44]	376,000 [36]	41,000 [31]	–––	1060	6·6	F,H,Pr
Harvest mouse	1,425,000 [5]	1,415,000 [48]	?0 [20=]	10,000 [20=]	––	693	3·5	Cl,F?,H,P?
Hedgehog	1,555,000 [4]	1,100,000 [45]	310,000 [32]	145,000 [35]	––	1980	8·9	H?,Pr?R?
Water shrew	1,900,000 [4]	1,200,000 [46]	400,000 [37]	300,000 [38]	±?	654	6·6	H
Pipistrelle	2,000,000 [3]	1,250,000 [47]	550,000 [38]	200,000 [36]	–––	1438	5·5	H,P

Table 14 continued

	Population size (Total)	England	Scotland	Wales	Changing status (see footnote)	British range (see footnote)	European status (see footnote)	Population threats (see footnote)
Grey squirrel	2,520,000 [3]	2,000,000 [49]	200,000 [31]	320,000 [39]	++	1476 [2]	98.0	–
House mouse	>5,192,000 [5]	4,535,000 [50]	657,000 [39]	206,000 [37]	– –	851	8.7	C?,K,P
Common rat	>6,790,000 [4]	5,240,000 [52]	870,000 [40]	680,000 [40]	– –	1380	6.6	H,K,P
Pygmy shrew	8,600,000 [4]	4,800,000 [51]	2,300,000 [42]	1,500,000 [41]	±	948	5.6	H?,P?
Bank vole	23,000,000 [3]	17,750,000 [54]	3,500,000 [43]	1,750,000 [42]	±	1062	6.6	–
Mole	31,000,000 [3]	19,750,000 [56]	8,000,000 [44]	3,250,000 [43]	±	2223	8.6	K?,P?
Rabbit	37,500,000 [3]	24,500,000 [57]	9,500,000 [45]	3,500,000 [44=]	++	2249	6.0	D
Wood mouse	38,000,000 [3]	19,500,000 [55]	15,000,000 [47]	3,500,000 [44=]	±	1362	6.4	P?
Common shrew	41,700,000 [3]	26,000,000 [58]	11,500,000 [46]	4,200,000 [46]	±	1429	7.8	H?,P?
Field vole	75,000,000 [4]	17,500,000 [53]	41,000,000 [48]	16,500,000 [47]	–	1301	6.2	H

Population size: the estimated number of animals at the beginning of the breeding season.

Changing status: population changes over the last 30 years. This is an assessment of recent population changes rather than current population trends. E extinct; ++ strong evidence of increase in numbers and/or range; + suggestions of increase; ± probably stable, or no clear evidence of change; – suggestions of decline; – – strong evidence of decline in numbers and/or range.

British range: number of 10 x 10 km squares from which the species has been recorded since 1960, excluding the Channel Islands and the Isle of Man (Arnold 1993). + indicates that this species is under represented, because many records did not differentiate between this and a very similar species (there were 245 records of whiskered/Brandt's bat and 896 of 'long-eared bats' in addition to records that identified the actual species); [1] post-1975 records only; [2] all 10 x 10 km square records.

European status: approximate percentage of western European range that is contributed by the British range (or, * where possible, the population similarly estimated).

Population threats: factors which are known or believed may currently affect population size, or which may affect population size in the future. C - competitors; Cl - climate changes and/or adverse weather conditions; D - disease; F - population fragmentation or isolation; H - habitat changes; I - interbreeding; K - deliberate killing by people, particularly hunting, gamekeepers, pest control, poaching; P - pesticides, pollution, poisoning or the use of other chemicals; Pr - predation; R - road casualties; – no known threats; ? - unclear if that factor posed a serious threat.

Table 15. Status and protection of British mammals.

	Biogeographical status in Britain (see footnote)	Conservation status in Britain (see footnote)	Legal protection in Britain (see footnote)	EC Directive (Annex/es) (see footnote)	Bern Convention (Appendix) (see footnote)	CITES (Appendix) (see footnote)
Marsupialia						
Red-necked wallaby	I	V	Schedule 9	-	-	-
Insectivora						
Hedgehog	N	C	Schedule 6	-	III	-
Mole	N	C	-	-	-	-
Common shrew	N	C	Schedule 6	-	III	-
Pygmy shrew	N	C	Schedule 6	-	III	-
Water shrew	N	LC	Schedule 6	-	III	-
Lesser white-toothed shrew	I	LC	Schedule 6	-	III	-
Chiroptera						
Greater horseshoe bat	N	V	Schedule 5, 6	IIa, IVa	II	-
Lesser horseshoe bat	N	V	Schedule 5, 6	IIa, IVa	II	-
Whiskered bat	N	V?	Schedule 5, 6	IVa	II	-
Brandt's bat	N	V?	Schedule 5, 6	IVa	II	-
Natterer's bat	N	LC	Schedule 5, 6	IVa	II	-
Bechstein's bat	N	R	Schedule 5, 6	IIa, IVa	II	-
Greater mouse-eared bat	N	Ex	Schedule 5, 6	IIa, IVa	II	-
Daubenton's bat	N	LC	Schedule 5, 6	IVa	II	-
Particoloured bat	V	R	Schedule 5, 6	IVa	II	-
Serotine	N	V	Schedule 5, 6	IVa	II	-
Northern bat	V	R	Schedule 5, 6	IVa	II	-
Noctule	N	V?	Schedule 5, 6	IVa	II	-
Leisler's bat	N	V?	Schedule 5, 6	IVa	II	-
Pipistrelle	N	C	Schedule 5, 6	IVa	II	-
Nathusius' pipistrelle	M	R	Schedule 5, 6	IVa	II	-
Barbastelle	N	R	Schedule 5, 6	IIa, IVa	III	-
Brown long-eared bat	N	LC	Schedule 5, 6	IVa	II	-
Grey long-eared bat	N	E	Schedule 5, 6	IVa	II	-

Table 15 continued

	Biogeographical status in Britain (see footnote)	Conservation status in Britain (see footnote)	Legal protection in Britain (see footnote)	EC Directive (Annex/es) (see footnote)	Bern Convention (Appendix) (see footnote)	CITES (Appendix) (see footnote)
Lagomorpha						
Rabbit	I	C	-1,2	-	-	-
Brown hare	I	C	-1,3	-	-	-
Mountain hare	N	LC	-1,3	V	III	-
Rodentia						
Red squirrel	N	V	Schedule 5, 6	-	III	-
Grey squirrel	I	C	Schedule 9[4]	-	-	-
Bank vole	N	C	-	-	-	-
Skomer vole	N	LC	-	-	-	-
Field vole	N	C	-	-	-	-
Orkney vole	I	LC	-	-	-	-
Water vole	N	V	-	-	-	-
Wood mouse	N	C	-	-	-	-
Yellow-necked mouse	N	LC	-	-	-	-
Harvest mouse	I(?)	LC	-	-	-	-
House mouse	I	C	-	-	-	-
Common rat	I	C	-	-	-	-
Ship rat	I	E	Schedule 9	-	-	-
Common dormouse	N	V	Schedule 5, 6	IVa	III	-
Fat dormouse	I	LC	Schedule 6, 9	-	III	-
Coypu	I	Ex	Schedule 9[5]	-	-	-
Carnivora						
Red fox	N	C	-	-	-	-
Pine marten	N	LC	Schedule 5, 6	Va	III	-
Stoat	N	C	-	-	III	III[11]
Weasel	N	C	-	-	III	-
Polecat	N	LC	Schedule 6	Va	III	-
Feral ferret	I	R	-	-	-	-

Table 15 continued

	Biogeographical status in Britain (see footnote)	Conservation status in Britain (see footnote)	Legal protection in Britain (see footnote)	EC Directive (Annex/es) (see footnote)	Bern Convention (Appendix) (see footnote)	CITES (Appendix) (see footnote)
American mink	I	C	Schedule 9[6]	-	-	-
Badger	N	C	Schedule 6[7]	-	III	-
Otter	N	LC	Schedule 5, 6	IIa, IVa	II	I
Wildcat	N	LC	Schedule 5, 6	IVa	II	II
Feral cat	I	C	-	-	-	-
Pinnipedia						
Common seal	N	LC	Seals Act, 1970[8]	IIa	III	-
Grey seal	N	LC	Seals Act, 1970[8]	IIa	III	-
Ringed seal	V	R	-	Va	III	-
Harp seal	V	R	-	Va	III	-
Bearded seal	V	R	-	Va	III	-
Hooded seal	V	R	-	Va	III	-
Walrus	V	R	Schedule 5	-	II	III
Artiodactyla						
Red deer	N	LC	Deer Act, 1991[10]	-	III	-
Sika deer	I	LC	Deer Act, 1991[10]	-	III	-
Fallow deer	I	LC	Deer Act, 1991[10]	-	III	-
Roe deer	N	C	Deer Act, 1991[10]	-	III	-
Chinese muntjac	I	LC	Deer Act, 1991[10]	-	III	-
Chinese water deer	I	R	Deer Act, 1991[10]	-	III	-
Reindeer	N	R	Deer Act, 1991[10]	-	III	-
Park cattle	N	R	-	-	-	-
Feral goat	I	R	-	-	II	-
Feral sheep	I	V	-	-	-	-

Biogeographical status: this assessment refers to the species as a whole, although there may have been substantial restocking of some native species with animals from abroad. I = introduced (22 species); M = migrant (one species); N = native (41 species and one subspecies); V = vagrant (seven species).

137

Table 15 continued

Conservation status in Britain: these are subjective assessments based on the data presented in this review. C = common (20 species); E = endangered, species threatened with extinction (two species); Ex = believed to be extinct in the wild (two species); LC = locally common, species with relatively large populations but a limited distribution (20 species and one subspecies); R = rare (15 species); V = vulnerable, species whose populations are either small or threatened (12 species).

Legal protection in Britain: Schedules refer to the Wildlife and Countryside Act 1981 and its subsequent amendments. Those species protected under Schedule 5 cannot be intentionally killed, injured or taken. Species covered by Schedule 6 of the Act are not fully protected, but there are prohibitions of certain methods of killing and taking. Schedule 9 lists established species for which further releases to the wild are prohibited without a licence. Other relevant British legislation is listed as follows: [1] except for the provisions of the Ground Game Act 1880; [2] an amendment to the Pests Act 1954 makes it an offence to release a rabbit with signs of myxomatosis where other rabbits may become infected; [3] except for the limitations on periods when they can be sold, as laid out in the Hare Preservation Act 1892; [4] the Grey Squirrel (Prohibition of Importation and Keeping) Order 1937 makes it an offence to keep this species in captivity without a licence from the Ministry of Agriculture, Fisheries and Food; [5] the keeping of coypu is banned under the Coypu (Prohibition on Keeping) Order 1987; [6] the keeping of American mink requires a licence under the Mink (Keeping) Order 1987; [7] badgers are protected by a series of legislation - the Badgers Act 1973 (plus amendments in the Wildlife and Countryside Act 1981 and the Wildlife and Countryside (Amendment) Act 1985), and the Protection of Badgers Act 1992; [8] the Conservation of Seals Act 1970 provides separate close seasons for both common and grey seals during their pupping periods, and section 3 orders can be used to extend these close seasons as necessary e.g. as was done during the recent phocine distemper virus epizootic; [9] no statutory close seasons; [10] The Deer Act 1991 only applies to England and Wales; for Scotland the main legislation is the Deer (Scotland) Act 1959, the Deer (Amendment) (Scotland) Act 1982 and the Deer (Close Seasons) (Scotland) Order 1984. For a fuller account of the legal status of British mammals, see Harris & Jefferies (1991).

EC Directive 92/43/EEC on the conservation of natural habitats and wild fauna and flora: Annex II - designation of protected areas for that species, although there are no designated priority species in Britain; Annex IV - special protection for the species; Annex V - exploitation of that species to be subject to management.

Bern Convention on the Conservation of European Wildlife and Natural Habitats: Appendix II - strict protection for that species; Appendix III - exploitation of that species to be subject to regulation.

CITES (Convention on international trade in endangered species): Appendix I - trade only in exceptional circumstances; Appendix II - trade subject to licensing; Appendix III - trade subject to limited licensing. [11] UK reservation.

Acknowledgements

This project was funded by the Joint Nature Conservation Committee, and for the Schedule 5 and 6 species drew on data compiled by P. Morris for a project funded by the Vincent Wildlife Trust. We are grateful to both these organizations. S. Harris would also like to thank the Dulverton Trust for additional financial support. Many people made their data available to us, produced population or density estimates, and/or commented on drafts of the manuscript; without their generous help, this review would not have been possible. Thus we are extremely grateful to H.R. Arnold, S. Baker, D. Balharry, D.R. Bancroft, R.J. Berry, J.D.S. Birks, P.R.S. Blandford, W.N. Bonner, P.W. Bright, D. Brown, A.P. Buckle, S. Bullion, D.J. Bullock, E. Calcott, A. Chadwick, P.R.F. Chanin, N.G. Chapman, P. Chapman, C.L. Cheeseman, M. Clarke, K. Claydon, M. Claydon, A.S. Cooke, G.B. Corbet, L.K. Corbett, D.P. Cowan, J. Cubby, A.J. de Nahlik, B.A.C. Don, C. Duck, R.I.M. Dunbar, N. Dunstone, A. Dymond, R. Engeldow, L. Farrell, J.R. Flowerdew, R.M.A. Gill, B. Gilliam, M.L. Gorman, L.M. Gosling, J. Green, R. Green, A. Gudgion, J. Gurnell, S.J.G. Hall, F.G.L. Hartley, T.D. Healing, J. Herman, R. Hewson, M. Hicks, J.L. Holm, J.H.D. Hooper, M. Hutchings, A.M. Hutson, P. James, D.J. Jefferies, A.L. Johnson, T. Johnson, G. Jones, L.M. Jones-Walters, A. Jowitt, R.E. Kenward, C.M. King, A.C. Kitchener, H.H. Kolb, H. Kruuk, J. Langbein, J. Latham, I. Linn, J. Livingstone, R. Lovegrove, V.P.W. Lowe, A. Lucas, A. MacColl, H.C. Mallorie, C. Mann, C.F. Mason, B. Mayle, S. McOrist, A.P. Meehan, J. Messenger, A. Meyer, A.J. Mitchell-Jones, W.I. Montgomery, P.J. Moors, I.K. Morgan, M. Oates, R.J.C. Page, S. Parr, I.J. Patterson, J.M. Pemberton, H.W. Pepper, M.R. Perrow, S.M.C. Poulton, R.J. Putman, R.J. Quy, P.A. Racey, R. Ramage, S.E. Randolph, R.D. Ransome, P.R. Ratcliffe, N.D. Redgate, J.C. Reynolds, P.W. Richardson, D. Roberts, R. Scott, Sea Mammal Research Unit, A. Shankster, G. Shaw, C.B. Shedden, R.F. Shore, E. Smith, P.A. Smith, J.R. Speakman, B. Staines, R.E. Stebbings, I.R. Stevenson, R. Strachan, S.C. Tapper, F. Tattersall, N. Teall, T.E. Tew, S. Thirgood, C.M. Todd, J.M. Tonkin, R.C. Trout, G.I. Twigg, K.C. Walton, H. Warwick, R. Whitta, C.J. Wilson, G.L. Woodroffe, D.E. Woods and S. Wroot. Finally, we owe a great debt of gratitude to Debra Young for all her hard work typing the many drafts of this review, to R.G.H. Bunce and D.C. Howard for their help and encouragement with this project, and to T.E. Tew for his help, encouragement and support throughout this project.

References

Adams, L.E. 1913. The harvest mouse. *Wild Life, London, 2*: 7-18.

Alibhai, S.K., & Gipps, J.H.W. 1985. The population dynamics of bank voles. *Symposia of the Zoological Society of London, 55*: 277-313.

Alibhai, S.K., & Gipps, J.H.W. 1991. Bank vole *Clethrionomys glareolus*. In: *The handbook of British mammals*, ed. by G.B. Corbet & S. Harris, 192-203. Blackwell Scientific Publications, Oxford.

Allen, N. 1990. *Exmoor's wild red deer*. Dulverton Exmoor Press.

Anderson, D., & Cham, S.A. 1987. Muntjac deer (*Muntiacus reevesi*) - the early years. *Bedfordshire Naturalist, 42*: 14-18.

Anderson, P., & Yalden, D.W. 1981. Increased sheep numbers and the loss of heather moorland in the Peak District. *Biological Conservation, 20*: 195-213.

Anderson, S.H. 1990. *Seals*. Whittet, London.

Andrews, E., & Crawford, A.K. 1986. *Otter survey of Wales 1984-85*. Vincent Wildlife Trust, London.

Anon. 1887. On the present condition of the existing herds of British wild white cattle. *Zoologist*, third series, *11*: 401-414.

Anon. 1963. Oxford Lundy expedition - 1962. *Bulletin of the Mammal Society of the British Isles, 20*: 26-28.

Anon. 1989. Report of Council 1989. *Otters, Journal of the Otter Trust, 2*(3), 1-4.

Anon. 1993. Vaynol cattle return to the Vaynol estate. *Ark, 20*: 38.

Arnold, H.R. 1984. *Distribution maps of the mammals of the British Isles*. Institute of Terrestrial Ecology, Abbots Ripton.

Arnold, H.R. 1993. *Atlas of mammals in Britain*. Her Majesty's Stationery Office, London.

Attuquayefio, D.K., Gorman, M.L., & Wolton, R.J. 1986. Home range sizes in the wood mouse *Apodemus sylvaticus*: habitat, sex and seasonal differences. *Journal of Zoology, London, 210A*: 45-53.

Baker, S.J. 1990. Escaped exotic mammals in Britain. *Mammal Review, 20*: 75-96.

Balharry, D. 1993. *Factors affecting the distribution and population density of pine martens (*Martes martes*) in Scotland*. PhD Thesis, University of Aberdeen.

Balharry, E., Staines, B.W., Marquiss, M., & Kruuk, H. 1994. *Hybridisation in British mammals*. JNCC report no. 154. Joint Nature Conservation Committee, Peterborough.

Barnes, R.F.W., & Tapper, S.C. 1985. A method for counting hares by spotlight. *Journal of Zoology, London, 206A*: 273-276.

Barnes, R.F.W., & Tapper, S.C. 1986. Consequences of the myxomatosis epidemic in Britain's rabbit (*Oryctolagus cuniculus* L.) population on the numbers of brown hares (*Lepus europaeus* Pallas). *Mammal Review, 16*: 111-116.

Barr, C.J., Bunce, R.G.H., Clarke, R.T., Fuller, R.M., Furse, M.T., Gillespie, M.K., Groom, G.B., Hallam, C.J., Hornung, M., Howard, D.C. & Ness, M.J. 1993. *Countryside survey 1990 - main report*. Department of the Environment, London.

Barrett-Hamilton, G.E.H., & Hinton, M.A.C. 1910-1921. *A history of British mammals*. Gurney & Jackson, London.

Batten, H.M. n.d. *British wild animals*. Odhams Press, London.

Batten, L.A., Bibby, C.J., Clement, P., Elliott, G.D., & Porter, R.F., eds. 1990. *Red Data birds in Britain - action for rare, threatened and important species*. Poyser, London.

Bell, D.J., & Webb, N.J. 1991. Effects of climate on reproduction in the European wild rabbit (*Oryctolagus cuniculus*). *Journal of Zoology, London, 224*: 639-648.

Bell, T. 1874. *A history of British quadrupeds.* Van Voorst, London.

Bentley, E.W. 1959. The distribution and status of *Rattus rattus* L. in the United Kingdom in 1951 and 1956. *Journal of Animal Ecology, 28*: 299-308.

Bentley, E.W. 1964. A further loss of ground by *Rattus rattus* L. in the United Kingdom during 1956-61. *Journal of Animal Ecology, 33*: 371-373.

Benzal, J., de Paz, O., & Gisbert, J. 1991. Los murcielagos de la peninsula Iberica y Balearas. Patrones biogeograficos de sec distribucion. In: *Les murcielagos de Españay Portugal,* ed. by J. Benzal & O. de Paz, 37-162. ICONA, Madrid.

Bergman, A., & Olsson, M. 1986. Pathology of Baltic grey seal and ringed seal females with special reference to adrenocortical hyperplasia: is environmental pollution the cause of a widely distributed disease syndrome? *Finnish Game Research, 44*: 47-62.

Berry, R.J. 1968. The ecology of an island population of the house mouse. *Journal of Animal Ecology, 37*: 445-470.

Berry, R.J. 1969. History in the evolution of *Apodemus sylvaticus* (Mammalia) at one edge of its range. *Journal of Zoology, London, 159*: 311-328.

Berry, R.J. 1991. House mouse *Mus domesticus.* In: *The handbook of British mammals,* ed. by G.B. Corbet & S. Harris, 239-247. Blackwell Scientific Publications, Oxford.

Berry, R.J., Berry, A.J., Anderson, T.J.C., & Scriven, P. 1992. The house mice of Faray, Orkney. *Journal of Zoology, London, 228*: 233-246.

Berry, R.J., Cuthbert, A., & Peters, J. 1982. Colonization by house mice: an experiment. *Journal of Zoology, London, 198*: 329-336.

Berry, R.J., & Jakobson, M.E. 1975. Ecological genetics of an island population of the house mouse (*Mus musculus*). *Journal of Zoology, London, 175*: 523-540.

Berry, R.J., & Rose, F.E.N. 1975. Islands and the evolution of *Microtus arvalis* (Microtinae). *Journal of Zoology, London, 177*: 395-409.

Berry, R.J., & Tricker, B.J.K. 1969. Competition and extinction: the mice of Foula, with notes on those of Fair Isle and St Kilda. *Journal of Zoology, London, 158*: 247-265.

Beven, G. 1965. The food of tawny owls in London. *London Bird Report for 1964, 29*: 56-72.

Beven, G. 1967. The food of tawny owls in Surrey. *Surrey Bird Report for 1966,* 32-38.

Beven, G. 1982. Further observations on the food of tawny owls in London. *London Naturalist, 61*: 88-94.

Birks, J.D.S. 1989. What regulates the numbers of feral mink? *Nature in Devon, 10*: 45-61.

Birks, J. 1990. Feral mink and nature conservation. *British Wildlife, 1*: 313-323.

Birks, J.D.S., & Dunstone, N. 1991. Mink *Mustela vison.* In: *The handbook of British mammals,* ed. by G.B. Corbet & S. Harris, 406-415. Blackwell Scientific Publications, Oxford.

Birks, J.D.S., & Linn, I.J. 1982. Studies of home range of the feral mink, *Mustela vison. Symposia of the Zoological Society of London, 49*: 231-257.

Blandford, P.R.S. 1987. Biology of the polecat *Mustela putorius*: a literature review. *Mammal Review, 17*: 155-198.

Blandford, P.R.S., & Walton, K.C. 1991. Polecat *Mustela putorius.* In: *The handbook of British mammals,* ed. by G.B. Corbet & S. Harris, 396-405. Blackwell Scientific Publications, Oxford.

Blomkvist, G., Roos, A., Jensen, S., Bignert, A., & Olsson, M. 1992. Concentrations of SDDT and PCB in seals from Swedish and Scottish waters. *Ambio, 21*: 539-545.

Boelter, W.R. 1909. *The rat problem.* Bale, London.

Bonner, W.N. 1972. The grey seal and common seal in European waters.

Oceanography and Marine Biology Annual Review, 10: 461-507.

Bonner, W.N. 1975. Population increase of grey seals at the Farne Islands. *Rapport et procès-verbaux des réunions. Conseil Permanent International pour l'Exploration de la Mer, 169*: 366-370.

Bonner, W.N. 1976. The stocks of grey seals (*Halichoerus grypus*) and common seals (*Phoca vitulina*) in Great Britain. *Natural Environment Research Council Publications Series C, 16*: 1-16.

Bonner, W.N. 1981. Grey Seal *Halichoerus grypus* Fabricius, 1791. In: *Handbook of Marine mammals, Vol. 2. Seals*, ed. by S.H. Ridgway & R.J. Harrison, 111-144. Academic Press, London.

Bonner, W.N. 1982. *Seals and man - a study of interactions*. University of Washington, Seattle.

Bonner, W.N. 1989a. *The natural history of seals*. Christopher Helm, London.

Bonner, W.N. 1989b. Seals and man - a changing relationship. *Biological Journal of the Linnean Society, 38*: 53-60.

Bonner, W.N., & Thompson, P.M. 1991. Common seal *Phoca vitulina*. In: *The handbook of British mammals*, ed. by G.B. Corbet & S. Harris, 462-471. Blackwell Scientific Publications, Oxford.

Bonner, W.N., Vaughan, R.W., & Johnston, L. 1973. The status of common seals in Shetland. *Biological Conservation, 5*: 185-190.

Booth, C., & Booth, J. 1994. *The mammals of Orkney*. Orcadian Press, Kirkwall.

Bowman, N. 1980a. The food of barn owls (*Tyto alba*) at a long-used Pembrokeshire site. *Nature in Wales, 17*: 106-108.

Bowman, N. 1980b. The food of the barn owl (*Tyto alba*) in mid-Wales. *Nature in Wales, 17*: 84-88.

Boyd, I.L. 1981. Population changes and the distribution of a herd of feral goats (*Capra* sp.) on Rhum, Inner Hebrides, 1960-78. *Journal of Zoology, London, 193*: 287-304.

Boyd, I.L., Myhill, D.G., & Mitchell-Jones, A.J. 1988. Uptake of Gamma-HCH (Lindane) by pipistrelle bats and its effect on survival. *Environmental Pollution, 51*: 95-111.

Boyd, I.L., & Stebbings, R.E. 1989. Population changes of brown long-eared bats (*Plecotus auritus*) in bat boxes at Thetford Forest. *Journal of Applied Ecology, 26*: 101-112.

Boyd, J.M. 1974. Introduction. In: *Island survivors: the ecology of the Soay sheep of St Kilda*, ed. by P.A. Jewell, C. Milner & J.M. Boyd, 1-7. Athlone Press, London.

Bright, P.W. 1993. Habitat fragmentation - problems and predictions for British mammals. *Mammal Review, 23*: 101-111.

Bright, P.W., Mitchell, P., & Morris, P.A. 1994. Dormouse distribution: survey techniques, insular ecology and selection of sites for conservation. *Journal of Applied Ecology, 31*: 329-339.

Bright, P., & Morris, P. 1989. *A practical guide to dormouse conservation*. Mammal Society, London.

Bright, P.W., & Morris, P.A. 1990. Habitat requirements of dormice *Muscardinus avellanarius* in relation to woodland management in southwest England. *Biological Conservation, 54*: 307-326.

Bright, P., & Morris, P. 1992. *The dormouse*. Mammal Society, London.

Bright, P.W., & Morris, P.A. 1993. Foraging behaviour of dormice *Muscardinus avellanarius* in two contrasting habitats. *Journal of Zoology, London, 230*: 69-85.

Brockless, M., & Tapper, S. 1993. Small mammals on Loddington set-aside. *Game Conservancy Review, 24*: 47-48.

Brown, L.E. 1954. Small mammal populations at Silwood Park Field Centre, Berkshire, England. *Journal of Mammalogy, 35*: 161-176.

Brown, R.W. 1980. Small mammal populations of the moors. In: *Moorland research 1977-79*, 23. North York Moors National Park, Helmsley.

Buckley, J., & Goldsmith, J.G. 1985. The prey of the barn owl (*Tyto alba alba*) in east Norfolk. *Mammal Review, 5*: 13-16.

Buckner, C.H. 1969. Some aspects of the population ecology of the common shrew, *Sorex araneus*, near Oxford, England. *Journal of Mammalogy, 50*: 326-332.

Bullock, D.J. 1991. Feral goat *Capra hircus*. In: *The handbook of British mammals*, ed. by G.B. Corbet & S. Harris, 541-547. Blackwell Scientific Publications, Oxford.

Bunce, R.G.H., Barr, C.J., & Whittaker, H.A. 1981a. An integrated system of land classification. In: *Annual Report of the Institute of Terrestrial Ecology* for *1980*: 28-33.

Bunce, R.G.H., Barr, C.J., & Whittaker, H.A. 1981b. *Land classes in Great Britain: preliminary descriptions for users of the Merlewood method of land classification*. Institute of Terrestrial Ecology, Grange-over-Sands.

Burnham, K.P., Anderson, D.R., & Laake, J.L. 1980. Estimation of density from line transect sampling of biological populations. *Wildlife Monographs, 72*: 1-202.

Burton, M. 1969. *The hedgehog*. André Deutsch, London.

Butterfield, J., Coulson, J.C., & Wanless, S. 1981. Studies on the distribution, food, breeding biology and relative abundance of the pygmy and common shrews (*Sorex minutus* and *S. araneus*) in upland areas of northern England. *Journal of Zoology, London, 195*: 169-180.

Cadman, W.A. 1957. Vole damage in Wales 1956/7. *Nature in Wales, 3*: 504-507.

Callander, R.F., & MacKenzie, N.A. 1991. *The management of wild red deer in Scotland*. Rural Forum, Perth.

Campbell, R.N. 1974. St Kilda and its sheep. In: *Island survivors: the ecology of the Soay sheep of St Kilda*, ed. by P.A. Jewell, C. Milner, & J.M. Boyd, 8-35. Athlone Press, London.

Cassola, F. 1985. Management and conservation of the Sardinian moufflon (*Ovis musimon* Schreber). An outline. In: *The biology and management of mountain ungulates*, ed. by S. Lovari, 197-203. Croom Helm, Beckenham.

Cats Protection League. 1993. *A report on cat welfare*. Cats Protection League, Horsham.

Carter, S.D., Hughes, D.E., Taylor, V.J., & Bell, S.C. 1992. Immune responses in common and grey seals during the seal epizootic. *Science of the Total Environment, 115*: 83-91.

Chanin, P.R.F. 1976. *The ecology of the feral mink (*Mustela vison *Schreber) in Devon*. PhD Thesis, University of Exeter.

Chanin, P. 1981. The feral mink - natural history, movements and control. *Nature in Devon, 2*: 33-54.

Chanin, P. 1991. Otter *Lutra lutra*. In: *The handbook of British mammals*, ed. by G.B. Corbet & S. Harris, 424-431. Blackwell Scientific Publications, Oxford.

Chanin, P. 1992. The otter in Britain from 1900-1990. In: *Proceedings of the National Otter Conference Cambridge, September 1992*, ed. by P.A. Morris, 6-11. Mammal Society, Bristol.

Chanin, P.R.F., & Jefferies, D.J. 1978. The decline of the otter *Lutra lutra* L. in Britain: an analysis of hunting records and discussion of causes. *Biological Journal of the Linnean Society, 10*: 305-328.

Chapman, D.I. 1977. Deer of Essex. *Essex Naturalist*, new series, *1*: 1-50.

Chapman, D.I., & Chapman, N. 1969. Observations on the biology of fallow deer (*Dama dama*) in Epping Forest, Essex, England. *Biological Conservation, 2*: 55-62.

Chapman, D.I., Chapman, N.G., & Dansie, O. 1984. The periods of conception and parturition in feral Reeves' muntjac (*Muntiacus reevesi*) in southern England, based upon age of juvenile animals. *Journal of Zoology, London, 204*: 575-578.

Chapman, N.G. 1991. Chinese muntjac *Muntiacus reevesi*. In: *The handbook of British mammals*, ed. by G.B. Corbet & S. Harris, 526-532. Blackwell Scientific Publications, Oxford.

Chapman, N.G., Claydon, K., Claydon, M., & Harris, S. 1985. Distribution and habitat selection by muntjac and other species of deer in a coniferous forest. *Acta Theriologica, 30*: 283-303.

Chapman, N., Harris, S., & Stanford, A. 1994. Reeves' muntjac *Muntiacus reevesi* in Britain: their history, spread, habitat selection, and the role of human intervention in accelerating their dispersal. *Mammal Review, 24*: 113-160.

Chapman, N.G., & Putman, R.J. 1991. Fallow deer *Dama dama*. In: *The handbook of British mammals*, ed. by G.B. Corbet & S. Harris, 508-518. Blackwell Scientific Publications, Oxford.

Churchfield, S. 1984. An investigation of the population ecology of syntopic shrews inhabiting water-cress beds. *Journal of Zoology, London, 204*: 229-240.

Churchfield, S. 1991a. Common shrew *Sorex araneus*. In: *The handbook of British mammals*, ed. by G.B. Corbet & S. Harris, 51-58. Blackwell Scientific Publications, Oxford.

Churchfield, S. 1991b. Pygmy shrew *Sorex minutus*. In: *The handbook of British mammals*, ed. by G.B. Corbet & S. Harris, 60-64. Blackwell Scientific Publications, Oxford.

Churchfield, S. 1991c. Water shrew *Neomys fodiens*. In: *The handbook of British mammals*, ed. by G.B. Corbet & S. Harris, 64-68. Blackwell Scientific Publications, Oxford.

Churchfield, S., & Brown, V.K. 1987. The trophic impact of small mammals in successional grassland. *Biological Journal of the Linnean Society, 31*: 273-290.

Clark, M., & Summers, S. 1980. Seasonal population movements of brown rats and house mice in Hertfordshire. *Transactions of the Hertfordshire Natural History Society, 28*: 17-19.

Clarkson, K., & Whiteley, D. 1985. The distribution of the Daubenton's bat in Sheffield. *Sorby Record, 23*: 17-20.

Claydon, K., Claydon, M., & Harris, S. 1986. Estimating the number of muntjac deer (*Muntiacus reevesi*) in a commercial coniferous forest. *Bulletin of the British Ecological Society, 17*: 185-189.

Clements, E.D., Neal, E.G., & Yalden, D.W. 1988. The national badger sett survey. *Mammal Review, 18*: 1-9.

Clinging, V., & Whiteley, D. 1980. Mammals of the Sheffield area. *Sorby Record Special Series, 3*: 1-48.

Clutton-Brock, T.H., & Albon, S.D. 1989. *Red deer in the Highlands*. BSP Professional Books, Oxford.

Clutton-Brock, T.H., Price, O.F., Albon, S.D., & Jewell, P.A. 1991. Persistent instability and population regulation in Soay sheep. *Journal of Animal Ecology, 60*: 593-608.

Clutton-Brock, T.H., Price, O.F., Albon, S.D., & Jewell, P.A. 1992. Early development and population fluctuations in Soay sheep. *Journal of Animal Ecology, 61*: 381-396.

Conroy, J. 1992. Otter mortality and survival. In: *Proceedings of the National Otter Conference, Cambridge, September 1992*, ed. by P.A. Morris, 21-24. Mammal Society, Bristol.

Corbet, G.B. 1960. *The distribution, variation and ecology of voles in the Scottish Highlands*. PhD Thesis, University of St Andrews.

Corbet, G.B. 1978. *The mammals of the Palaearctic region - a taxonomic review*. British Museum (Natural History), London.

Corbet, G.B., & Harris, S., eds. 1991. *The handbook of British mammals*. 3rd ed.

Blackwell Scientific Publications, Oxford.

Corbett, L.K. 1979. *Feeding ecology and social organisation of wildcats (*Felis silvestris*) and domestic cats (*Felis catus*) in Scotland*. PhD Thesis, University of Aberdeen.

Corke, D. 1977. A combination of extensive and intensive survey techniques for the study of the occurrence of *Apodemus flavicollis* in Essex. *Journal of Zoology, London, 182*: 171-175.

Corke, D., & Harris, S. 1972. The small mammals of Essex. *Essex Naturalist, 33*: 32-59.

Coulson, J.C. 1981. A study of the factors influencing the timing of breeding in the grey seal *Halichoerus grypus*. *Journal of Zoology, London, 194*: 553-571.

Coulson, J.C., & Hickling, G. 1964. The breeding biology of the grey seal, *Halichoerus grypus* (Fab.), on the Farne Islands, Northumberland. *Journal of Animal Ecology, 33*: 485-512.

Cowan, D.P. 1984. The use of ferrets (*Mustela furo*) in the study and management of the European wild rabbit (*Oryctolagus cuniculus*). *Journal of Zoology, London, 204*: 570-574.

Cowan, D.P. 1991. Rabbit *Oryctolagus cuniculus*. In: *The handbook of British mammals*, ed. by G.B. Corbet & S. Harris, 146-154. Blackwell Scientific Publications, Oxford.

Cramp, S., Conder, P.J., & Ash, J.S. 1962. *Deaths of birds and mammals from toxic chemicals: January - June 1961*. Royal Society for the Protection of Birds, Sandy.

Cresswell, P., Harris, S., Bunce, R.G.H., & Jefferies, D.J. 1989. The badger (*Meles meles*) in Britain: present status and future population changes. *Biological Journal of the Linnean Society, 38*: 91-101.

Cresswell, P., Harris, S., & Jefferies, D.J. 1990. *The history, distribution, status and habitat requirements of the badger in Britain*. Nature Conservancy Council, Peterborough.

Cresswell, W.J., Harris, S., Cheeseman, C.L., & Mallinson, P.J. 1992. To breed or not to breed: an analysis of the social and density-dependent constraints on the fecundity of female badgers (*Meles meles*). *Philosophical Transactions of the Royal Society of London, series B, 338*: 393-407.

Cuthbert, J.H. 1973. The origin and distribution of feral mink in Scotland. *Mammal Review, 3*: 97-103.

Daan, S. 1980. Long term changes in bat populations in the Netherlands: a summary. *Lutra, 22*: 95-118.

Dards, J. 1981. Habitat utilisation by feral cats in Portsmouth dockyard. In: *The ecology and control of feral cats*, 30-46. Universities Federation for Animal Welfare, Potters Bar.

Davis, R.A. 1955. Small mammals caught near London. *London Naturalist, 35*: 88-89.

Davis, T.A.W. 1975. Food of the kestrel in winter and early spring. *Bird Study, 22*: 85-91.

de Winton, W.E. 1894. On a neglected species of British field mouse, *Mus flavicollis*, Melchoir. *Zoologist*, third series, *18*: 441-445.

Delany, M.J. 1957. The small mammals of a Dumbartonshire oakwood. *Glasgow Naturalist, 17*: 272-278.

Delany, M.J. 1961. The ecological distribution of small mammals in north-west Scotland. *Proceedings of the Zoological Society of London, 137*: 107-126.

Dickman, C.R., & Doncaster, C.P. 1987. The ecology of small mammals in urban habitats. I. Populations in a patchy environment. *Journal of Animal Ecology, 56*: 629-640.

Doncaster, C.P. 1992. Testing the role of intraguild predation in regulating hedgehog populations. *Proceedings of the Royal Society of London, series B, 249*: 113-117.

Drummond, D.C. 1985. Developing and monitoring urban rodent control programmes. *Acta Zoologica Fennica*, *173*: 145-148.

Drummond, D.C., Taylor, E.J., & Bond, M. 1977. Urban rat control: further experimental studies at Folkestone. *Environmental Health*, *85*: 265-267.

Duff, J.P., Chasey, D., Munro, R., & Wooldridge, M. 1994. European brown hare syndrome in England. *Veterinary Record*, *134*: 669-673.

Dunstone, N. 1993. *The mink*. Poyser, London.

Dunstone, N., & Birks, J.D.S. 1983. Activity budget and habitat usage by coastal-living mink (*Mustela vison* Schreber). *Acta Zoologica Fennica*, *174*: 189-191.

Dunstone, N., & Birks, J.D.S. 1985. The comparative ecology of coastal, riverine and lacustrine mink *Mustela vison* in Britain. *Zeitshcrift für Angewandte Zoologie*, *72*: 59-70.

Easterbee, N., Hepburn, L.V., & Jefferies, D.J. 1991. *Survey of the status and distribution of the wildcat in Scotland, 1983-1987*. Nature Conservancy Council for Scotland, Edinburgh.

Edwards, C.A., & Lofty, J.R. 1972. *Biology of earthworms*. Chapman & Hall, London.

Eldridge, J. 1971. Some observations on the dispersion of small mammals in hedgerows. *Journal of Zoology, London*, *165*: 530-534.

Ellis, J.C.S. 1946. Notes on the food of the kestrel. *British Birds*, *39*: 113-115.

Elton, C. 1942. *Voles, mice and lemmings: problems in population dynamics*. Clarendon Press, Oxford.

Farrell, L., & Cooke, A. 1991. Chinese water deer *Hydropotes inermis*. In: *The handbook of British mammals*, ed. by G.B. Corbet & S. Harris, 532-537. Blackwell Scientific Publications, Oxford.

Ferns, P. 1979. Growth, reproduction and residency in a declining population of *Microtus agrestis*. *Journal of Animal Ecology*, *48*: 739-758.

Fielding, D.C. 1966. The identification of skulls of the two British species of

Apodemus. *Journal of Zoology, London*, *150*: 498-500.

Flowerdew, J.R. 1991. Wood mouse *Apodemus sylvaticus*. In: *The handbook of British mammals*, ed. by G.B. Corbet & S. Harris, 220-229. Blackwell Scientific Publications, Oxford.

Flux, J.E.C. 1970. Life history of the mountain hare (*Lepus timidus scoticus*) in north-east Scotland. *Journal of Zoology, London*, *161*: 75-123.

Flux, J.E.C., & Fullagar, P.J. 1992. World distribution of the rabbit *Oryctolagus cuniculus* on islands. *Mammal Review*, *22*: 151-205.

Foster-Turley, P., Macdonald, S., & Mason, C. 1990. *Otters - an action plan for their conservation*. International Union for Conservation of Nature and Natural Resources, Gland.

Fraser, C. 1988. Hopewell House farm study. *Imprint*, *11*: 2-11.

French, D.D., Corbett, L.K., & Easterbee, N. 1988. Morphological discriminants of Scottish wildcats (*Felis silvestris*), domestic cats (*F. catus*) and their hybrids. *Journal of Zoology, London*, *214*: 235-259.

Fullagar, P.J., Jewell, P.A., Lockley, R.M., & Rowlands, I.W. 1963. The Skomer vole (*Clethrionomys glareolus skomerensis*) and long-tailed field mouse (*Apodemus sylvaticus*) on Skomer Island, Pembrokeshire, in 1960. *Proceedings of the Zoological Society of London*, *140*: 295-314.

Gaisler, J. 1989. The *r-K* selection model and life-history strategies in bats. In: *European bat research 1987*, ed. by V. Hanák, I. Horácek & J. Gaisler, 117-124. Charles University Press, Prague.

Gaisler, J., Hanák, V., & Horácek, I. 1991. Remarks on the current status of bat populations in Czechoslovakia. *Myotis*, *18-19*: 68-75.

Gavier-Widén, D., & Mörner, T. 1991. Epidemiology and diagnosis of the European brown hare syndrome in

Scandinavian countries: a review. *Revue Scientifique et Technique-Office International des Epizooties, 10*: 453-458.

Geraci, J.R. 1990. Physiologic and toxic effects on cetaceans. In: *Sea mammals and oil: confronting the risks*, ed. by J.R. Geraci & D.J. St Aubin, 167-197. Academic Press, London.

Gibbons, D.W., Reid, J.B., & Chapman, R.A., eds. 1993. *The new atlas of breeding birds in Britain and Ireland: 1988-1991*. Poyser, London.

Gibbs, E.P.J., Herniman, K.A.J., Lawman, M.J.P., & Sellers, R.F. 1975. Foot-and-mouth disease in British deer: transmission of the virus to cattle, sheep and deer. *Veterinary Record, 96*: 558-563.

Gibson, J.A. 1973. The distribution of voles on the Clyde Islands. *Western Naturalist, 2*: 40-44.

Gill, R. 1990. *Monitoring the status of European and North American cervids*. Global, United Nations Environment Programme, Nairobi.

Gill, R.M.A. 1992. A review of damage by mammals in north temperate forests: 1. Deer. *Forestry, 68*: 145-169.

Gipps, J.H.W., & Alibhai, S.K. 1991. Field vole *Microtus agrestis*. In: *The handbook of British mammals*, ed. by G.B. Corbet & S. Harris, 203-208. Blackwell Scientific Publications, Oxford.

Gliksten, E.M. 1993. Fallow deer farming in Britain. In: *Proceedings of the first world forum on fallow deer farming, Mudgee, NSW, Australia*, ed. by G.W. Asher, 53-57. Australian Fallow Deer Society and New Zealand Fallow Deer Society.

Glue, D.E. 1974. Food of the barn owl in Britain and Ireland. *Bird Study, 21*: 200-210.

Glue, D.E. 1977. Feeding ecology of the short-eared owl in Britain and Ireland. *Bird Study, 24*: 70-78.

Glue, D.E., & Hammond, G.J. 1974. Feeding ecology of the long-eared owl in Britain and Ireland. *British Birds, 67*: 361-369.

Gorman, M.L. 1991. Orkney and Guernsey voles *Microtus arvalis*. In: *The handbook of British mammals*, ed. by G.B. Corbet & S. Harris, 208-211. Blackwell Scientific Publications, Oxford.

Gorman, M.L., & Reynolds, P. 1993. The impact of land-use change on voles and raptors. *Mammal Review, 23*: 121-126.

Gorman, M.L., & Zubaid, A.M.A. 1993. A comparative study of the ecology of woodmice *Apodemus sylvaticus* in two contrasting habitats: deciduous woodland and maritime sand dunes. *Journal of Zoology, London, 229*: 385-396.

Gosling, L.M., & Baker, S.J. 1989. The eradication of muskrats and coypus from Britain. *Biological Journal of the Linnean Society, 38*: 39-51.

Gosling, L.M., & Baker, S.J. 1991. Coypu *Myocastor coypus*. In: *The handbook of British mammals*, ed. by G.B. Corbet & S. Harris, 267-275. Blackwell Scientific Publications, Oxford.

Gosling, L.M., Watt, A.D., & Baker, S.J. 1981. Continuous retrospective census of the East Anglian coypu population between 1970 and 1979. *Journal of Animal Ecology, 50*: 885-901.

Government Statistical Service. 1988. *Agricultural statistics. United Kingdom 1986*. Her Majesty's Stationery Office, London.

Government Statistical Service. 1992. *The digest of agricultural census statistics. United Kingdom 1991*. Her Majesty's Stationery Office, London.

Green, J., & Green, R. 1980. *Otter survey of Scotland 1977-1979*. Vincent Wildlife Trust, London.

Green, J., & Green, R. 1987. *Otter survey of Scotland 1984-85*. Vincent Wildlife Trust, London.

Green, J., & Green, R. 1994. Mammals. In: *The freshwaters of Scotland: a national resource of international significance*, ed. by P.S. Maitland, P.J. Boon and D.S. McLusky, 251-259. Wiley, Chichester.

Green, J., Green, R., & Jefferies, D.J. 1984. A radio-tracking survey of otters *Lutra lutra* on a Perthshire river system. *Lutra, 27*: 85-145.

Green, R. 1979. The ecology of wood mice (*Apodemus sylvaticus*) on arable farmland. *Journal of Zoology, London, 188*: 357-377.

Greenaway, F., & Hill, J.E. 1987. A British record of the northern bat (*Eptesicus nilssonii*). *Bat News, 10*: 1-2.

Greig, J.C. 1969. *The ecology of feral goats in Scotland*. MSc Thesis, University of Edinburgh.

Greig-Smith, P.W. 1988. Wildlife hazards from the use, misuse and abuse of pesticides. *Aspects of Applied Biology, 17*: 247-256.

Griffiths, H.I. 1991. *On the hunting of badgers: an enquiry into the hunting and conservation of the Eurasian badger* Meles meles *(L.) in the western part of its range*. Piglet Press, Brynna.

Griffiths, H.I., & Kryštufek, M. 1993. Hunting pressures and badgers *Meles meles*: patterns and possible futures. *Lutra, 36*: 49-61.

Griffiths, H.I., & Thomas, D.H. 1993. The status of the badger *Meles meles* (L., 1758) (Carnivora, Mustelidae) in Europe. *Mammal Review, 23*: 17-58.

Griffiths, I.R., & Whitwell, K.E. 1993. Leporine dysautonomia: further evidence that hares suffer from grass sickness. *Veterinary Record, 132*: 376-377.

Gulland, F.M.D. 1991. *Nematodirus species* on St Kilda. *Veterinary Record, 128*: 576.

Gurnell, J. 1983. Squirrel numbers and the abundance of tree seeds. *Mammal Review, 13*: 133-148.

Gurnell, J. 1987. *The natural history of squirrels*. Croom Helm, Beckenham.

Gurnell, J. 1989. Demographic implications for the control of grey squirrels. In: *Mammals as pests*, ed. by R.J.

Putman, 131-143. Chapman & Hall, London.

Gurnell, J. 1991a. Red squirrel *Sciurus vulgaris*. In: *The handbook of British mammals*, ed. by G.B. Corbet & S. Harris, 177-186. Blackwell Scientific Publications, Oxford.

Gurnell, J. 1991b. Grey squirrel *Sciurus carolinensis*. In: *The handbook of British mammals*, ed. by G.B. Corbet & S. Harris, 186-191. Blackwell Scientific Publications, Oxford.

Gurnell, J., & Pepper, H. 1993. A critical look at conserving the British red squirrel *Sciurus vulgaris*. *Mammal Review, 23*: 127-137.

Haddow, J.F. 1992. Recorded distribution of bats in Scotland. In: *Scottish bats*, vol.1, ed. by J.F. Haddow & J.S. Herman, 49-52. South-east Scotland Bat Groups, Edinburgh.

Haddow, J., Herman, J., & Hewitt, S. 1989. *Myotis mystacinus* and *M. brandtii* in Scotland. *Batchat, 12*: 1-2.

Hall, A.J., Law, R.J., Wells, D.E., Harwood, J., Ross, H.M., Kennedy, S., Allchin, C.R., Campbell, L.A., & Pomeroy, P.P. 1992. Organochlorine levels in common seals (*Phoca vitulina*) which were victims and survivors of the 1988 phocine distemper epizootic. *Science of the Total Environment, 115*: 145-162.

Hall, A.J., Pomeroy, P.P., & Harwood, J. 1992. The descriptive epizootiology of phocine distemper in the UK during 1988/89. *Science of the Total Environment, 115*: 31-44.

Hall, S.J.G. 1991. Park cattle *Bos taurus*. In: *The handbook of British mammals*, ed. by G.B. Corbet & S. Harris, 538-541. Blackwell Scientific Publications, Oxford.

Hall, S.J.G., & Hall, J.G. 1988. Inbreeding and population dynamics of the Chillingham cattle (*Bos taurus*). *Journal of Zoology, London, 216*: 479-493.

Hall, S.J.G., & Moore, G.F. 1986. Feral cattle of Swona, Orkney Islands. *Mammal Review, 16*: 89-96.

Hansson, L. 1985. The food of bank voles, wood mice and yellow-necked mice. *Symposia of the Zoological Society of London, 55*: 141-168.

Harding, S.P. 1986. *Aspects of the ecology and social organisation of the muntjac deer* Muntiacus reevesi. DPhil Thesis, University of Oxford.

Hardy, E. 1933. The disappearing harvest-mouse. *Field, London, 162*: 45.

Hardy, P. 1975. *A lifetime of badgers.* Newton Abbot, David & Charles.

Harriman, R., & Morrison, B.R.S. 1982. Ecology of streams draining forested and non forested catchments in an area of central Scotland and subject to acid precipitation. *Hydrobiologia, 88*: 251-263.

Harrington, R. 1982. The hybridization of red deer (*Cervus elaphus* L. 1758) and Japanese sika deer (*Cervus nippon* Temminck 1838). *Transactions of the International Congress of Game Biologists, 14*: 559-571.

Harris, S. 1973/74. The history and distribution of squirrels in Essex. *Essex Naturalist, 33*: 64-78.

Harris, S. 1979a. History, distribution, status and habitat requirements of the harvest mouse (*Micromys minutus*) in Britain. *Mammal Review, 9*: 159-171.

Harris, S. 1979b. *The secret life of the harvest mouse*. Hamlyn, London.

Harris, S. 1979c. Breeding season, litter size and nestling mortality of the harvest mouse, *Micromys minutus* (Rodentia: Muridae), in Britain. *Journal of Zoology, London, 188*: 437-442.

Harris, S. 1981. An estimation of the number of foxes (*Vulpes vulpes*) in the city of Bristol, and some possible factors affecting their distribution. *Journal of Applied Ecology, 18*: 455-465.

Harris, S. 1993. The status of the badger (*Meles meles*) in Britain, with particular reference to East Anglia. *Transactions of the Suffolk Naturalists' Society, 29*: 104-112.

Harris, S., Cresswell, W., Reason, P., & Cresswell, P. 1992. An integrated approach to monitoring badger (*Meles meles*) population changes in Britain. In: *Wildlife 2001: populations*, ed. by D.R. McCullough & R.H. Barrett, 945-953. Elsevier Applied Science, London.

Harris, S., & Jefferies, D.J. 1991. Working within the law: guidelines for veterinary surgeons and wildlife rehabilitators on the rehabilitation of wild mammals. *British Veterinary Journal, 147*: 1-17.

Harris, S., & Lloyd, H.G. 1991. Fox *Vulpes vulpes*. In: *The handbook of British mammals*, ed. G.B. Corbet & S. Harris, 351-367. Blackwell Scientific Publications, Oxford.

Harris, S., & Rayner, J.M.V. 1986a. Urban fox (*Vulpes vulpes*) population estimates and habitat requirements in several British cities. *Journal of Animal Ecology, 55*: 575-591.

Harris, S., & Rayner, J.M.V. 1986b. Models for predicting urban fox (*Vulpes vulpes*) numbers in British cities and their application for rabies control. *Journal of Animal Ecology, 55*: 593-603.

Harris, S., & Rayner, J.M.V. 1986c. A discriminant analysis of the current distribution of urban foxes (*Vulpes vulpes*) in Britain. *Journal of Animal Ecology, 55*: 605-611.

Harris, S., & Saunders, G. 1993. The control of canid populations. *Symposia of the Zoological Society of London, 65*: 441-464.

Harris, S., & Smith, G.C. 1987a. The use of sociological data to explain the distribution and numbers of urban foxes (*Vulpes vulpes*) in England and Wales. *Symposia of the Zoological Society of London, 58*: 313-328.

Harris, S., & Smith, G.C. 1987b. Demography of two urban fox (*Vulpes vulpes*) populations. *Journal of Applied Ecology, 24*: 75-86.

Harris, S., & Trout, R.C. 1991. Harvest mouse *Micromys minutus*. In: *The handbook of British mammals*, ed. by G.B. Corbet & S. Harris, 233-239.

Blackwell Scientific Publications, Oxford.

Harris, S., & Woollard, T. 1990. The dispersal of mammals in agricultural habitats in Britain. In: *Species dispersal in agricultural habitats*, ed. by R.G.H. Bunce & D.C. Howard, 159-188. Belhaven Press, London.

Harting, J.E. 1887. On the bank vole, *Arvicola glareolus* (Schreber). *Zoologist*, third series, *11*: 361-371.

Harting, J.E. 1888. The whiskered bat, *Vespertilio mystacinus. Zoologist*, third series, *12*: 161-166.

Harting, J.E. 1889a. Natterer's bat, *Vespertilio nattereri. Zoologist*, third series, *13*: 241-248.

Harting, J.E. 1889b. Daubenton's bat, *Vespertilio daubentonii*, Leisler. *Zoologist*, third series, *13*: 161-166.

Harvie-Brown, J.A. 1881a. Early chapters in the history of the squirrel in Great Britain. Part II. - Mythological, heraldic and historical evidence in Scotland. *Proceedings of the Royal Physical Society of Edinburgh, 6*: 31-63.

Harvie-Brown, J.A. 1881b. Late chapters in the history of the squirrel in Great Britain. Part III. - Restoration, resuscitation, and dispersal of the species through Scotland. *Proceedings of the Royal Physical Society of Edinburgh, 6*: 115-182.

Harwood, J., Carter, S.D., Hughes, D.E., Bell, S.C., Baker, J.R., & Cornwell, H.J.C. 1989. Seal disease predictions. *Nature, London, 339*: 670.

Harwood, J., & Greenwood, J.J.D. 1985. Competition between British grey seals and fisheries. In: *Marine mammals and fisheries*, ed. by J.R. Beddington, R.J.H. Beverton & D.M. Lavigne, 153-169. George Allen & Unwin, London.

Harwood, J., & Grenfell, B. 1990. Long term risks of recurrent seal plagues. *Marine Pollution Bulletin, 21*: 284-287.

Harwood, J., & Hall, A. 1990. Mass mortality in marine mammals: its implications for population dynamics and genetics.

Trends in Ecology and Evolution, 5: 254-257.

Harwood, J., Hiby, L., Thompson, D., & Ward, A. 1991. Seal stocks in Great Britain - surveys conducted between 1986 and 1989. *NERC News, 16*: 11-15.

Harwood, J., & Prime, J.H. 1978. Some factors affecting the size of British grey seal populations. *Journal of Applied Ecology, 15*: 401-411.

Healing, T.D., Jewell, V.T., Jewell, P.A., Rowlands, I.W., & Gipps, J.H.W. 1983. Populations of the bank vole (*Clethrionomys glareolus*) and long-tailed field mouse (*Apodemus sylvaticus*) on Skomer Island, Dyfed. *Journal of Zoology, London, 199*: 447-460.

Heaver, S. 1987. The status of the lesser horseshoe bat (*Rhinolophus hipposideros*). *Bat News, 10*: 5-7.

Heide-Jørgensen, M.-P., Härkönen, T., & Ålberg, P. 1992. Long-term effects of epizootic in harbor seals in the Kattegat-Skagerrak and adjacent areas. *Ambio, 21*: 511-516.

Heide-Jørgensen, M.-P., Härkönen, T., Dietz, R., & Thompson, P.M. 1992. Retrospective of the 1988 European seal epizootic. *Diseases of Aquatic Organisms, 13*: 37-62.

Hellawell, T.C. 1992. *Aspects of the ecology and management of the feral goat (Capra hircus L.) populations of the Rhinogau and Maentwrog area, North Wales*. PhD Thesis, University of Wales, Cardiff.

Herman, J.S. 1992. The earliest record of Nathusius' pipistrelle from the British Isles. In: *Scottish bats*, vol.1, ed. by J.F. Haddow & J.S. Herman, 48. South-east Scotland Bat Groups, Edinburgh.

Hewson, R. 1951. Some observations on the Orkney vole *Microtus o. orcadensis* (Millais). *Northwestern Naturalist, 23*: 7-10.

Hewson, R. 1984a. Mountain hare, *Lepus timidus*, bags and moor management.

Journal of Zoology, London, 204: 563-565.

Hewson, R. 1984b. Changes in the numbers of foxes (*Vulpes vulpes*) in Scotland. *Journal of Zoology, London, 203:* 561-569.

Hewson, R. 1986. Distribution and density of fox breeding dens and the effects of management. *Journal of Applied Ecology, 23:* 531-538.

Hewson, R. 1990a. Behaviour, population changes, and dispersal of mountain hares (*Lepus timidus*) in Scotland. *Journal of Zoology, London, 220:* 287-309.

Hewson, R. 1990b. *Predation upon lambs by foxes in the absence of control.* League Against Cruel Sports, London.

Hewson, R. 1991. Mountain hare/Irish hare *Lepus timidus.* In: *The handbook of British mammals,* ed. by G.B. Corbet & S. Harris, 161-167. Blackwell Scientific Publications, Oxford.

Hewson, R., & Kolb, H.H. 1973. Changes in the numbers and distribution of foxes (*Vulpes vulpes*) killed in Scotland from 1948-1970. *Journal of Zoology, London, 171:* 345-365.

Hewson, R., & Taylor, M. 1975. Embryo counts and length of the breeding season in European hares in Scotland from 1960 - 1972. *Acta Theriologica, 20:* 247-254.

Hiby, L., Duck, C., & Thompson, D. 1993. Seal stocks in Great Britain: surveys conducted in 1991. *NERC news, 24:* 30-31.

Hingston, F. 1988. *Deer parks and deer of Great Britain.* Sporting and Leisure Press, Buckingham.

Hinton, M.A.C. 1920. *Rats and mice as enemies of mankind.* British Museum (Natural History), London.

Hirons, G. 1984. The diet of tawny owls (*Strix aluco*) and kestrels (*Falco tinnunculus*) in the New Forest, Hampshire. *Proceedings of the Hampshire Field Club and Archaeological Society, 40:* 21-26.

Holm, J.L. 1990. *The ecology of red squirrels* Sciurus vulgaris *in deciduous*

woodlands. PhD Thesis, University of London.

Hoodless, A., & Morris, P.A. 1993. An estimate of population density of the fat dormouse (*Glis glis*). *Journal of Zoology, London, 230:* 337-340.

Hooper, J.H.D. 1983. The study of horseshoe bats in Devon caves: a review of progress, 1947-1982. *Studies in Speleology, 4:* 59-70.

Hooper, J.H.D., & Hooper, W.M. 1956. Habits and movements of cave-dwelling bats in Devonshire. *Proceedings of the Zoological Society of London, 127:* 1-26.

Howes, C.A. 1979. A review of the food and mortality of water voles in Yorkshire. *Naturalist, 104:* 71-74.

Hubbard, A.L., McOrist, S., Jones, T.W., Boid, R., Scott, R., & Easterbee, N. 1992. Is survival of European wildcats *Felis silvestris* in Britain threatened by interbreeding with domestic cats? *Biological Conservation, 61:* 203-208.

Hudson, W.H. 1898. *Birds in London.* Longmans, Green & Co., London.

Hudson, P., & Cox, R. 1989. Mink problems in the Outer Hebrides: a pilot study. *Game Conservancy Review of 1988, 20:* 133-135.

Hurrell, E., & McIntosh, G. 1984. Mammal Society dormouse survey, January 1975 - April 1979. *Mammal Review, 14:* 1-18.

Hutson, A.M. 1993. *Action plan for the conservation of bats in the United Kingdom.* Bat Conservation Trust, London.

Insley, H. 1977. An estimate of the population density of the red fox (*Vulpes vulpes*) in the New Forest, Hampshire. *Journal of Zoology, London, 183:* 549-553.

Jefferies, D.J. 1969. Causes of badger mortality in eastern counties of England. *Journal of Zoology, London, 157:* 429-436.

Jefferies, D.J. 1972. Organochlorine insecticide residues in British bats and their significance. *Journal of Zoology, London, 166:* 245-263.

Jefferies, D.J. 1987. The effects of angling interests on otters with particular reference to disturbance. In: *Angling and wildlife in fresh waters*, ed. by P.S. Maitland and A.K. Turner, 23-30. Institute of Terrestrial Ecology, Grange-over-Sands.

Jefferies, D.J. 1989. The changing otter population of Britain 1700-1989. *Biological Journal of the Linnean Society, 38*: 61-69.

Jefferies, D.J. 1992. Polecats *Mustela putorius* and pollutants in Wales. *Lutra, 35*: 28-39.

Jefferies, D.J., Green, J., & Green, R. 1984. *Commercial fish and crustacean traps: a serious cause of otter* Lutra lutra *(L.) mortality in Britain and Europe*. Vincent Wildlife Trust, London.

Jefferies, D.J., & Hanson, H.M. 1987. The Minsmere otter release and information gained from a detailed examination and analysis of the two casualties. *Otters, Journal of the Otter Trust, 2*: 19-29.

Jefferies, D.J., & Mitchell-Jones, A.J. 1993. Recovery plans for British mammals of conservation importance, their design and value. *Mammal Review, 23*: 155-166.

Jefferies, D.J., Morris, P.A., & Mulleneux, J.E. 1989. An enquiry into the changing status of the water vole *Arvicola terrestris* in Britain. *Mammal Review, 19*: 111-131.

Jefferies, D.J., & Pendlebury, J.B. 1968. Population fluctuations of stoats, weasels and hedgehogs in recent years. *Journal of Zoology, London, 156*: 513-517.

Jefferies, D.J., Stainsby, B., & French, M.C. 1973. The ecology of small mammals in arable fields drilled with winter wheat and the increase in their dieldrin and mercury residues. *Journal of Zoology, London, 171*: 513-539.

Jefferies, D.J., Wayre, P., Jessop, R.M., & Mitchell-Jones, A.J. 1986. Reinforcing the native otter *Lutra lutra* population in East Anglia: an analysis of the behaviour and range development of the first release group. *Mammal Review, 16*: 65-79.

Jenkins, D. 1962. The present status of the wildcat (*Felis silvestris*) in Scotland. *Scottish Naturalist, 70*: 126-138.

Jensen, S., Kihlstrom, J.E., Olsson, M., Lundberg, C., & Orberg, J. 1977. Effects of PCB and DDT on mink (*Mustela vison*) during the reproductive season. *Ambio, 6*: 239.

Jessop, R.M. 1992 The re-introduction of the European otter *Lutra lutra* into lowland England carried out by the Otter Trust 1983-92: a progress report. In: *Proceedings of the National Otter Conference Cambridge, September 1992*, ed. by P.A. Morris, 12-16. Mammal Society, Bristol.

Jewell, P.A., Milner, C., & Boyd, J.M. 1974. *Island survivors: the ecology of the Soay sheep of St Kilda*. Athlone Press, London.

Johnson, I.P., Flowerdew, J.R., & Hare, R. 1991. Effects of broadcasting and of drilling methiocarb molluscicide pellets on field populations of wood mice, *Apodemus sylvaticus*. *Bulletin of Environmental Contamination and Toxicology, 46*: 84-91.

Johnson, T.H. 1984. *Habitat and social organisation of roe deer* (Capreolus capreolus). PhD Thesis, University of Southampton.

Johnston, S.D. 1974. Wild mink in Northumberland. *Transactions of the Natural History Society of Northumberland, Durham and Newcastle-upon-Tyne, 41*: 165-178.

Jones, G., & van Parijs, S.M. 1993. Bimodal echolocation in pipistrelle bats: are cryptic species present? *Proceedings of the Royal Society of London, series B, 251*: 119-125.

Jones-Walters, L.M., & Corbet, G.B. 1991. Fat dormouse *Glis glis*. In: *The handbook of British mammals*, ed. by G.B. Corbet & S. Harris, 264-267. Blackwell Scientific Publications, Oxford.

Kelsall, J.E. 1887. The distribution in Great Britain of the lesser horse-shoe bat. *Zoologist, third series, 11*: 89-93.

Kenward, R.E., & Holm, J.L. 1989. What future for British red squirrels? *Biological Journal of the Linnean Society, 38*: 83-89.

Kenward, R.E., & Holm, J.L. 1993. On the replacement of the red squirrel in Britain: a phytotoxic explanation. *Proceedings of the Royal Society of London, series B, 251*: 187-194.

Kenward, R.E., & Parish, T. 1986. Bark-stripping by grey squirrels (*Sciurus carolinensis*). *Journal of Zoology, London, 210A*: 473-481.

Kenward, R.E., & Tonkin, J.M. 1986. Red and grey squirrels: some behavioural and biometric differences. *Journal of Zoology, London, 209A*: 279-281.

Keymer, I.F., Wells, G.A.H., Mason, C.F., & Macdonald, S.M. 1988. Pathological changes and organochlorine residues in tissues of wild otters (*Lutra lutra*). *Veterinary Record, 122*: 153-155.

King, C. 1989. *The natural history of weasels and stoats.* Christopher Helm, London.

King, C.M. 1991a. Stoat *Mustela erminea.* In: *The handbook of British mammals*, ed. by G.B. Corbet & S. Harris, 377-387. Blackwell Scientific Publications, Oxford.

King, C.M. 1991b. Weasel *Mustela nivalis.* In: *The handbook of British mammals*, ed. by G.B. Corbet & S. Harris, 387-396. Blackwell Scientific Publications, Oxford.

Kitchener, A. 1992. The Scottish wildcat *Felis silvestris*: decline and recovery. In: *Cats*, ed. by P. Mansard), 21-41. Ridgeway Trust for Endangered Cats, Hastings.

Kolb, H.H. 1991a. Use of burrows and movements by wild rabbits (*Oryctolagus cuniculus*) on an area of sand dunes. *Journal of Applied Ecology, 28*: 879-891.

Kolb, H.H. 1991b. Use of burrows and movements of wild rabbits (*Oryctolagus cuniculus*) in an area of hill grazing and forestry. *Journal of Applied Ecology, 28*: 892-905.

Kolb, H.H. 1994. Rabbit *Oryctolagus cuniculus* populations in Scotland since the introduction of myxomatosis. *Mammal Review, 24*: 41-48.

Kolb, H.H., & Hewson, R. 1980. A study of fox populations in Scotland from 1971 to 1976. *Journal of Applied Ecology, 17*: 7-19.

Kristiansson, H. 1990. Population variables and causes of mortality in a hedgehog (*Erinaceous* [sic] *europaeus*) population in southern Sweden. *Journal of Zoology, London, 220*: 391-404.

Kruuk, H. 1978. Spatial organization and territorial behaviour of the European badger *Meles meles. Journal of Zoology, London, 184*: 1-19.

Kruuk, H., & Conroy, J.W.H. 1991. Mortality of otters (*Lutra lutra*) in Shetland. *Journal of Applied Ecology, 28*: 83-94.

Kruuk, H., Carss, D.N., Conroy, J.W.H., & Durbin, L. 1993. Otter (*Lutra lutra* L.) numbers and fish productivity in rivers in north-east Scotland. *Symposia of the Zoological Society of London, 65*: 171-191.

Kruuk, H., Moorhouse, A., Conroy, J.W.H., Durbin, L., & Frears, S. 1989. An estimate of numbers and habitat preferences of otters (*Lutra lutra*) in Shetland, UK. *Biological Conservation, 49*: 241-254.

Kruuk, H.H., & Parish, T. 1987. Changes in the size of groups and ranges of the European badger (*Meles meles* L.) in an area of Scotland. *Journal of Animal Ecology, 56*: 351-364.

Langbein, J., & Putman, R.J. 1992. *Conservation and management of deer on Exmoor and the Quantocks.* Unpublished report, The National Trust.

Langley, P.J.W., & Yalden, D.W. 1977. The decline of the rarer carnivores in Great Britain during the nineteenth century. *Mammal Review, 7*: 95-116.

Larkin, P.A. 1948. *Ecology of mole* Talpa europaea *L. populations*. DPhil Thesis, University of Oxford.

Laver, H. 1898. *The mammals, reptiles and fishes of Essex*. Essex Field Club, Buckhurst Hill.

Law, R.J., Allchin, C.R., & Harwood, J. 1989. Concentrations of organochlorine compounds in the blubbers of seals from eastern and north-eastern England. *Marine Pollution Bulletin, 20*: 110-115.

Law, R.J., Fileman, C.F., Hopkins, A.D., Baker, J.R., Harwood, J., Jackson, D.B., Kennedy, S., Martin, A.R., & Morris, R.J. 1991. Concentrations of trace metals in the livers of marine mammals (seals, porpoises and dolphins) from waters around the British Isles. *Marine Pollution Bulletin, 22*: 183-191.

Lawton, J.H., & Woodroffe, G.L. 1991. Habitat and the distribution of water voles: why are there gaps in a species' range? *Journal of Animal Ecology, 60*: 79-91.

Lazenby, S., Johnson, S., & Whiteley, D. 1986. Small mammals in Limb Valley - progress report 1984 and 1985. *Sorby Record, 24*: 49-52.

Lenton, E.J., Chanin, P.R.F., & Jefferies, D.J. 1980. *Otter survey of England 1977-79*. Nature Conservancy Council, London.

Lever, C. 1977. *The naturalized animals of the British Isles*. Hutchinson, London.

Lilford, Lord. 1887. A few words on European bats. *Zoologist, third series, 11*: 61-67.

Limpens, H.J.G.A., Helmer, W., van Winden, A., & Mostert, K. 1989. Vleermuizen (Chiroptera) en lintvormige landschapselementen - een overzicht van de huidige kennis van het belang van lintvormige landschapselementen voor vleermuizen. *Lutra, 32*: 1-20.

Linder, G., & Richmond, M.E. 1990. Feed aversion in small mammals as a potential source of hazard reduction for environmental chemicals: agrichemical case studies.

Environmental Toxicology and Chemistry, 9: 95-105.

Linn, I., & Scott, H. 1980. Food of the barn owl *Tyto alba* in Devon and Jersey. *Nature in Devon, 1*: 28-46.

Linn, I., & Stevenson, J.H.F. 1980. Feral mink in Devon. *Nature in Devon, 1*: 7-27.

Lloyd, E.R. 1975. *The wild red deer of Exmoor*. Exmoor Press, Dulverton.

Lloyd, H.G. 1970. Post-myxomatosis rabbit populations in England and Wales. *European Plant Protection Organisation Public series A, 58*: 197-215.

Lloyd, H.G. 1980. *The red fox*. Batsford, London.

Lloyd, H.G. 1983. Past and present distributions of red and grey squirrels. *Mammal Review, 13*: 69-80.

Lockie, J.D. 1956. After myxomatosis - notes on the food of some predatory animals in Scotland. *Scottish Agriculture, 36*: 65-69.

Lockie, J.D. 1964. Distribution and fluctuations of the pine marten, *Martes martes* (L.), in Scotland. *Journal of Animal Ecology, 33*: 349-356.

Lockie, J.D. 1966. Territory in small carnivores. *Symposia of the Zoological Society of London, 18*: 143-165.

Lockley, R.M. 1966. *Grey seal, common seal*. André Deutsch, London.

Lord, J.C. 1961. Some further results of trapping for small mammals at Bookham Common. *London Naturalist, 40*: 73-80.

Loudon, A. 1982. Too many deer for the trees? *New Scientist, 93*: 708-711.

Lowe, V.P.W. 1993. The spread of the grey squirrel (*Sciurus carolinensis*) into Cumbria since 1960 and its present distribution. *Journal of Zoology, London, 231*: 663-667.

Lowe, V.P.W., & Gardiner, A.S. 1974. A re-examination of the subspecies of red deer (*Cervus elaphus*) with particular reference to the stocks in Britain. *Journal of Zoology, London, 174*: 185-201.

Lowe, V.P.W., & Gardiner, A.S. 1975. Hybridization between red deer (*Cervus elaphus*) and sika deer (*Cervus nippon*) with particular reference to the stocks in N.W. England. *Journal of Zoology, London, 177*: 553-566.

Lowe, V.P.W., & Gardiner, A.S. 1983. Is the British squirrel (*Sciurus vulgaris leucourus* Kerr) British? *Mammal Review, 13*: 57-67.

Lundberg, K. 1989. *Social organisation and survival of the pipistrelle bat* Pipistrellus pipistrellus *and a comparison of advertisement behaviour in three polygynous bat species*. PhD Thesis, University of Lund.

Macdonald, D.W. 1991. Feral cat *Felis catus*. In: *The handbook of British mammals*, ed. by G.B. Corbet & S. Harris, 437-440. Blackwell Scientific Publications, Oxford.

Macdonald, D.W., & Apps, P.J. 1978. The social behaviour of a group of semi-dependent farm cats, *Felis catus*: a progress report. *Carnivore Genetics Newsletter, 3*: 256-268.

Macdonald, D.W., Apps, P.J., Carr, G.M., & Kerby, G. 1987. Social dynamics, nursing coalitions, and infanticide among farm cats, *Felis catus*. *Advances in Ethology, 28*: 1-66.

Macdonald, D.W., Bunce, R.G.H., & Bacon, P.J. 1981. Fox populations, habitat characterization and rabies control. *Journal of Biogeography, 8*: 145-151.

MacDonald, I.C. 1989. *Social organisation and behaviour of free-living European rabbits* Oryctolagus cuniculus *L*. PhD Thesis, University of Newcastle-upon-Tyne.

Macdonald, S., & Mason, C.F. 1976. The status of the otter (*Lutra lutra* L.) in Norfolk. *Biological Conservation, 9*: 119-124.

Macdonald, S.M., & Mason, C.F. 1983. Some factors influencing the distribution of otters (*Lutra lutra*). *Mammal Review, 13*: 1-10.

MacGillivray, A. 1994. *Environmental measures: indicators for the UK environment*. Environment Challenge Group, London.

Maisels, F. 1988. *The feeding ecology of the Cyprus mouflon*, Ovis orientalis Gmelina, *1774, in the Paphos Forest, Cyprus*. PhD Thesis, University of Edinburgh.

Malcolm, S., Piatkowski, A., Morgan, D., Little, D., Turner, K., & Crabtree, K. 1984. *Exmoor red deer survey, 1981-1982: a comparison of lowland and upland habitats*. Devon Trust for Nature Conservation, Exeter.

Mallorie, H.C., & Flowerdew, J.R. 1994. Woodland small mammal population ecology in Britain: a preliminary review of the Mammal Society survey of wood mice *Apodemus sylvaticus* and bank voles *Clethrionomys glareolus*, 1982-1987. *Mammal Review, 24*: 1-15.

Mann, J.C.E. 1983. *The social organisation and ecology of the Japanese sika deer* Cervus nippon *in southern England*. PhD Thesis, University of Southampton.

Marchant, J.H., Hudson, R., Carter, S.P., & Whittington, P. 1990. *Population trends in British breeding birds*. British Trust for Ornithology, Tring.

Mason, C.F. 1989. Water pollution and otter distribution: a review. *Lutra, 32*: 97-131.

Mason, C.F. 1991. Acidification of freshwaters - a problem for otters? In: *Proceedings of the V. International Otter Colloquium*, ed. by C. Reuther & R. Röchert, 235-236. Gruppe Naturschutz GmbH, Hankensbüttel.

Mason, C.F. 1992. Do otter releases make sense? The experience in Britain. In: *Otterschutz in Deutschland*, ed. by C. Reuther, 157-161. Gruppe Naturschutz GmbH, Hankensbüttel.

Mason, C.F. 1993. Regional trends in PCB and pesticide contamination in northern Britain as determined in otter (*Lutra lutra*) scats. *Chemosphere, 26*: 941-944.

Mason, C.F., & Macdonald, S.M. 1986. *Otters - ecology and conservation*. Cambridge University Press, Cambridge.

Mason, C.F., & Macdonald, S.M. 1989. Acidification and otter (*Lutra lutra*) distribution in Scotland. *Water, Air and Soil Pollution, 43*: 365-374.

Mason, C.F., & Macdonald, S.M. 1992. Pollution and otter conservation in a European context. In: *Proceedings of the National Otter Conference, Cambridge, September 1992*, ed. by P.A. Morris, 17-20. Mammal Society, Bristol.

Mason, C.F., & Macdonald, S.M. 1993a. Impact of organochlorine pesticide residues and PCBs on otters (*Lutra lutra*): a study from western Britain. *Science of the Total Environment, 138*: 127-145.

Mason, C.F., & Macdonald, S.M. 1993b. *PCB and organochlorine pesticide residues in otter spraints: their significance for regional otter conservation strategies*. Unpublished report, World Wide Fund for Nature U.K.

Mason, C.F., & Macdonald, S.M. 1993c. Impact of organochlorine pesticide residues and PCBs on otters (*Lutra lutra*) in eastern England. *Science of the Total Environment, 138*: 147-160.

Mason, C.F., & Macdonald, S.M. 1993d. PCBs and organochlorine pesticide residues in otter (*Lutra lutra*) spraints from Welsh catchments and their significance to otter conservation strategies. *Aquatic Conservation: Marine and Freshwater Ecosystems, 3*: 43-51.

Mason, C.F., & Madsen, A.B. 1990. Mortality and condition in otters *Lutra lutra* from Denmark and Great Britain. *Natura Jutlandica, 22*: 217-220.

Matheson, C. 1944. The domestic cat as a factor in urban ecology. *Journal of Animal Ecology, 13*: 130-133.

Matheson, C. 1962. *Brown rats*. Sunday Times, London.

Mayle, B.A. 1990. A biological basis for bat conservation in British woodlands - a review. *Mammal Review, 20*: 159-195.

McOrist, S., & Kitchener, A.C. 1994. Current threats to the European wildcat, *Felis silvestris*, in Scotland. *Ambio, 23*: 243-245.

McOrist, S., Boid, R., Jones, T.W., Easterbee, N., Hubbard, A.L., & Jarrett, O. 1991. Some viral and protozoal diseases of the European wildcat (*Felis silvestris*). *Journal of Wildlife Diseases, 27*: 693-696.

Meyer, A.N., & Drummond, D.C. 1980. Improving rodent control strategies in Lambeth. *Environmental Health, 88*: 77-81.

Mickleburgh, S. 1988. Bat records from the London area during 1987. *London Naturalist, 67*: 161-170.

Middleton, A.D. 1931. *The grey squirrel*. Sidgwick & Jackson, London.

Millais, J.G. 1904a. On the first occurrence of the noctule in Scotland. *Zoologist, fourth series, 8*: 425.

Millais, J.G. 1904b. On a new British vole from the Orkney islands. *Zoologist, fourth series, 8*: 241-246.

Millais, J.G. 1904-1906. *The mammals of Great Britain and Ireland*. Longmans, Green & Co., London.

Milner, C., & Ball, D.F. 1970. Factors affecting the distribution of the mole (*Talpa europaea*) in Snowdonia (North Wales). *Journal of Zoology, London, 162*: 61-69.

Ministry of Agriculture and Fisheries. 1932. *Rats and how to exterminate them*. His Majesty's Stationery Office, London.

Mitchell-Jones, A.J., Cooke, A.S., Boyd, I.L., & Stebbings, R.E. 1989. Bats and remedial timber treatment chemicals - a review. *Mammal Review, 19*: 93-110.

Mitchell-Jones, A.J., Hutson, A.M., & Racey, P.A. 1993. The growth and development of bat conservation in Britain. *Mammal Review, 23*: 139-148.

Mitchell-Jones, A.J., Jefferies, D.J., Stebbings, R.E., & Arnold, H.R. 1986. Public concern about bats (Chiroptera) in

Britain: an analysis of enquiries in 1982-83. *Biological Conservation, 36*: 315-328.

Moller, H. 1986. Red squirrels (*Sciurus vulgaris*) feeding in a Scots pine plantation in Scotland. *Journal of Zoology, London, 209A*: 61-83.

Montgomery, W.I. 1978. Studies on the distributions of *Apodemus sylvaticus* (L.) and *A. flavicollis* (Melchior) in Britain. *Mammal Review, 8*: 177-184.

Montgomery, W.I. 1980. Population structure and dynamics of sympatric *Apodemus* species (Rodentia: Muridae). *Journal of Zoology, London, 192*: 351-377.

Montgomery, W.I. 1985. Interspecific competition and the comparative ecology of two congeneric species of mice. In: *Case studies in population biology*, ed. by L.M. Cook, 126-187. Manchester University Press, Manchester.

Montgomery, W.I. 1989. Population regulation in the wood mouse, *Apodemus sylvaticus*. I. Density dependence in the annual cycle of abundance. *Journal of Animal Ecology, 58*: 465-475.

Montgomery, W.I. 1991. Yellow-necked mouse *Apodemus flavicollis*. In: *The handbook of British mammals*, ed. by G.B. Corbet & S. Harris, 229-233. Blackwell Scientific Publications, Oxford.

Montgomery, W.I., & Dowie, M. 1993. The distribution of the wood mouse *Apodemus sylvaticus* and the house mouse *Mus domesticus* on farmland in north-east Ireland. *Irish Naturalists Journal, 24*: 199-203.

Moors, P.J. 1974. *The annual energy budget of a weasel* Mustela nivalis *population in farmland*. PhD Thesis, University of Aberdeen.

Morgan, I.K. 1992-1993. Interim notes on the status of the pine marten in south and mid Wales. *Llanelli Naturalists Newsletter, winter 1992-93*. 11-22.

Morris, P. 1970. The study of small mammal remains from discarded bottles. *School Natural Science Society Publications, 41*: 1-8.

Morris, P.A. 1984. An estimate of the minimum body weight necessary for hedgehogs (*Erinaceus europaeus*) to survive hibernation. *Journal of Zoology, London, 203*: 291-294.

Morris, P.A. 1988. A study of home range and movements in the hedgehog (*Erinaceus europaeus*). *Journal of Zoology, London, 214*: 433-449.

Morris, P.A. 1991. Hedgehog *Erinaceus europaeus*. In: *The handbook of British mammals*, ed. by G.B. Corbet & S. Harris, 37-43. Blackwell Scientific Publications, Oxford.

Morris, P.A. 1993a. British mammals - their status, research needs and likely future. *Mammal Review, 23*: 167-176.

Morris, P.A. 1993b. *A red data book for British mammals*. Mammal Society, London.

Morris, P.A., Munn, S., & Craig-Wood, S. 1993. The effects of releasing captive hedgehogs (*Erinaceus europaeus*) into the wild. *Field Studies, 8*: 89-99.

Mulder, J.L. 1990. The stoat *Mustela erminea* in the Dutch dune region, its local extinction, and a possible cause: the arrival of the fox *Vulpes vulpes*. *Lutra, 33*: 1-21.

Nadachowski, A. 1989. Origin and history of the present rodent fauna in Poland based on fossil evidence. *Acta Theriologica, 34*: 37-53.

National Rivers Authority. 1991. *The quality of rivers, canals and estuaries in England and Wales: report of the 1990 survey*. National Rivers Authority, Bristol.

Natural Environment Research Council. 1982. Seal stocks in Great Britain: surveys conducted in 1981. *NERC Newsjournal, 3*(1), 8-10.

Nature Conservancy. 1963. *Grey seals and fisheries - report of the consultative committee on grey seals and fisheries*. Her Majesty's Stationery Office, London.

Nature Conservancy Council. 1983. *The ecology and conservation of amphibian and reptile species endangered in Britain.* Nature Conservancy Council, London.

Nature Conservancy Council. 1986. *Nature conservation and afforestation in Britain.* Nature Conservancy Council, Peterborough.

Nau, B.S. 1992. Chinese water deer in Bedfordshire. *Bedfordshire Naturalist, 46*: 17-27.

Neville, P.F. 1989. Feral cats: management of urban populations and pest problems by neutering. In: *Mammals as pests,* ed. by R.J. Putman, 261-267. Chapman & Hall, London.

Niethammer, J., & Krapp, F., eds. 1978-1990. *Handbuch der Saügethiere Europas.* Akademische Verlagsgesellschaft, Wiesbaden.

Norris, J.D. 1967. A campaign against feral coypus (*Myocastor coypus* Molina) in Great Britain. *Journal of Applied Ecology, 4*: 191-199.

Novotny, J., & Pankova, M. 1981. *The Orbis pocket encyclopaedia of the world.* Orbis, London.

O'Connor, R.J., & Shrubb, M. 1986. *Farming and birds.* Cambridge University Press, Cambridge.

Office of Population Censuses and Surveys. 1984. *Census 1981 key statistics for urban areas Great Britain.* Her Majesty's Stationery Office, London.

Okubo, A., Maini, P.K., Williamson, M.H., & Murray, J.D. 1989. On the spatial spread of the grey squirrel in Britain. *Proceedings of the Royal Society of London, series B, 238*: 113-125.

Olney, N.J., & Garthwaite, D.G. 1990. *Pesticide usage survey report 95: rodenticide usage in England on farms growing arable crops 1990.* Unpublished report, Ministry of Agriculture, Fisheries and Food.

Olsson, M., Karlson, B., & Ahnland, E. 1992. Seals and seal protection: a presentation of a Swedish research project. *Ambio, 21*: 494-496.

Paget, R.J., & Patchett, P.N. 1978. National badger survey: report for south and west Yorkshire. *Naturalist, Leeds, 946*: 103-104.

Pemberton, J.M., & Smith, R.H. 1985. Lack of biochemical polymorphism in British fallow deer. *Heredity, 55*: 199-207.

Pernetta, J.C. 1973. The ecology of *Crocidura suaveolens cassiteridum* (Hinton) in a coastal habitat. *Mammalia, 37*: 241-256.

Pernetta, J.C. 1977. Population ecology of British shrews in grassland. *Acta Theriologica, 22*: 279-296.

Phillips, W.W.A., & Blackmore, M. 1970. Mouse-eared bats *Myotis myotis* in Sussex. *Journal of Zoology, London, 162*: 520-521.

Pickvance, T.J., & Chard, J.S.R. 1960. Midland mammals survey 1. Feral muntjac deer (*Muntiacus* spp.) in the West Midlands, with special reference to Warwickshire. *Proceedings of the Birmingham Natural History and Philosophical Society, 19*: 1-8.

Plant, C.W. 1979. The status of the hedgehog *Erinaceus europaeus* in the London boroughs of Barking, Newham, Redbridge and Waltham Forest. *London Naturalist, 58*: 27-37.

Pocock, R.I. 1932. Ferrets and polecats. *Scottish Naturalist, 196*: 97-108.

Pollard, E., & Relton, J. 1970. Hedges. V. A study of small mammals in hedges and cultivated fields. *Journal of Applied Ecology, 7*: 549-557.

Pucek, Z. ed. 1981. *Keys to vertebrates of Poland: mammals.* PWN, Warsaw.

Putman, R.J. 1986. *Grazing in temperate ecosystems - large herbivores and the ecology of the New Forest.* Croom Helm, London.

Putman, R.J., & Hunt, E.J. 1993. Hybridisation between red and sika deer in Britain. *Deer, 9*: 104-110.

Quy, R.J., Cowan, D.P., & Swinney, T. 1993. Tracking as an activity index to measure gross changes in Norway rat populations. *Wildlife Society Bulletin, 21*: 122-127.

Racey, P.A. 1991. Particoloured bat *Vespertilio murinus*. In: *The handbook* of British mammals, ed. by G.B. Corbet & S. Harris, 111-112. Blackwell Scientific Publications, Oxford.

Racey, P.A., & Swift, S.M. 1986. The residual effects of remedial timber treatments on bats. *Biological Conservation, 35*: 205-214.

Rae, B.B. 1960. *Seals and Scottish fisheries.* Her Majesty's Stationery Office, Edinburgh.

Ransome, R.D. 1989. Population changes of greater horseshoe bats studied near Bristol over the past twenty-six years. *Biological Journal of the Linnean Society of London, 38*: 71-82.

Ransome, R.D. 1991a. Greater horseshoe bat *Rhinolophus ferrumequinum*. In: *The handbook of British mammals,* ed. by G.B. Corbet & S. Harris, 88-94. Blackwell Scientific Publications, Oxford.

Ransome, R.D. 1991b. Lesser horseshoe bat *Rhinolophus hipposideros*. In: *The handbook of British mammals*, ed. by G.B. Corbet & S. Harris, 95-97. Blackwell Scientific Publications, Oxford.

Ratcliffe, P.R. 1984. Population dynamics of red deer (*Cervus elaphus* L.) in Scottish commercial forests. *Proceedings of the Royal Society of Edinburgh, 82B*: 291-302.

Ratcliffe, P.R. 1987. Distribution and current status of sika deer, *Cervus nippon*, in Great Britain. *Mammal Review, 17*: 39-58.

Ratcliffe, P.R., Peace, A.J., Hewison, A.J.M., Hunt, E.J., & Chadwick, A.H. 1991. The origins and characterization of Japanese sika deer populations in Great Britain. In: *Wildlife conservation - present trends and perspectives for the 21st century*, ed. by N. Maruyama, B. Bobek, Y. Ono, W. Regelin, L. Bartos & P.R. Ratcliffe, 185-190. Tsukuba & Yokohama, Tokyo.

Reason, P., Harris, S., & Cresswell, P. 1993. Estimating the impact of past persecution and habitat changes on the numbers of badgers *Meles meles* in Britain. *Mammal Review, 23*: 1-15.

Rees, P. 1981. The ecological distribution of feral cats and the effects of neutering a hospital colony. In: *The ecology and control of feral cats*, 12-22. Universities Federation for Animal Welfare, Potters Bar.

Reeve, N.J. 1982. The home range of the hedgehog as revealed by a radio tracking study. *Symposia of the Zoological Society of London, 49*: 207-230.

Reeve, N. 1994. *Hedgehogs.* Poyser, London.

Reichholf, J. 1983. Nehmen die Strassenverkehrsverluste Einfluss auf die Bestandsentwicklung des Igels (*Erinaceus europaeus*)? *Spixiana, 6*: 87-91.

Reijnders, P.J.H. 1986. Reproductive failure in common seals feeding on fish from polluted coastal waters. *Nature, London, 324*: 456-457.

Reijnders, P.J.H., & Lankester, K. 1990. Status of marine mammals in the North Sea. *Netherlands Journal of Sea Research, 26*: 427-435.

Rennison, B.O., & Drummond, D.C. 1984. Monitoring and improving rodent control progress in non-agricultural premises in England and Wales. *Environmental Health, 92*: 287-297.

Rennison, B.D., & Shenker, A.M. 1976. Rodent infestation in some London boroughs in 1972. *Environmental Health, 84*: 9-10, 12-13.

Reynolds, J.C. 1981. *The interaction of red and grey squirrels.* PhD Thesis, University of East Anglia.

Reynolds, J.C. 1985. Details of the geographic replacement of the red squirrel (*Sciurus vulgaris*) by the grey squirrel (*Sciurus carolinensis*) in eastern England. *Journal of Animal Ecology, 54*: 149-162.

Reynolds, J., & Tapper, S. 1994. Are foxes on the increase? *Game Conservancy Review of 1993, 25*: 94-96.

Rice-Oxley, S.B. 1993. Caching behaviour of red squirrels *Sciurus vulgaris* under conditions of high food availability. *Mammal Review, 23*: 93-100.

Richards, C.G.J. 1985. The population dynamics of *Microtis agrestis* in Wytham, 1949 to 1978. *Acta Zoologica Fennica, 173*: 35-38.

Richards, C.G.J. 1989. The pest status of rodents in the United Kingdom. In: *Mammals as pests*, ed. by R.J. Putman, 21-33. Chapman & Hall, London.

Ritchie, J. 1920. *The influence of man on animal life in Scotland: a study in faunal evolution*. Cambridge University Press, Cambridge.

Roberts, J.L., & Bowman, N. 1986. Diet and ecology of short-eared owls *Asio flammeus* breeding on heather moor. *Bird Study, 33*: 12-17.

Rope, G.T. 1885. On the range of the dormouse in England and Wales. *Zoologist*, third series, *9*: 201-213.

Ross, J. 1982. Myxomatosis: the natural evolution of the disease. *Symposia of the Zoological Society of London, 50*: 77-95.

Ross, J., & Sanders, M.F. 1984. The development of genetic resistance to myxomatosis in wild rabbits in Britain. *Journal of Hygiene, Cambridge, 92*: 255-261.

Rothschild, M. 1963. A rise in the flea-index on the hare (*Lepus europaeus* Pallas) with relevant notes on the fox (*Vulpes vulpes* (L.)), and wood-pigeon (*Columba palumbus* L.) at Ashton, Peterborough. *Proceedings of the Zoological Society of London, 140*: 341-346.

Rowe, F.P., Swinney, T., & Quy, R.J. 1983. Reproduction of the house mouse (*Mus musculus*) in farm buildings. *Journal of Zoology, London, 199*: 259-269.

Rowe, F.P., & Taylor, E.J. 1964. The numbers of harvest-mice (*Micromys minutus*) in corn-ricks. *Proceedings of the Zoological Society of London, 142*: 181-185.

Rowe, F.P., Taylor, E.J., & Chudley, A.H.J. 1963. The numbers and movements of house mice (*Mus musculus* L.) in the vicinity of four corn-ricks. *Journal of Animal Ecology, 32*: 87-97.

Saint Girons, M-C. 1973. *Les mammifères de France et du Benelux*. Doin, Paris.

Scott, H. 1985. *Otters on the Somerset Levels and Moors 1983-84: summary of report*. Vincent Wildlife Trust, London.

Scottish Development Department. 1990. *The Scottish environment - statistics*. Scottish Office, Edinburgh.

Shaw, G., & Livingstone, J. 1992. The pine marten - its reintroduction and subsequent history in the Galloway Forest Park. *Transactions of the Dumfries and Galloway Natural History and Antiquarian Society*, third series, *67*, 1-7.

Shawyer, C.R. 1987. *The barn owl in the British Isles - its past, present and future*. The Hawk Trust, London.

Shedden, C.B. 1993. Roe deer in Scotland. *Shooting & Conservation, Spring 1993*: 43-44.

Shillito, J.F. 1960. *The general ecology of the common shrew* Sorex araneus L. PhD Thesis, University of Exeter.

Shillito, J.F. 1963a. Observations on the range and movements of a woodland population of the common shrew *Sorex araneus* L. *Proceedings of the Zoological Society of London, 140*: 533-546.

Shillito, J.F. 1963b. Field observations on the water shrew (*Neomys fodiens*). *Proceedings of the Zoological Society of London, 140*: 320-322.

Shore, R.F. 1988. *Effects of variation in environmental calcium availability on wild rodent populations*. PhD Thesis, University of Manchester.

Shore, R.F., & Mackenzie, S. 1993. The effects of catchment liming on shrews *Sorex* spp. *Biological Conservation, 64*: 101-111.

Shorten, M. 1954. *Squirrels*. Collins, London.

Shorten, M. 1962. *Squirrels, their biology and control*. Her Majesty's Stationery Office, London.

Shorten, M., & Courtier, F.A. 1955. A population study of the grey squirrel (*Sciurus carolinensis*) in May 1954. *Annals of Applied Biology, 43*: 494-510.

Simms, C. 1961. Indications of the food of the kestrel in upland districts of Yorkshire. *Bird Study, 8*: 148-151.

Sinclair, G. 1992. *The lost land - land use change in England 1945-1990.* Council for the Protection of Rural England, London.

Skinner, C., Skinner, P., & Harris, S. 1991. The past history and recent decline of badgers *Meles meles* in Essex: an analysis of some of the contributory factors. *Mammal Review, 21*: 67-80.

Smal, C.M. 1993. The national badger survey: preliminary results for the Irish Republic. In: *The badger*, ed. by T.J. Hayden, 9-22. Royal Irish Academy, Dublin.

Smallshire, D., & Davey, J.W. 1989. Feral Himalayan porcupines in Devon. *Nature in Devon, 10*: 62-69.

Smith, E.A. 1966. A review of the world's grey seal population. *Journal of Zoology, London, 150*: 463-489.

Smith, I., & Lyle, A. 1979. *Distribution of freshwaters in Great Britain.* Institute of Terrestrial Ecology, Edinburgh.

Smith, P.A. 1985. Ship rats on Lundy, 1983. *Report of the Lundy Field Society, 36*: 35-38.

Smith, P.A., Smith, J.A., Tattersall, F.H., Lancaster, V., Natynczuk, S.E., & Seymour, R.S. 1993. The ship rat (*Rattus rattus*) on Lundy, 1991. *Journal of Zoology, London, 231*: 689-695.

Snow, D.W. 1968. Movements and mortality of British kestrels *Falco tinnunculus*. *Bird Study, 15*: 65-83.

South, G.R. 1966. Food of long-eared owls in south Lancashire. *British Birds, 59*: 493-497.

Southern, H.N. 1954. Tawny owls and their prey. *Ibis, 96*: 384-410.

Southern, H.N. 1970. The natural control of a population of tawny owls (*Strix aluco*). *Journal of Zoology, London, 162*: 197-285.

Southern, H.N., & Laurie, E.M.O. 1946. The house mouse (*Mus musculus*) in corn ricks. *Journal of Animal Ecology, 15*: 134-149.

Spagnesi, M., Cagnolaro, L., Perco, F., & Scala, C. 1986. La capra di Montecristo (*Capra aegagrus hircus* Linnaeus, 1758). *Ricerche di Biologia della Selvaggina, 76*: 1-147.

Speakman, J.R. 1991. The impact of predation by birds on bat populations in the British Isles. *Mammal Review, 21*: 123-142.

Speakman, J.R., Webb, P.I., & Racey, P.A. 1991. Effects of disturbance on the energy expenditure of hibernating bats. *Journal of Applied Ecology, 28*: 1087-1104.

Speakman, J.R., Racey, P.A., Catto, C.M.C., Webb, P.I., Swift, S.M., & Burnett, A.M. 1991a. Minimum summer populations and densities of bats in N.E. Scotland, near the northern borders of their distributions. *Journal of Zoology, London, 225*: 327-345.

Speakman, J.R., Racey, P.A., Hutson, A.M., Webb, P.I., & Burnett, A.M. 1991b. Status of Nathusius' pipistrelle (*Pipistrellus nathusii*) in Britain. *Journal of Zoology, London, 225*: 685-690.

Spencer, J.W., & Kirby, K.J. 1992. An inventory of ancient woodland for England and Wales. *Biological Conservation, 62*: 77-93.

Spencer-Booth, Y. 1956. Shrews (*Crocidura cassiteridum*) on the Scilly Isles. *Proceedings of the Zoological Society of London, 126*: 167-170.

Spencer-Booth, Y. 1963. A coastal population of shrews (*Crocidura suaveolens cassiteridum*). *Proceedings of the Zoological Society of London, 140*: 322-326.

Springthorpe, G.D., & Myhill, N.G. 1985. *Forestry Commission Wildlife Rangers Handbook.* Forestry Commission, Edinburgh.

Staines, B. 1986. The spread of grey squirrels (*Sciurus carolinensis* Gm) into northeast Scotland. *Scottish Forestry, 40*: 190-196.

Staines, B.W. 1991. Red deer *Cervus elaphus*. In: *The handbook of British mammals*, ed. by G.B. Corbet & S. Harris, 492-504. Blackwell Scientific Publications, Oxford.

Staines, B.W., & Ratcliffe, P.R. 1987. Estimating the abundance of red deer (*Cervus elaphus* L.) and roe deer (*Capreolus capreolus* L.) and their current status in Great Britain. *Symposia of the Zoological Society of London, 58*: 131-152.

Staines, B.W., & Ratcliffe, P.R. 1991. Roe deer *Capreolus capreolus*. In: *The handbook of British mammals*, ed. by G.B. Corbet & S. Harris, 518-525. Blackwell Scientific Publications, Oxford.

Stebbings, R.E. 1988. *Conservation of European bats*. Christopher Helm, London.

Stebbings, R.E. 1989a. Conservation of the greater horseshoe bat - is the long-term survival of the greater horseshoe bat a viable concept? *British Wildlife, 1*: 14-19.

Stebbings, R.E. 1989b. The Bechstein's bat (*Myotis bechsteinii*) in Dorset and Britain 1800-1989. *Proceedings of the Dorset Natural History and Archaeological Society, 110*: 178-180.

Stebbings, R.E. 1992. Mouse-eared bat - extinct in Britain? *Bat News, 26*: 2-3.

Stebbings, R.E., & Arnold, H.R. 1987. Assessment of trends in size and structure of a colony of the greater horseshoe bat. *Symposia of the Zoological Society of London, 58*: 7-24.

Stebbings, R.E., & Arnold, H.R. 1989. Preliminary observations of 20th century changes in distribution and status of *Rhinolophus ferrumequinum* in Britain. In: *European bat research 1987*, ed. by V. Hanák, I. Horácek & J. Gaisler, 559-563. Charles University Press, Praha.

Stebbings, R.E., & Griffith, F. 1986. *Distribution and status of bats in Europe*. Institute of Terrestrial Ecology, Abbots Ripton.

Stebbings, R.E., & Hutson, A.M. 1991. Mouse-eared bat *Myotis myotis*. In: *The handbook of British mammals*, ed. by G.B. Corbet & S. Harris, 107-108. Blackwell Scientific Publications, Oxford.

Stebbings, R.E., & Robinson, M.F. 1991. The enigmatic serotine bat - a case of human dependency. *British Wildlife, 2*: 261-265.

Stebbings, R.E., & Walsh, S.T. 1991. *Bat boxes*. Bat Conservation Trust, London.

Stewart, L.K. 1985. Red deer. In: *Vegetation management in northern Britain*, ed. by R.B. Murray, 45-50. British Crop Protection Council, Croydon.

Stoate, C. 1993. The 1992 BFSS hare survey. *Game Conservancy Review of 1992, 24*: 100-101.

Stocker, L. 1987. *The complete hedgehog*. Chatto & Windus, London.

Stone, R.D. 1986. *The social ecology of the European mole (*T. europaea L.*) and the Pyrenean desman (*Galemys pyrenaicus G.*): a comparative study*. PhD Thesis, University of Aberdeen.

Stone, R.D., & Gorman, M.L. 1991. Mole *Talpa europaea*. In: *The handbook of British mammals*, ed. by G.B. Corbet & S. Harris, 44-49. Blackwell Scientific Publications, Oxford.

Storch, G. 1978. *Glis glis* (Linnaeus, 1766) - Siebenschläfer. In: *Handbuch der Säugethiere Europas* 1(1), ed. by J.B. Niethammer & F. Krapp, 243-258. Akademische Verkigsgesellschaft, Wiesbaden.

Strachan, R., Birks, J.D.S., Chanin, P.R.F., & Jefferies, D.J. 1990. *Otter survey of England 1984-1986*. Nature Conservancy Council, Peterborough.

Strachan, R., & Jefferies, D.J. 1993. *The water vole* Arvicola terrestris *in Britain 1989-1990: its distribution and changing status*. Vincent Wildlife Trust, London.

Stroud, D.A., & Glue, D. 1991. *Britain's birds in 1989-90: the conservation and monitoring review.* British Trust for Ornithology & Nature Conservancy Council, Thetford.

Summers, C.F. 1978. Trends in the size of British grey seal populations. *Journal of Applied Ecology, 15*: 395-400.

Summers, C.F. 1979. The scientific background to seal stock management in Great Britain. *Natural Environment Research Council Publications, Series C, 21*: 1-14.

Summers, C.F., & Harwood, J. 1979. The grey seal 'problem' in the Outer Hebrides. *Proceedings of the Royal Society of Edinburgh, 77B*: 495-503.

Sumption, K.J., & Flowerdew, J.R. 1985. The ecological effects of the decline in rabbits (*Oryctolagus cuniculus* L.) due to myxomatosis. *Mammal Review, 15*: 151-186.

Sutcliffe, A.J., & Kowalski, K. 1976. Pleistocene rodents of the British Isles. *Bulletin of the British Museum (Natural History) Geology, 27*: 31-147.

Tabor, R. 1981. General biology of feral cats. In: *The ecology and control of feral cats,* 5-11. Universities Federation for Animal Welfare, Potters Bar.

Tapper, S. 1979. The effect of fluctuating vole numbers (*Microtus agrestis*) on a population of weasels (*Mustela nivalis*) on farmland. *Journal of Animal Ecology, 48*: 603-617.

Tapper, S. 1982. Using estate records to monitor population trends in game and predator species, particularly weasels and stoats. *Transactions of the International Union of Game Biologists, 14*: 115-120.

Tapper, S. 1987. Cycles in game-bag records of hares and rabbits in Britain. *Symposia of the Zoological Society of London, 58*: 79-98.

Tapper, S. 1992. *Game heritage - an ecological review from shooting and gamekeeping records.* Game Conservancy Ltd., Fordingbridge.

Tapper, S.C., & Barnes, R.F.W. 1986. Influence of farming practice on the ecology of the brown hare (*Lepus europaeus*). *Journal of Applied Ecology, 23*: 39-52.

Tapper, S., & Parsons, N. 1984. The changing status of the brown hare (*Lepus capensis* L.) in Britain. *Mammal Review, 14*: 57-70.

Tapper, S.C., Potts, G.R., & Brockless, M. 1991. The Salisbury Plain predation experiment: the conclusion. *The Game Conservancy Review of 1990, 22*: 87-91.

Tapper, S., & Stoate, C. 1992. Surveys galore - but how many hares? *Game Conservancy Review of 1991, 23*: 63-64.

Tapper, S., & Stoate, C. 1994. Hares - the game management connection. *Game Conservancy Review of 1993, 25*: 102-103.

Tarrant, K.A., & Westlake, G.E. 1988. Laboratory evaluation of the hazard to wood mice, *Apodemus sylvaticus*, from the agricultural use of methiocarb molluscicide pellets. *Bulletin of Environmental Contamination and Toxicology, 40*: 147-152.

Tarrant, K.A., Johnson, I.P., Flowerdew, J.R., & Greig-Smith, P.W. 1990. Effects of pesticide applications on small mammals in arable fields, and the recovery of their populations. In: *Proceedings of the 1990 British crop protection conference - pests and diseases,* 173-182. British Crop Protection Council, Farnham.

Tattersall, F. 1992. *The ecology of the house mouse (Mus domesticus), with particular reference to interaction with the woodmouse (Apodemus sylvaticus).* PhD Thesis, University of Reading.

Taylor, I.R., Dowell, A., Irving, T., Langford, I.K., & Shaw, G. 1988. The distribution and abundance of the barn owl *Tyto alba* in south-west Scotland. *Scottish Birds, 15*: 40-43.

Taylor, J.C., & Blackmore, D.K. 1961. A short note on the heavy mortality in foxes during the winter 1959-60. *Veterinary Record, 73*: 232-233.

Taylor, K.D. 1978. Range of movement and activity of common rats (*Rattus norvegicus*) on agricultural land. *Journal of Applied Ecology, 15*: 663-677.

Taylor, K.D., Fenn, M.G., & Macdonald, D.W. 1991. Common rat *Rattus norvegicus*. In: *The handbook of British mammals*, ed. by G.B. Corbet & S. Harris, 248-255. Blackwell Scientific Publications, Oxford.

Taylor, K.D., Quy, R.J., & Gurnell, J. 1981. Comparison of three methods for estimating the numbers of common rats (*Rattus norvegicus*). *Mammalia, 45*: 403-413.

Taylor, W.L. 1946. The wildcat (*Felis silvestris*) in Great Britain. *Journal of Animal Ecology, 15*: 130-133.

Teagle, W.G. 1963. Analysis of barn owl pellets from Claremont, Esher, Surrey. *London Naturalist, 42*: 59-61.

Tew, T.E. 1989. *The behavioural ecology of the wood mouse in the cereal field ecosystem*. DPhil Thesis, University of Oxford.

Tew, T.E. 1992. Radio-tracking arable-dwelling woodmice. In: *Wildlife telemetry: remote monitoring and tracking of animals*, ed. by I.G. Priede & S.M. Swift, 561-569. Ellis Horwood, Chichester.

Tew, T.E. 1994. Farmland hedgerows: habitat, corridors or irrelevant? A small mammal's perspective. In: *Hedgerow management and nature conservation*, ed. by T.A. Watt & G.P. Buckley, 80-94. Wye College Press, Wye.

Tew, T.E., & Macdonald, D.W. 1993. The effects of harvest on arable wood mice *Apodemus sylvaticus. Biological Conservation, 65*: 279-283.

Tew, T.E., Macdonald, D.W., & Rands, M.R.W. 1992. Herbicide application affects microhabitat use by arable wood mice (*Apodemus sylvaticus*). *Journal of Applied Ecology, 29*: 532-539.

Thirgood, S.J. 1990. *Variation in social systems of fallow deer*. PhD Thesis, University of Southampton.

Thompson, H.V. 1956. The origin and spread of myxomatosis, with particular reference to Great Britain. *Terre et la Vie, 103*: 137-151.

Thompson, H.V. 1964. Wild mink. *Agriculture, 26*: 564-567.

Thompson, H.V. 1968. British wild mink. *Annals of Applied Biology, 61*: 345-349.

Thompson, H.V., & Peace, T.R. 1962. The grey squirrel problem. *Quarterly Journal of Forestry, 56*: 33-42.

Thompson, H.V., & Worden, A.N. 1956. *The rabbit*. Collins, London.

Thompson, P.M. 1989. Seasonal changes in the distribution and composition of common seal (*Phoca vitulina*) haul-out groups. *Journal of Zoology, London, 217*: 281-294.

Thompson, P.M. 1992. The conservation of marine mammals in Scottish waters. *Proceedings of the Royal Society of Edinburgh, 100B*: 123-140.

Thompson, P.M., & Hall, A.J. 1993. Seals and epizootics - what factors might affect the severity of mass mortalities? *Mammal Review, 23*: 149-154.

Thompson, P.M., & Harwood, J. 1990. Methods for estimating the population size of common seals, *Phoca vitulina. Journal of Applied Ecology, 27*: 924-938.

Thompson, P.M., & Miller, D. 1992. Phocine distemper virus outbreak in the Moray Firth common seal population: an estimate of mortality. *Science of the Total Environment, 115*: 57-65.

Thompson, P.M., Fedak, M.A., McConnel, B.J., & Nicholas, K.S. 1989. Seasonal and sex-related variation in the activity patterns of common seals (*Phoca vitulina*). *Journal of Applied Ecology, 26*: 521-535.

Thompson, P.M., Cornwell, H.J.C., Ross, H.M., & Miller, D. 1992. Serologic study of phocine distemper in a population of harbor seals in Scotland.

Journal of Wildlife Diseases, 28: 21-27.

Thorburn, A. 1920. *British mammals.* Longmans, Green & Co., London.

Tittensor, A.M. 1977. Red squirrel *Sciurus vulgaris.* In: *The handbook of British mammals*, ed. by G.B. Corbet & H.N. Southern, 153-164. Blackwell Scientific Publications, Oxford.

Tittensor, A.M. 1981. Rabbit population trends in southern England. In: *Proceedings of the World Lagomorph Conference, Guelph, Ontario 1979*, ed by K. Myers, 629-632. University of Guelph, Ontario.

Toms, M.P. 1990. *An investigation into the distribution of small mammal species in different year classes of sweet chestnut coppice.* BSc Thesis, University of Southampton.

Tonkin, J.M. 1983. *Ecology of the red squirrel* Sciurus vulgaris *L.* in mixed woodland. PhD Thesis, University of Bradford.

Trewhella, W.J., & Harris, S. 1988. A simulation model of the pattern of dispersal in urban fox (*Vulpes vulpes*) populations and its application for rabies control. *Journal of Applied Ecology, 25*: 435-450.

Triggs, G.S. 1991. The population ecology of house mice (*Mus domesticus*) on the Isle of May, Scotland. *Journal of Zoology, London, 225*: 449-468.

Trout, R.C. 1978. A review of studies on populations of wild harvest mice (*Micromys minutus* (Pallas)). *Mammal Review, 8*: 143-158.

Trout, R.C., Tapper, S.C., & Harradine, J. 1986. Recent trends in the rabbit population in Britain. *Mammal Review, 16*: 117-123.

Tubbs, C.R. 1986. *The New Forest.* Collins, London.

Twigg, G.I. 1961. Infestations of the brown rat (*Rattus norvegicus*) in drift mines of the British Isles. *Journal of Hygiene, Cambridge, 59*: 271-284.

Twigg, G. 1975. *The brown rat.* David & Charles, Newton Abbot.

Twigg, G.I. 1992. The black rat *Rattus rattus* in the United Kingdom in 1989. *Mammal Review, 22*: 33-42.

Ueckermann, E. 1984. Zur situation des Damwildes (*Cervus dama*) in Europe. In: *The fallow deer*, 29-35. International Council for Game and Wildlife Conservation, Budapest.

Usher, M.B., Crawford, T.J., & Banwell, J.L. 1992. An American invasion of Great Britain: the case of the native and alien squirrel (*Sciurus*) species. *Conservation Biology, 6*: 108-115.

Vaughan, R.W. 1978. A study of common seals in the Wash. *Mammal Review, 8*: 25-34.

Velander, K.A. 1983. *Pine marten survey of Scotland, England and Wales 1980-1982.* Vincent Wildlife Trust, London.

Velander, K.A. 1991. Pine marten *Martes martes.* In: *The handbook of British mammals*, ed. by G.B. Corbet & S. Harris, 368-376. Blackwell Scientific Publications, Oxford.

Venables, L.S.V., & Leslie, P.H. 1942. The rat and mouse populations of corn ricks. *Journal of Animal Ecology, 11*: 44-68.

Vesey-Fitzgerald, B. 1965. *Town fox, country fox.* André Deutsch, London.

Village, A. 1981. The diet and breeding of long-eared owls in relation to vole numbers. *Bird Study, 28*: 215-224.

Village, A., & Myhill, D. 1990. Estimating small mammal abundance for predator studies: snap-trapping versus sign indices. *Journal of Zoology, London, 222*: 681-689.

Walsh, A.L., Harris, S., & Hutson, A.M. 1995. Abundance and habitat selection of foraging vespertilionid bats in Britain: a landscape scale approach. *Symposia of the Zoological Society of London, 67*: in press.

Walsh, S.T., Stebbings, R.E., & Thompson, M.J.A. 1987. Distribution and abundance of the pipistrelle bat *Pipistrellus pipistrellus. Annual Report of the Vincent Wildlife Trust, 1987*: 43-46.

Walton, K.C. 1964. The distribution of the polecat (*Putorius putorius*) in England, Wales and Scotland, 1959-62. *Proceedings of the Zoological Society of London, 143*: 333-336.

Walton, K.C. 1968. The distribution of the polecat, *Putorius putorius* in Great Britain, 1963-67. *Journal of Zoology, London, 155*: 237-240.

Walton, K.C. 1970. The polecat in Wales. In: *Welsh wildlife in trust*, ed. by W.S. Lacey, 98-108. North Wales Naturalists' Trust, Bangor.

Ward, A.J., Thompson, D., & Hiby, A.R. 1987. Census techniques for grey seal populations. *Symposia of the Zoological Society of London, 58*: 181-191.

Watson, A., & Hewson, R. 1963. *Mountain hares*. Sunday Times, London.

Wauters, L., & Dhondt, A.A. 1990. Red squirrel (*Sciurus vulgaris* Linnaeus, 1758) population dynamics in different habitats. *Zeitschrift für Säugetierkunde, 55*: 161-175.

Wayre, P. 1989. History and known results of the Otter Trust re-introduction programme 1983-1989. *Otters, Journal of the Otter Trust, 2*(3): 26-27.

Weber, D. 1987. *Zur Biologie des Iltisses* (Mustela putorius *L.*) *und den Ursachen seines Rückganges in der Schweiz*. PhD Thesis, Naturhistorisches Museum, Basel.

Webster, J.A. 1973. Seasonal variation in mammal contents of barn owl castings. *Bird Study, 20*: 185-196.

Weir, A., McLeod, J., & Adams, C.E. 1995. The winter diet and parasitic fauna of a population of red-necked wallabies *Macropus rufogriseus* recently introduced to Scotland. *Mammal Review, 25*: in press.

Whitaker, J. 1892. *A descriptive list of the deer-parks and paddocks of England*. Ballantyne, Hanson & Co., London.

Whitehead, G.K. 1964. *The deer of Great Britain and Ireland - an account of their history, status and distribution*. Routledge & Regan Paul, London.

Whitehead, G.K. 1972. *The wild goats of Great Britain and Ireland*. David & Charles, Newton Abbot.

Whiteley, D. 1985. Sheffield bat report 1981-1985. *Sorby Record, 23*: 3-11.

Whiteley, D., & Clarkson, K. 1985. Leisler's bats in the Sheffield area - 1985. *Sorby Record, 23*: 12-16.

Whiteley, D., & Yalden, D.W. 1976. Small mammals in the Peak District. *Naturalist, 101*: 89-101.

Whitwell, K.E. 1991. Do hares suffer from grass sickness? *Veterinary Record, 128*: 395-396.

Williamson, M.H., & Brown, K.C. 1986. The analysis and modelling of British invasions. *Philosophical Transactions of the Royal Society of London, series B, 314*: 505-522.

Wilson, P. 1982. A survey of the Irish fox population. *Irish Veterinary Journal, 35*: 31-33.

Wilson, W.L., Montgomery, W.I., & Elwood, R.W. 1993. Population regulation in the wood mouse, *Apodemus sylvaticus*. *Mammal Review, 23*: 73-92.

Wolton, R.J. 1985. The ranging and nesting behaviour of wood mice, *Apodemus sylvaticus* (Rodentia, Muridae), as revealed by radio-tracking. *Journal of Zoology, London, 206A*: 203-224.

Woodroffe, G.L. 1988. *Ecology of riverside mammals in the North Yorkshire Moors National Park*. MPhil Thesis, University of York.

Woodroffe, G.L., Lawton, J.H., & Davidson, W.L. 1990a. Patterns in the production of latrines by water voles (*Arvicola terrestris*) and their use as indices of abundance in population surveys. *Journal of Zoology, London, 220*: 439-445.

Woodroffe, G.L., Lawton, J.H., & Davidson, W.L. 1990b. The impact of feral mink *Mustela vison* on water voles *Arvicola terrestris* in the North Yorkshire Moors National Park. *Biological Conservation, 51*: 49-62.

Yalden, D.W. 1974. Population density in the common shrew, *Sorex araneus*.

Journal of Zoology, London, 173: 262-264.

Yalden, D.W. 1980. Urban small mammals. *Journal of Zoology, London, 191*: 403-406.

Yalden, D.W. 1981. The occurrence of the pigmy shrew *Sorex minutus* on moorland, and the implications for its presence in Ireland. *Journal of Zoology, London, 195*: 147-156.

Yalden, D.W. 1984a. The status of the mountain hare, *Lepus timidus*, in the Peak District. *Naturalist, 109*: 55-59.

Yalden, D.W. 1984b. The yellow-necked mouse, *Apodemus flavicollis*, in Roman Manchester. *Journal of Zoology, London, 203*: 285-288.

Yalden, D.W. 1985. Dietary separation of owls in the Peak District. *Bird Study, 32*: 122-131.

Yalden, D.W. 1988. Feral wallabies in the Peak District, 1971-1985. *Journal of Zoology, London, 215*: 369-374.

Yalden, D.W. 1990. Recreational disturbance of large mammals in the Peak District. *Journal of Zoology, London, 221*: 293-298.

Yalden D.W. 1991. Red-necked wallaby *Macropus rufogriseus*. In: *The handbook of British mammals*, ed. by G.B. Corbet & S. Harris, 563-566. Blackwell Scientific Publications, Oxford.

Yalden, D.W. 1992. Changing distribution and status of small mammals in Britain. *Mammal Review, 22*: 97-106.

Yalden, D.W. 1993. Chad's shrews. *Naturalist, 118*: 65-67.

Yalden, D.W., & Shore, R.F. 1991. Yellow-necked mice *Apodemus flavicollis* at Woodchester Park, 1968-1989. *Journal of Zoology, London, 224*: 329-332.

Yalden, D.W., & Warburton, A.B. 1979. The diet of the kestrel in the Lake District. *Bird Study, 26*: 163-170.

Zeuner, F.E. 1963. *A history of domesticated animals*. Hutchinson, London.

Zhang, Z., & Usher, M.B. 1991. Dispersal of wood mice and bank voles in an agricultural landscape. *Acta Theriologica, 36*: 239-245.

Appendix: vagrant species recorded since 1900

Order: Chiroptera

Particoloured bat *Vespertilio murinus*

Status: Vagrant; very rare.

Distribution: There are occasional records throughout Britain from south coast of England to Shetland and the North Sea.

Records: There are only seven records this century (Brighton, East Sussex, March 1986; Cambridge, Cambridgeshire, November 1985; North Sea 270 km east of Berwick, June 1965; Shetland, March 1927, November 1981, November 1984) (Racey 1991), and Chadwell Heath, Essex, October 1994 (J. Dobson pers. comm.).

Northern bat *Eptesicus nilssonii*

Status: Vagrant; very rare.

Records: There is only one record, of a single specimen found in a hibernaculum at Betchworth, Surrey, in January 1987 (Greenaway & Hill 1987).

Order: Pinnipedia

Ringed seal *Phoca hispida*

Status: Occasional sightings in British waters; very rare.

Records: There are very few records from British waters this century (Aberdeen 1901; Shetland, occasional animals taken by common seal hunters in 1960s; Northumberland, 1991; Orkney, 1992) (Sea Mammal Research Unit pers. comm.).

Harp seal *Phoca groenlandica*

Status: Occasional sightings in British waters, especially when the species extends its range further south into the northern part of the North Sea. Very rare.

Records: There are thirty-one records from United Kingdom waters since about 1800; there are records this century from Teignmouth, Devon, 1902; Firth of Forth, 1903; Shetland, two in 1987; River Humber, 1987; Boston, Lincolnshire, 1988; Medway, Kent, 1988; Flamborough Head, Yorkshire, 1988 (Sea Mammal Research Unit pers. comm.).

Bearded seal *Erignathus barbatus*

Status: Occasional sightings in British waters; very rare.

Records: There are very few records from British waters: recent records include Shetland, two records in 1977; Mid Yell, Shetland, 1981; Ronas Voe, Shetland, 1986; Shetland, two records in 1987 and a sighting from Orkney could be the same animal as seen in Shetland two days earlier; Orkney, 1988; Shetland - two in 1988 (Sea Mammal Research Unit pers. comm.).

Hooded seal *Cystophora cristata*

Status: Occasional sightings in British waters; very rare.

Records: There are very few records from the British Isles, and many seem to be of young animals: records this century from Elgin, 1903; Haaf Gruney, Shetland, 1980; Felixstowe, Suffolk, 1989; Shetland, 1993 (Sea Mammal Research Unit pers. comm.).

Walrus *Odobenus rosmarus*

Status: Occasional sightings in British waters; very rare.

Records: Between 1815 and 1954, there were 26 records in British waters; all records were from off the Scottish coasts, except one in the Severn in 1839. Since 1954 there have been the following reports: the Isle of Arran, 1981; Shetland, 1981; the Wash, 1981; Pentland Firth, 1984; Orkney, 1986; Shetland, two in 1986 (Sea Mammal Research Unit pers. comm.).